Warren Brown is the award-winning editorial cartoonist and writer for the *Daily Telegraph*, and is well known for his appearances on television and radio.

He has a passion for both motoring and history. He co-conceived the recreation of the Peking to Paris race of 1907, using five original cars and, with co-driver Lang Kidby, was awarded the *Australian Geographic* Spirit of Adventure Award.

Since 2006 Warren has been the overnight host at Gallipoli on Anzac Day; and in 2010 was appointed a member of the National Commission on the Commemoration of the Anzac Centenary. He is currently serving on two committees for the upcoming Anzac Centenary.

Warren lives in Sydney with his wife Tanya and son Oliver.

FRANCIS BIRTLES

FRANCIS BIRTLES

WARREN BROWN

hachette
AUSTRALIA

People of Aboriginal or Torres Strait Islander heritage are advised that this book contains names, descriptions and images of people who are deceased or who may be deceased.

[] hachette
AUSTRALIA

Published in Australia and New Zealand in 2012
by Hachette Australia
(an imprint of Hachette Australia Pty Limited)
Level 17, 207 Kent Street, Sydney NSW 2000
www.hachette.com.au

National Library of Australia
Cataloguing-in-Publication data

Brown, Warren, 1965-

Francis Birtles / Warren Brown.

9780733628672 (pbk.)

Birtles, Francis, 1881-1941 – Travel.
Adventure and adventurers – Australia – Biography.
Explorers – Australia – Biography.
Australia – Description and travel.
Asia – Description and travel.
Europe – Description and travel.

910.92

Cover design by Blue Cork
Cover photograph from author's private collection
Text design by Bookhouse, Sydney
Typeset in Simoncini Garamond
Printed and bound in Australia by Griffin Press, Adelaide, an Accredited ISO AS/NZS 14001:2009 Environmental Management System printer

MIX
Paper from
responsible sources
FSC® C009448

The paper this book is printed on is certified against the Forest Stewardship Council® Standards. Griffin Press holds FSC chain of custody certification SGS-COC-005088. FSC promotes environmentally responsible, socially beneficial and economically viable management of the world's forests.

For beautiful Tanya and Oliver –
every day is an adventure

Contents

Author's Note

In this book I have tried to tell the *story* of Francis Birtles – not present a detailed, comprehensive record of his life. It is a true story: dialogue has been taken from contemporary accounts, and the events described did happen.

His life did not run in a linear fashion. It ran in all directions at once. It seemed that the more information I uncovered, the more confusing and intriguing the Francis Birtles story became.

The main sources of information on Birtles' life and travels were his own books and articles – and accounts by his contemporaries. None of these is unbiased – all push one line or another. However, I have tried to pick my way through them and present an account of his doings which is authentic in its colour and framework.

When you look at the maps of his trips across Australia and the world, you wonder how on earth this adventurer crammed all these brutal, long-distance excursions into one lifetime. It was no secret. He just did not stop. Ever. He devoted himself to a life of adventure and 'hard living' that saw him perpetually – relentlessly – on the move. Frank had no responsibilities. He had no home. He had no dependants. He had no job. He made his money by regaling theatre audiences with thrilling accounts of his outback exploits, showing moving pictures and magic-lantern slides and from selling photographs of his adventures to anyone who'd listen. As far as he was concerned his sole responsibility was to stay alive. As long as he was on the move – often with a dog to accompany him – Frank Birtles was in his element careering back and forth across the Australian wilds.

That such an extraordinary Australian is little remembered today might seem surprising but when you follow Frank Birtles' story, it is perhaps not surprising. Certainly the world left him behind. His tireless overlanding career was eclipsed and then obliterated with the emergence of a new breed of adventurer – the aviator. And perhaps there was more to Francis Birtles that made it difficult to place him on a pedestal. For all his brilliance, he was a flawed character. As can happen in Australia, sometimes he was 'too-clever-by-half'. On more than one occasion he overstepped the mark with the wrong people, clumsily meddling in politics, pushing others aside – and at times he could be described as a bit of a rogue, every now and then flirting with the law.

Yet he possessed all the qualities that counted for being an Australian of his era: he was resourceful, fearless, ingenious, determined. But above all, he was unstoppable. If there was ever a tough decision for Frank Birtles to make, there was no doubt on which side the coin would land. 'My motto's "Chance it" . . .' he was famous for saying.

What I hope I have achieved in this book is to bring his story alive – and introduce him to a modern generation of Australians.

Warren Brown
Sydney, 2012

Preface

Among Frank Birtles' papers held by the Mitchell Library in Sydney is a hand-drawn map of the Australian continent on which the 'overlander' detailed his seemingly countless odysseys across and around the continent. Drawn with a paintbrush dipped in Indian ink and highlighted in red watercolour, the routes Francis Birtles has depicted trace his accomplishments with bicycle and later with motor cars through the dead heart, up to the Gulf of Carpentaria, down Australia's west coast and across the Nullarbor.

At first glance the map is startling – blood-red lines crisscross the continent from all directions like a network of veins connecting to the arteries that are Australia's ports. The freehand style in which Frank – as the artist – has drawn the map gives the illustration a kind of energy that professional charts drawn by cartographers simply don't have. It's as though a mad person has furiously scrawled red lines back and forth, up and down, diagonally, latitudinally, longitudinally, all over a crude and simple outline of the Australian continent.

This very personal and energetic record of Frank's travels tends to suggest the exploits depicted might be as imprecise as his hand-drawn Australian coastline. Yet a detailed study of every line drawn across the map reveals a specific escapade documented and accounted for during the period from 1906 through to 1921. Every line represents a real adventure.

Exactly how many times Francis Birtles traversed Australia isn't known. He made countless forays into the interior for the 20 years after the map was drawn. When he grew tired and intolerant of city life – which was frequently – he'd just pack up and head bush for months or even years. Sometimes it was reported he'd crossed Australia 70 times; other accounts claimed as many as 88. As Frank's journeys melded into a lifetime of continuous travel, it may have been difficult even for him to differentiate one adventure from another.

But the precise number of his transcontinental expeditions doesn't really matter. Even today, one cycle ride across Australia would be considered the experience of a lifetime. But to run your finger along the red line following Frank's adventure in cycling across the Nullarbor Plain in 1906 gives a chilling insight as to what an undertaking it must have been. There was nothing out there. No highway. No road. No track. No guarantee of finding food or water.

And then to follow another of the map's many red lines retracing his 16,000 kilometre cycling trip from Sydney to Darwin and down the west coast of Australia, and another line from Sydney to Darwin and then south to Alice Springs, and then more lines heading in all directions throughout Australia reinforces just what Frank accomplished.

It was these cycling and motoring feats that made Francis Birtles famous in Australia. This young, fit, bronzed adventurer seemed to embody the excitement and optimism of a new country flourishing in a new century. This was a golden age where man was developing a relationship with machines, and people wondered whether Frank Birtles' partnership with his trusty bicycle and cars might somehow finally lead to the subjugation of an untameable Australia.

He was seen at this time as a sort of conquering hero – a son-of-the-soil bushman about to take on the heartless forces of nature and the elements, giving no quarter. Newspaper advertisements for various products sometimes depicted a brave broad-brimmed-hat-wearing Birtles-esque figure riding a bicycle or driving a car. Readers knew who the figure was supposed to be because the cyclist was wearing shorts – a fashion Francis Birtles adopted while serving in South Africa and was said to have introduced to Australia.

The public held their breath when Frank waved farewell from the GPO in Sydney or Melbourne or Brisbane or Perth. His preparedness to undertake breathtakingly long rides into the never-never helped to foster a new-found interest in the Australian interior and began to demystify its reputation. Frank's hand-drawn map provides some idea of the distances involved in his expeditions, but gives little insight into just how desolate and punishing Australia's interior really was.

To put his exploits in true perspective, Australia during Frank Birtles' time can't be viewed through a 21st century prism. It was a vastly different world. Australia might have been brought together as a single, united nation during its Federation in 1901 but the sheer size of the continent meant the major ports and cities dotted around the coast might as well have been on the other side of the planet. Perth on Australia's west coast and Port Darwin at the top end were completely isolated from the rest of Australia and only accessible by sea.

To travel to these destinations from the eastern cities required booking a long sea voyage. Travelling overland to Perth or Darwin was out of the question. There was only endless desert and hopelessness. Even travelling along the eastern seaboard was problematic. The railways required changing trains at borders because of variations in rail gauges, so travel by sea was the preferred option for anyone travelling between Brisbane, Sydney, Melbourne and Adelaide. Travelling by road wasn't even a consideration.

Someone needed to turn their back on the sea as the way Australians interacted with each other and start figuring out how to use the nation's interior. Someone needed to get out there and get cracking to start forging paths overland. That someone was Francis Birtles – adventurer.

1
North-Western Burma – 1928

There are 60 mountains between the village of Palel and the Kabaw Valley on the edge of the Chindwin River in north-western Burma. They are at the southern end of the Naga Hills, a formidable mountain range that rises from a maze of swirling tributaries and rivulets, in places soaring almost vertically to heights of up to 1,600 metres.

The mountains are covered in thick, dark, leech-infested jungle, concealing a lethal world that harbours some of Asia's most deadly wildlife – snakes such as the black-banded Asiatic krait and the king cobra, and, of course, there was the silent, ever-present menace of tigers lurking in the bamboo forests. During the monsoon season the region is pounded mercilessly by torrential rains, the rivers and creeks building into vast, churning highways of brown water that rip south, ultimately dumping into Burma's greatest river, the Irrawaddy. During the summer, the humidity is, at best, unbearable, the air thick with malaria-carrying mosquitoes and the forest floor home to an astonishing array of scorpions and giant spiders.

For centuries, the Naga Hills were regarded as an impenetrable barrier between India and Burma. There were no roads in or out, only single-file tracks that meandered through near-vertical scrub, worn through over many years by animals and the elusive and frightening Naga Hillmen, well known to British colonials for their practice of souveniring the hacked-off heads and genitals of those who had unfortunately wandered into their territory. It was not a world for outsiders. If, in 1928, you had chartered a plane to fly over the area, it would have looked very much as it does today – deep valleys, rugged gorges, swirling rivers, towering peaks and impenetrable jungle, a broad olive-green mountain-scape stretching as far as the eye can see.

Yet, during February and March that year, hidden somewhere under the thick forest canopy was an unexpected and extraordinarily incongruous sight. Here, deep in the Burmese jungle, balanced precariously on the edge of a high cliff, rested a scarlet, torpedo-bodied racing car, suspended at an alarming angle, with well-worn ropes wrapped through its wire wheels and lashed to the trunks of two teak trees. The ropes were all that held the machine from sliding off the cliff's edge and plunging into the river far below, where it would have been smashed and swept south into the churning Irrawaddy.

There had never been an automobile in this part of the world before, let alone one as unusual as this. It looked like the type of machine one would have expected to see hurtling along the banked racing circuit at Brooklands, weaving through a roaring pack of Bentleys and Bugattis. Its battered bodywork was long and sleek, tapering to a vertical edge, a tiny two-seater cockpit situated midway along it with a copper exhaust running almost the full length of the passenger side. Signwritten logos announced various company sponsorships including Shell Motor Spirit and Dunlop Tyres, two of which were roped to the rear.

Closer examination of the car would reveal some curious idiosyncrasies. The brass radiator cap was topped with the figure of an upright kangaroo. The car's weathered paintwork was adorned with rough depictions of the Australian continent, along with kookaburras and boomerangs. Crudely painted in cursive along both sides of the hinged bonnet was the name of the car's manufacturer, Bean, and above that the car's nickname: 'Sundowner'.

•

Only eighteen months earlier, this car had smashed the intercity speed record from Darwin to Melbourne, where 10,000 people had crowded to see it cross the finish line at the Melbourne GPO.

In 1928, it was Australia's most famous motor car. And now, here it was – shabby and weather-beaten – stranded in the pitiless jungle of northern Burma. Sitting silently on a rock nearby were two malnourished white men, their dishevelled beards matted with grit and grease, the creases in their faces filled with grime – a mixture of sump oil and jungle dirt. They'd been trapped in the roadless jungle with this car for more than a month and were now living on what little tea, flour and rice they had left. Due to the humidity, their clothes had begun to rot apart at the seams and disintegrate. Their boots had split, which meant the leeches no longer needed to work their way through the bootlace holes to reach the flesh.

The pair had been sitting exhausted without saying a word for nearly two hours now while the tropical sun overhead brought the jungle's temperature up to simmer as it had done every day for weeks. Both had a look of grim resignation – their eyes morose, almost soulless, as if whatever suggestion of life there might be flickering within was at any second about to be extinguished.

The younger of the two, Percy Stollery, was a Canadian traveller about twenty years old who had been roaming the world in hope of high adventure. However, instead of being able to look forward to one day regaling his family and friends with his tales of his wild experiences abroad, he had suddenly – somehow – found himself in a Burmese jungle about to die. Here in the stifling humidity and raucous din of insects, any hope of a fulfilled life where he might have had a job, a girlfriend or a wife and maybe even children was rapidly vanishing.

The older man looked as though he'd had ten lifetimes of scrapes and close calls – his gaunt, ravaged, leathery face belied his 47 years. A severe gash scored across the back of his right hand had begun to turn septic. Yet this warhorse had been through worse. Since he was a boy, he had lived a life of non-stop adventure – in his time he'd been shot at, almost drowned at sea, almost burned alive, almost perished of thirst, almost died of fever, almost frozen to death. He'd sailed around the world twice by the time he was nineteen. He'd fought in a war. He'd crisscrossed Australia countless times on bicycles and in motor cars. He was a pioneer aviator. He'd written books and painted pictures, taken photographs and made films. He'd lived in the farthest-flung regions of the outback with the Aborigines. He knew the Australian continent like the back of his hand. In Australia, he was what you might call a household name – 'The King of Arnheim Land' (sic) he called himself. Others knew him as 'the Overlander'. To many he was best known as Australia's most famous motorist. His passport announced him as Francis Edwin Birtles. Occupation: Explorer.

Yet, in all his scrapes, this one was shaping up as one of the worst. Birtles and Stollery had manhandled the ton-and-a-half of motor car through the roadless jungle mountain range for over a month, cutting through the undergrowth, hacking out some form of road on which to haul the car up a mountainside, only to lower it down another. They were averaging a few kilometres a day.

That morning, they had only just saved the car from sliding sideways over the precipice, taking Birtles with it. The section of makeshift track they'd spent two days carving out of the yellow mud gave way on the outer edge. With the brakes locked and Birtles helpless at the wheel, the car slipped down an embankment, but was stopped miraculously at the cliff's edge by Stollery, who'd hung on to a guide rope.

Birtles was here in Burma as a result of a failed four-way marriage between himself as Australia's best-known motorist, the badly organised Bean Car Company, an irascible, paranoid Sydney newspaper journalist and a textile engineer prone to concocting grand schemes.

It was intended to be a monumentally important achievement – to take a British motor car and drive overland across the world from England to Australia, linking these two disparate countries and thereby strengthening the bonds that held together the British Empire.

Only seven months earlier, Birtles had been part of another attempt to drive from England to Australia, which had ended disastrously. The whole expedition – and the car – was scrapped by the time it reached India. When everything had fallen apart, Birtles should have just walked away, but it was his own single-mindedness, perhaps pig-headedness, that saw him take up another challenge. Once again, Francis Birtles was facing death – but now this young Canadian fella was about to perish with him.

Having secured the car to the trees, the pair sat solemnly, taking stock of the situation. They had made a pact weeks earlier. Either the car was going through the mountains, or it wasn't coming back at all. Losing it to the jungle now would be catastrophic – the struggle to maintain the expedition's momentum was actually keeping them alive.

2

Blind Date with the Motor Car

In bleak circumstances, even the most emotionally hardened can suddenly find themselves reflecting on the report card of their lifetime experiences. No question, Frank Birtles had had more than his share. That very year, 1928, marked the 20th anniversary of his relationship with the motor car – the much-abused companion cobbled together from sheet steel, cast iron and rubber. Together they'd shared so many extraordinary adventures and, more often than not, depended on each other to survive. The tragedy now playing out on the side of this jungle-forested mountain in upper Burma marked a watershed in Birtles' incredible adventuring career. If he and Stollery were to survive, this was where everything Birtles was famous for would need to come into play: self-reliance, resilience, resourcefulness and stamina.

The past two decades of motoring adventure had in fact served as a necessary, if brutal, training ground for this trans-global drive. Birtles had accrued a knowledge of long-distance motoring that made him well equipped to handle catastrophic situations. He'd learned so much, and not only from a motoring perspective. Along the way, one of the many sobering lessons this Australian bushman learned was of the fickle, unreliable and untrustworthy nature of the human character, which unfortunately included his own. He was by no means perfect.

Joining the dots from one adventure to another through those years reveals that his life had been peppered with cameo appearances from some of the most extraordinary Australians of his era. Because of his unquestionable abilities, people were drawn to him: explorers, aviators, prime ministers, confidence tricksters, espionage agents, military men. They could all see something in Birtles they didn't understand, but could nevertheless appreciate.

His story reads almost like a Shakespearean play, where larger than life characters continually walk in and out of the limelight. When photographer Frank Hurley wanders off stage, he is replaced by Prime Minister Billy Hughes, who in turn is replaced by aviator Bert Hinkler. They all saw Frank as some sort of useful tool in helping their dreams and ambitions come to fruition. Whenever someone needed something done in the outback – a car tested, a survey completed, a speed record broken, a film made – Frank was the hired gun they would turn to.

Yet his knowledge and experience wasn't inherent – it was hard-earned. If you were to try to retrace the path of Birtles' motoring adventures from where he and Stollery were trapped perishing on the side of a Burmese mountain in 1928 to pinpoint the very first time this simple boy from Fitzroy in Victoria understood the astounding opportunities offered by the motor car, it would lead to a place on the map that was the antithesis of Burma's Naga Hills with its jungles and leeches, its headhunters and tigers.

•

Francis Birtles' extraordinary motoring career began in the winter of 1908 in the flat, arid wasteland of Australia's dead heart, only a stone's throw from the continent's geographical centre. It was a chance meeting that took place along the overland telegraph track 60 kilometres north of Alice Springs that paved the way for a world of adventure.

In 1908, there was no road north of Alice Springs, only a narrow, stony track following the iron telegraph poles dotted up through the dry desert scrub covering the MacDonnell Ranges on the town's outskirts. These rusted posts disappeared in a perfect line to the horizon conveying a single strand of 8 gauge galvanised wire 1,600 kilometres north to Port Darwin and 1,500 kilometres in the other direction to Adelaide.

The telegraph line was the only indication a human being had ever set foot in this part of the world. That the line existed at all was due to the perseverance and adaptability of the linesmen charged with its maintenance. Wooden posts first hammered into the desert soil back in 1872 had been completely devoured by voracious white ants within ten years. Iron was what ensured the telegraph's survival. Before long it would be motorised iron that would conquer Australia's dead heart.

In the early days of the colony, the centre of Australia offered the alluring notion that some wonderful discovery was lying in wait over the distant horizon – perhaps an inland sea or some arable, green farmland ripe for agriculture. The reality was altogether something else. Disappointed explorers like John McDouall Stuart staggered back from the wilderness with the grim news there was absolutely nothing out there except death for the ignorant and ill-prepared. Stuart, however, understood that the desert was more forgiving of explorers who travelled light and fast, and with his small band of companions he succeeded in traversing the continent from Adelaide to Darwin and back – but only just.

Those who attempted to attack the dead heart with grandiose expeditions the size of small armies could invoke the desert's wrath. Burke and Wills set out on what can only be viewed in hindsight as a naive and reckless attempt at a transcontinental crossing from south to north. Burke simply had no idea what he was doing other than operating along the lines that there would be safety in numbers.

The Australian interior was not to be treated flippantly. Burke and Wills lay dead under the baking sun. Along with the last skerrick of water from their canvas waterbag, decades of interest in exploring central Australia had evaporated to the point where travelling through the dead heart had become the domain of the hard-bitten long-distance outback cameleers.

Yet at the turn of the century, there was a change in the wind. In August 1908, three adventurers, Harry Dutton, Murray Aunger and Ernest Allchurch, were attempting to drive a car along the camel track that followed the 40-year-old overland telegraph line connecting Adelaide to Darwin. They were pioneer motorists embarking on Australia's first great automotive expedition – to complete a transcontinental crossing by motor car.

They were nursing a cumbersome yet robust Edwardian four-cylinder Talbot – one of the finest English cars available

– but still a bit of a worry when three lives were completely at the mercy of a piece of hand-crafted technology, miles from anywhere. This was in fact the second time Dutton and Aunger were having a crack at the challenge of the south–north Adelaide to Darwin crossing, and only a few days north of Alice Springs they were making painfully slow progress.

For all the allure and supposed romance of motoring, this was more of a 19th century covered-wagon-style saga, the three motorists constantly coaxing their overloaded machine like some faltering animal painfully jolting across the stony MacDonnell Ranges. To make matters worse, heavy rains had caused thick desert grasses to spring up which became entangled in the engine. It was a brutal drive.

Sharp spinifex ran to the horizon in every direction, concealing thousands of anthills possessing the strength and sympathy of concrete posts, each one capable of punching a hole through the sump, draining the oil, destroying the motor and ending the expedition then and there. For the three it was a never-ending ritual of climbing on and off the running boards, attempting to knock the anthills apart, hacking through the grass and pushing forward a yard at a time – progress being slowed to less than 10 miles per day. Only 1,000 miles to go.

What Dutton and Aunger were inadvertently doing was creating a template for motorised exploration in Australia – assembling a kind of unintended guidebook for later expeditions. They might have been making it up as they went along, but they were getting it right. For this attempt, the inclusion of Ernest Allchurch, a telegraph operator picked up in Alice Springs, was a masterstroke.

In an age with no telephones, radio or EPIRB, the overland telegraph line, with its lonely manned outposts dotted across the desert, was the expedition's lifeline to the outside world should things go wrong. If they simply followed the rambling telegraph line – and had someone with them who knew how to tap into it – they'd be safe. Nightly, Allchurch was able to access the line with his portable morse key, transmit their location and status and receive information from the other wireless operators about what they could expect further up the track. In 1908, this was about as close as you could get to GPS navigation.

The idea of driving across the Australian continent had taken hold of Dutton, a wealthy landowner always on the lookout for ways to open up the region north of Adelaide for agriculture. The possibility of exploring the full length of the state of South Australia from the Great Australian Bight to the Arafura Sea by motor car appealed enormously, particularly since Dutton was wealthy enough to finance a motorised expedition without the need of sponsorship.

Today we would think of a transcontinental crossing as perhaps running latitudinally from west to east. In the 19th and early 20th centuries, it was south to north that captured the public's imagination. For Australians, it pointed to Britain and the outside world, and the thin wire of the overland telegraph was the tangible connection.

Almost 30 years before the nation's Federation in 1901, the colony of South Australia accomplished an amazing feat with the construction of the 3,500 kilometre overland telegraph line connecting Adelaide to Darwin. From Darwin an underwater cable connected with Java and the rest of the world, making Adelaide, South Australia's capital, the nation's hub for international communication traffic. The idea of being able to drive that route strengthened that connection to the rest of the world.

For four weeks, Dutton and Aunger prepared the car for their first transcontinental motoring expedition. They fitted the Talbot out as if it were a sea-going vessel about to undertake an ocean voyage, overloading it with a wealth of provisions – fuel, shovels, axes, flour, rifles, ammunition, all covered with canvas sheeting and roped down to the chassis.

Planning was not without its problems, as they were facing situations Australian explorers had never had to deal with. Certainly water, for drinking, for cooking and washing, and filling up the car's radiator would be a major consideration when heading out into the desert. But now they needed to factor in the supply of petrol – or benzine as it was then called in Australia.

In 1908, there was no such thing as a petrol station. Petrol was simply supplied in tins in shops, and the Talbot would need to carry as much fuel as possible. But it couldn't carry enough for the whole 3,000 kilometre trip, so petrol needed to be sent ahead and deposited along the route.

They utilised the narrow-gauge Great Northern Railway that went as far as Oodnadatta, 1,000 kilometres north of Adelaide, depositing benzine at various railway stations and sidings along the line, and from there contracted cameleers would distribute the fuel to designated pick-up points along the overland telegraph track. Cameleers would also carry fuel along the track from the Oodnadatta railhead across the desert to Alice Springs – the town, never having seen a car before, had probably never seen petrol. Similarly, fuel would be brought south from Darwin.

Despite the careful planning, Dutton had made a potentially lethal mistake. Before leaving Adelaide, he'd been warned he was heading out at the wrong time of year, venturing headlong into blistering summer conditions, their lives at the mercy of such an unproven contraption as the motor car.

As predicted, once underway things went wrong – quickly. The gruelling terrain north proved far more difficult than either expected – countless stony washouts, vast sand hills and hundreds of kilometres of rocky terrain without any hint of water. Weary and almost out of fuel, the pair struggled on to finally arrive at their petrol dump at Coward Springs on the Oodnadatta Track where, to their horror, they discovered their supply had been left uncovered, and every fuel tin had burst due to the 50 degree heat.

Dutton and Aunger were forced to wait for days in the dead-flat desert by the railway line, ultimately loading the Talbot aboard the fortnightly train headed for the railhead at Oodnadatta, 300 kilometres north.

With the car refuelled, Dutton then made the decision to press on to Alice Springs (or Stuart, as it was then known). However, in reality the dream of a transcontinental expedition by motor car was over because a train had rescued them. Dutton should probably have called it quits at Oodnadatta. They were now faced with crossing the notorious Depot Hills, north of Finke River.

Continuing north, the Talbot's rear axle began to misbehave – at one point Aunger had to pull it all apart and replace the pinion and bearings. After they arrived at Stuart, Dutton was still insistent on pressing north to Darwin.

Then, in the blistering heat of Christmas Day 1907, it was all over. Sixty kilometres south of Tennant Creek, the Talbot became bogged in rough sand, the attempt to extricate the car breaking the differential.

The expedition was now finished. Not only were Dutton and Aunger forced to leave the car behind, but they were also faced with the grim reality they could well perish in the style of Burke and Wills. The pair were lucky. Retracing their tyre tracks beneath the telegraph line, they made it to the manned relay station at Barrow Creek.

For now, Dutton and Aunger were beaten. They returned to Oodnadatta by packhorse to begin the slow train journey back to Adelaide without their car – still stuck in the ground, thousands of kilometres away, near Tennant Creek.

Fortunately, Dutton, had enough money, drive and humility to try again, so seven months later, another farewell took place to mark his and Aunger's second attempt at crossing the continent. This time the feeling was more sober. Dutton had purchased an identical Talbot car and was determined to take up the fight and this time win. Understandably reserved, the president of the automobile club offered an optimistic if more measured toast: 'There is no doubt they will accomplish their object on this occasion.'

And now here they were with Ernest Allchurch, the morse telegraphist, motoring once again into Australia's dead heart. Once out of Alice Springs, the expedition was progressing well – if slowly. During one of his nightly telegraph communications, Allchurch received an unusual message from the office at Tennant Creek – the nearest town to the north, nearly 500 kilometres away – that another adventurer was heading south. Somewhere along the camel track meandering beneath the telegraph line the two parties would run into each other.

For the next few days, the Talbot, loaded to the gunnels, pressed on, plodding cautiously through the MacDonnell Ranges. Simply getting through the rocks and spinifex would be a huge relief. One day, out of the blue, something caught Dutton's eye – an aberration in the haze ahead. In a landscape of quivering mirages, a minuscule black speck, but one that seemed to be moving, broke the monotony of an otherwise stagnant horizon.

Dutton narrowed his eyes – the speck had gone. He was sure he'd seen something, but days of scanning the horizon meant his eyes occasionally played tricks. Then he saw it again. Dutton called out for Aunger to stop the car and fumbled for the field-glasses case.

He stood up, placing the binoculars to his eyes, his fingers adjusting the focusing dial. What on earth could it be? It wasn't a kangaroo – perhaps an emu? Whatever it was, it was moving towards them. In the haze, it appeared to have the shape of a human, but it was unlikely an Aborigine would be way out here alone, and besides – it was now moving with a peculiar gait – seeming to lope from side to side.

It then came into focus. Dutton slowly lowered the binoculars and turned to Aunger and Allchurch, his face a picture of disbelief. 'It's a bloke . . . on a *pushbike* . . .' Sure enough, the shimmering mirage began to take shape – a silhouette crowned with a broad-brimmed hat, making heavy work of the ride across the glistening gibber stones.

Stunned, the three motorists climbed out of the car and stood speechless at the sight pedalling towards them. As the cyclist drew closer, he swung his leg over the frame, got off his bicycle and wheeled it towards the car. He put out his hand and introduced himself as Frank Birtles.

Frank was about 5 feet 10 inches (178 centimetres) and slightly built, his skin leathery from exposure to the outback sun, so it was difficult to tell just how old he was – at a guess, somewhere in his mid-twenties. His face was thin, almost skeletal, and from it flashed a pair of grey eyes that gave him a startling and somewhat fierce presence. He sported a long moustache, which was matted with sweat and bulldust, as were his clothes – a well-worn bush jacket and trousers hacked off just above the knee. He wore puttees around his shins like a Boer War trooper.

As protocol demanded in those days, such an extraordinary meeting required brewing up some tea, and Allchurch set about removing a blackened tin billy wired to the tool chest on the Talbot's running board. In no time he had a small fire going.

Aunger, a noted cyclist in his day, took a keen interest in Frank's bicycle – a diamond-frame pushbike fitted with a headlight and small first-aid kit mounted on the handlebars; a canvas waterbag and two canvas panniers for basic foods, flour, tea and sugar; a brass water tank fitted under the main crossbar; a lightweight sleeping bag; and a Winchester lever-action rifle.

While the billy simmered away, Frank talked about the trouble he'd had with snakes on his travels south from Darwin – of how seemingly every snake he had seen attacked the bicycle. He said he thought the nickel-plated parts shining in the sun might have attracted them and that he'd been continually forced to get off the bike and find a stick or a stone so he could 'debate the question of ownership'.

The three motorists must have listened in disbelief. He'd pedalled a bicycle all the way from Darwin? That's 1,600 kilometres.

Then the obvious question: where on earth did Frank start?

Frank took his hat off and ran his hand through his thick, matted blond hair.

He began in the matter-of-fact way one might read a train timetable: well, he'd left Market Street in Sydney and then – let's see – cycled up through Armidale, Brisbane, Rockhampton, across to the Gulf country, Tennant Creek, up to Darwin – and now he was on his way to Adelaide.

Dutton, Aunger and Allchurch's eyes must have widened as Frank continued. Once he reached Adelaide, he warned, he had no intention of cycling across the Nullarbor – he'd already cycled from Fremantle to Sydney a couple of years ago.

Then it was Frank's turn – what were three men doing out here in a motor car?

Dutton explained – they were endeavouring to be the first to drive across the Australian continent. Frank told them he'd already seen the other Talbot stuck in the dirt north of Barrow Creek. It still looked fine, if a little bit rusty. Oh – and some birds had made a nest in it . . .

Frank then turned his interest towards the car, a leviathan compared with the bicycle. Unlike his own Spartan regime aboard the bicycle, the car seemed positively overloaded. He walked around, intrigued by the machine, feeling the Dunlop tyres, gigantic compared to those on his bike. He sat in the driver's seat and grasped the steering wheel. He placed his feet on the pedals. He shifted the long-throw gear lever through its gate. Then and there was the first time Francis Birtles had seen a motor car used as an exploration tool.

After they had taken photographs of each other with the pushbike alongside the Talbot, Frank climbed back on his bicycle and continued pedalling south, while the motorists packed up and headed north.

Yet years later they would look back on their bizarre chance encounter with a strange young cyclist way out in the dead heart, when the nation's first motorised transcontinental crossing bumped into Australia's greatest long-distance cyclist who would go on to achieve a motoring feat that would defy the imagination. Dutton, Aunger and Allchurch had met the amazing Francis Birtles.

As for Birtles – he'd met the motor car.

3

The Age of Overlanding

'Mr Birtles the indefatiguable (sic) cyclist reaches Melbourne and leaves soon after for Sydney . . .' read the inter-title caption in the silent 1910 Pathé newsreel, depicting grainy, flickering footage of Birtles in a broad-brimmed hat being farewelled by a cheering crowd in Collins Street.

'Indefatigable cyclist' was the perfect description for Francis Edwin Birtles, who in the space of three years had become a household name as the nation's foremost proponent of the bicycle. At the age of 28, Birtles was riding the crest of an international cycling wave.

At the turn of the 20th century, bicycling was beyond a craze. Before anyone had the remotest inkling of the impact the motor car would ultimately have on the world, for two decades the bicycle seemed to be carving its own unique path for the future of transport in Australia. The bicycle of the 1890s meant personal mobility for urban Australians. It was simple to operate and, other than the initial outlay to buy one, it cost nothing to run – save for a squirt of oil on the chain and the odd tyre inner-tube.

The bicycle as we know it appeared in the 1880s as the 'safety bicycle', or the 'diamond-frame bicycle', replacing its crude, cumbersome and now seemingly ludicrous ancestors, the penny-farthing and bone-shaker. The safety bicycle was distinguished by having two wheels of equal size and a chain drive, with a large sprocket connected to a smaller one. The different diameter sprockets meant a multiplication in the revolutions of the pedals, this 'gearing' allowing for smaller wheels. With the pedals positioned between the wheels, the safety bicycle had a low centre of gravity, giving the rider much greater control than earlier cycles, where the pedals were attached to the front wheel, which had the potential to throw the rider over the handlebars. But it was the advent of the pneumatic tyre over solid rubber tyres that gave the greatest impetus to the cycling phenomenon.

The development of the safety cycle created a worldwide cycling boom – especially in transport-obsessed Australia. Despite the romantic idea that colonial Australians lived in the rugged outback, the vast majority of the population were urban dwellers living in densely populated cities and suburbs on the coast. Those in cities generally had access to trains, trams and omnibuses, and the arrival of the bicycle improved individual transport considerably.

Before long, Australian cities were awash with clattering bicycles, giving a collective cyclist movement a considerable political voice which, in turn, was responsible for an increase in the improvement of roads. Probably Francis Birtles' first proper encounter with the bicycle occurred sometime in 1899 during his service as a dispatch rider in the Boer War, where cycles as an early form of mechanised military transport had begun service with field scouts and messengers. Eighteen-year-old Birtles was serving in a South African horse-mounted irregular infantry unit, but already the writing was on the wall for the long-serving horse's military career.

The safety bicycle was proving an impressive and promising addition to the future of military technology. With recent improvements in the manufacture of pneumatic tyres and stronger frame design, certain advantages of the bicycle over the horse were starting to emerge. For any armed force, mobility is crucial, and horses had been the key to all armies' mobility for thousands of years. Yet horses required tremendous logistical support – feed, water, shelter, farriers, veterinary care – and had limited range. There were places you simply could not go with a horse. Boggy ground, sharp rocky outcrops and sand were all places to avoid for mounted troops. The advent of the bicycle changed everything. It required minimal expertise to ride and maintain, and could be easily lifted and carried across terrain where no horse could hope to travel.

Military commanders began to see the potential of this lightweight, individual machine in specialist roles for which horses weren't really suitable, and by the end of the 19th century most European armies were raising cycling detachments. It was in the Boer campaign that the first known use of bicycles in combat took place. The bicycle had all sorts of applications during the Boer War – even railway lines were patrolled by specially constructed tandem bicycles fitted to the rails.

Both the British army and Boer farmers incorporated bicycles in various skirmishes and raids, the most conspicuous cycling infantry unit being the *Theron se Verkenningskorps* (Theron Reconnaissance Corps – the TVK) under the command of Daniël Johannes Stephanus Theron, a one-time school teacher and lawyer turned guerilla and commando. Theron's bicycle-driven guerilla campaign became legendary to both sides during the Boer conflict, his 105 revolver and carbine carrying cyclists regularly sneaking back and forth across British lines, relaying intelligence on British positions and tactics. The ancient and walrus-moustached British commander, Lord Roberts of Kandahar, described Theron as 'the hardest thorn in the flesh of the British advance'. Theron was so effective with his cycle-mounted infantry that Roberts placed a £1,000 bounty on his head – dead or alive – and sent 4,000 troops to hunt him down and destroy the TVK.

After his army service, Birtles returned briefly to Australia, and soon afterwards sailed back to South Africa, joining the Transvaal constabulary as a policeman. While serving in the police, he undertook his first great cycling feat, pedalling across the Great Karoo – a 400,000 square kilometre desert in western South Africa. In many ways, the Karoo Basin resembled Australia's outback regions.

For all of its extraordinary versatility and popularity in urban Australia, the bicycle had been proving a useful device for covering long distances. And Australia had some of the longest distances in the world. Even so, the excitement in cycling was elevated to a more extreme level. Frank was one of a new breed of adventurers involved in what we would probably pigeonhole today as an extreme sport – overlanding. In the early 1900s, 'overlanders' were the small but enthusiastic band of fit, young adventurers who would undertake extraordinary long-distance bicycle expeditions into the never-never. They would travel light and camp out, and would sometimes take months – even years – to complete their journey. Overlanders were a particular strain of adventurer – part endurance rider, part explorer, part athlete, part bushman and, because of mind-numbing and potentially soul-destroying loneliness and boredom, part philosopher.

Many overlanders would write of their wild adventures cycling across the outback, clearly compelled to offer some rationale as to why they would undertake such dangerous expeditions. Some confessed simply that they just had some sudden, inexplicable urge to cycle more than 3,000 kilometres across the continent, while others saw themselves serving a higher purpose, somehow opening up the continent for the betterment of the nation, formulating ideas on agriculture or defence.

Unwittingly, these tough adventurers, who suffered with every grinding turn of the pedals, were more or less true stoics – in a classical sense – who, despite enduring gruelling physical and psychological hardship, maintained control over their emotions. Any displays of emotion were seen as flaws, and therefore they were only weak when they allowed themselves to be. They cycled and suffered and put up with it. On top of all this, these cyclists generally travelled across the vast expanses of wilderness armed, not solely so they could hunt for food, but also because even in the 1890s they could still encounter hostile Aboriginal tribes.

Certainly Frank Birtles is the best remembered of the overlanders, and, probably through his own self-promotion, became known as 'Australia's greatest overlander', yet he had no shortage of like-minded, equally zealous contemporaries. And there were many who went before him. Birtles was by no means the first person to cycle across Australia, nor was he the first to circumnavigate the continent by bicycle. He was one in a line of these tough, obsessive, ultra-long-distance bike riders. He was in equally eccentric company.

In 1898, 34-year-old Jerome Murif became the first person to ride a bicycle across Australia, from Adelaide to Port Darwin, using a German Wertheim 'Electra' bicycle he called his 'kangaroo engine'. Murif couldn't really explain what had possessed him to undertake such a perilous journey; only that '. . . a vague longing to do "something" first flattered, then irritated, then oppressed me,' as he wrote in the foreword of his book, *From Ocean to Ocean*, describing the adventure. Newspaper reporters found Murif at the very least eccentric, describing him awkwardly as 'a queer customer'. And they were probably right. Photographs of Murif on the journey show him looking somewhat Hercule Poirot-esque, with a neatly trimmed beard and moustache and wearing a homburg hat. The rest of his attire was designed purely for comfort, and he rode the entire 74-day journey from Adelaide to Darwin wearing his pyjamas, the legs of which were tucked into high-topped boots to keep the sand out. He thought up the idea of riding from the seaside Adelaide suburb of Glenelg to Darwin while working as a waterpipe layer in Broken Hill, and since no-one wanted to ride with him he thought he'd go it alone.

His journey started out in secrecy, with only two friends aware of his attempt. Even though they tried to talk him out of it, they stayed with him while he went through the ceremony of dipping his bicycle in the sea at Glenelg, promising to do it again once he'd reached Darwin. Murif had all sorts of near-catastrophic difficulties on his ride, including bushfires, floods, and cuts and bruises from being flung over the handlebars, but he was just one of those people who took things in their stride. He wasn't interested in making money out of his achievement and he wanted no prize. He even painted over the Electra brand on the frame. He was not attempting any speed record, simply cycling at his own pace. His easy-going attitude made the 3,000 kilometre ride across the continent all sound deceptively easy.

On arrival in Darwin, Murif was feted by the outpost's entire population. His feat in crossing the continent on this tiny, two-wheeled, chain-driven, self-powered machine beggared belief. No cyclist had ever ridden further than 40 miles south of Darwin. The burgeoning cycling community in Darwin was ecstatic. As far as they were concerned, it was as if he had suddenly opened up a highway for cyclists through the dead heart. The Patron of the Northern Territory Athletic Association presented him with a certificate authenticating his ride. The bicycle itself was then examined by a mechanical engineer to determine what wear and tear it had received.

> The general condition of your Electra, from a mechanical point of view, is of such a nature that as a practical man I would not credit the statement that it had been used for the purpose of crossing the Australian continent had it not been for the authentic records which you carry with you.
>
> Thos. N. Messenger,
> Foreman Locomotive Works, Port Darwin

But not every cyclist had the psychological make-up to be an overlander. Soon after Murif's arrival, keen to emulate his success, a group of enthusiastic cyclists in Darwin set off south for Adelaide, soon finding themselves riding into blistering 40 degree winds. Some cyclists pegged out at only 30 kilometres out from Darwin. The remainder of the peloton pressed on until they'd run out of what little water they had. The group leader later described in a newspaper report that 'the thirsts of himself and his companions became uncontrollable'. The mission was abandoned. 'They reached 92 miles, when they became totally disabled, and would never have turned up if they had kept on.'

In 1899, Brazilian born Arthur Richardson became the first cyclist to complete a circumnavigation of the Australian continent, and in the process became the first person to cycle across the Nullarbor Plain, describing the temperature as '1,000 degrees in the shade'. He left Perth on 5 June, heading north carrying not much more than a few supplies and a pistol. Like the overlanders who followed him, Richardson had a fiercely independent, often extreme personality. (After the ride, he moved to South Africa, enlisting with Australian forces during the Boer War, then served in World War I, seeing action that left him physically incapacitated and mentally disturbed. In 1939, he died of gunshot wounds in a murder-suicide with his wife.)

Richardson's ride, which saw him fighting off attacks from 'hostile blacks', demonstrated how wild the outback still was even in the 1890s.

Richardson had in effect been racing a rival party of cyclists attempting to circumnavigate Australia in a counterclockwise direction. At the same time, 29-year-old Donald Mackay, together with brothers Alex and Frank White, also completed a circumnavigation of Australia by bicycle. Tough and well-travelled, Mackay was part owner of a cattle station at Yass in country New South Wales. At well over 6 feet tall and weighing over

13 stone, Mackay appeared especially formidable, being covered from head to foot with tattoos he'd commissioned while travelling through England and Japan. He first learned to ride a bicycle in 1889, his mount being an old bone-shaker that he still kept on the farm. Mackay wasn't interested in bicycle racing, and had never raced. Long-distance overlanding was his interest, but he was described as 'an all round athlete, being a good swimmer, boxer, shot, rider and runner'.

Constantly restless, in 1899 Mackay was '. . . seized with the idea of cycling around Australia "for the fun of it",' he told the *Australian Cyclist* in March 1906. Yet the experience dissuaded him from trying overlanding again. Mackay reckoned he'd tempted fate too many times on that journey, and he had decided he'd call it quits on overlanding. 'All I know is that main strength and stupidity pulled me through. When I got in a tangle, or was lost, I just went bull-headed whatever way seemed the easiest. Life is too short for such a trip, and I would not do it again for all the gold in the Indies.' Overlanding was unquestionably dangerous, generally requiring a spirit of bold recklessness that in an instant could flip to lethal stupidity.

'What advice would you give to the "tourist" who might like to circle Australia?' the *Australian Cyclist* asked Mackay, who replied, 'I would counsel him, on the Bible if he wanted it, that the trip is not worth the candle. The privations endured are worse than the trip from Earth to the Hellespont. The first thing to contend with is ordinary sickness; next malarial fever or dysentery; last, but not least, your bicycle smashing up, plus the awful perishes for want of food and water. Mosquitoes, ants, flies, heat, dirt, and other "entrees" are included without charge. These tell upon you, and I can assure you that, although I was never ill in my life, this trip has told upon my constitution. I am weaker in every way. My side aches, and my limbs are weary from the continuous riding and plugging over the weary, monotonous wastes of scrub, rock, and swamp. There is . . . nothing really worth seeing . . . No; there are plenty of other places where the cyclist can enjoy life, without regretting every day that he was ever born to be such a fool as to tempt his Creator.'

Mackay's summary of overlanding is one of the more truthful accounts – there are no flowery, deluded, romantic versions here. It's quite possible Mackay's adventure, published in 1906, had some influence on Francis Birtles, for six months later he was contemplating a transcontinental bicycle ride.

Frank had returned from Africa looking for 'opportunities for hard living and adventurous exploits', and he was about to embark on a mission that certainly boasted both of those features. After two years service with the Transvaal police, he'd been discharged after contracting blackwater fever (a serious complication of malaria that can often lead to kidney failure) and sailed home to Australia, unsure of his future. To try to regain his health he travelled to New Zealand, where he embarked on a cycling tour covering both islands. Returning to Melbourne, he worked briefly as a print and design artist in a lithographic studio, but life in an office wasn't for him.

Frank Birtles began formulating the plan for a transcontinental bicycle ride no-one had attempted before. Cyclists had crossed the Nullarbor a dozen times in the previous eight years but the restless Frank wanted to do something different. He wanted to cycle from Perth to Sydney the hard way.

On the eve of his departure from Fremantle in Western Australia, Birtles, who interestingly enough described himself to newspaper reporters as an artist and designer, gave a brief interview. 'It is ten years since I first left Victoria; my native state. During the whole time I have been a wanderer. For the last five years I have been in South Africa, and have travelled all over that country with the constabulary. I did a good deal of road-racing, and also crossed the Great Karoo desert from Calvinia to Naaupoort, a distance of nearly 800 miles. I am ambitious to try a long trip through Australia, and expect to reach Sydney in two to three months.'

It was then reported that 'Birtles will leave the railway at Laverton, proceeding through the unexplored portion of Central Australia to the overland telegraph line near Alice Springs, after which he will go through Adelaide, Ballarat, and Melbourne to Sydney. He has the latest information from the Survey Department regarding the route and water supply.'

Whatever information Frank had taken onboard from the Survey Department was either wrong or he simply ignored it. Frank was heading off in the blistering Western Australian summer, utilising the longer daylight hours and banking on an insignificant chance of rain. To ride a bicycle in an arc across the continent at this time of year was suicidal. The temperature at the tin-constructed goldmining town of Laverton on the edge of the Great Victoria Desert could reach 47 degrees Celsius, and the summer of 1906–07 turned out to be one of the hottest ever recorded.

Frank might have cycled across the Great Karoo, but his experience in the African desert was nothing like what he was about to face heading across Australia. He set off from the Esplanade in Fremantle on Boxing Day wearing a broad-brimmed hat, short-sleeved shirt and trousers hacked off at the

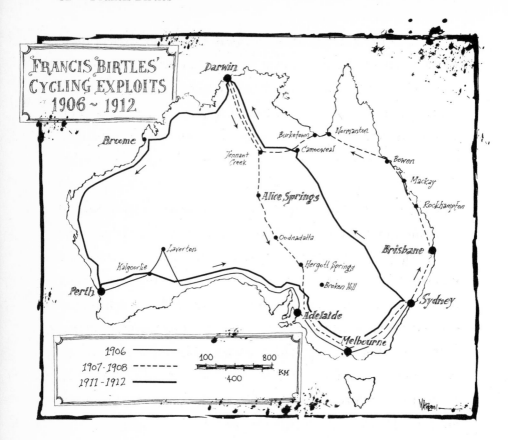

FRANCIS BIRTLES'
CYCLING EXPLOITS
1906 ~ 1912

1906 ——————
1907-1908 - - - - - -
1911-1912 ——————

100   800
400   KM

knees to cycle his way 1,000 kilometres north-east to Laverton, from where he struck out into the wilderness, confident of finding water at Minnie's Creek.

After five days riding through the heat, sand and spinifex, Frank arrived at the creek to discover it was bone-dry. He made for an Aboriginal well and discovered it too was waterless. After eleven days without finding a drop of water Frank, dehydrated and exhausted, limped back into Laverton's main street.

Cyclists gambled on finding water. For the same amount of water consumed by a pedestrian covering 40 kilometres, a cyclist could cover up to 160 kilometres. This ability to cover ground at such a rate meant cyclists would risk achieving distances they would never ordinarily consider attempting. However, if there was a mechanical failure beyond repair, an overlanding cyclist could find himself in a situation from which he might never recover. A 1909 report described how 'a cyclist had missed his way on the left bank, struck inland along a road which petered out in a back paddock, and had been found later lying dead of thirst with his clothes around him.'

After recuperating in Laverton for a few days, Frank decided to abandon his plan to cycle to Alice Springs, instead heading south for Eucla on the Great Australian Bight. It would be a lonely and dangerous ride. He reached the tiny goldmining town of Kurnalpi, some 300 kilometres from Laverton, and pressed on to a rock hole known as Gardunia, where he was able to scrounge a little water that lasted him another five days. But from here his luck ran out. There was no water anywhere. Frank had no option but to try and make it back to Gardunia and then return to Kurnalpi.

Whatever he experienced on the journey back certainly affected him. 'I had hoped to find water but there was none,' Frank wrote. 'There was nothing for it but to make back for Gardunia. I can't describe that journey. I could not obtain relief at the few rock holes along the way, because those that were not bone-dry were filled with the festering bodies of rabbits.' Finally reaching Gardunia, he was able to camp there for a few days, eking out a few pints of water before the long trip back to Kurnalpi.

Twice he'd cheated death in the desert. Yet, in what was to become a trademark character trait, these setbacks merely strengthened Frank's resolve even further. This time he was play- ing it safe, following the camel-train route south to Norseman and striking out to reach Eucla. Eventually regaining his confidence, he veered away from the coast to make for Port Augusta. Frank wrote that he was dealing with the problems of loneliness and the difficulties of the desert. However, his hardships were about to become worse.

Frank was riding headlong into a plague of march flies that attacked his face so fiercely he was almost rendered blind. In agony and unable to travel, Frank was forced to lay up for several days, the exposed parts of his body, face and head covered with sacking. Frank plastered his eyes with a poultice of flour and water mixed with diluted permanganate of potash.

•

On reaching Port Augusta, the worst of Frank's journey was over. The greatest obstacle he'd encounter was the occasional flood here and there, but he was never too far from help should he need it. Yet he'd been lucky to survive the desert, and he knew it. The key to overlanding was simple – never stop. 'No matter what happens, be it rain, dust, wind, missed waterhole, breakdown or sickness itself, the overlander must keep moving, for delay may mean death. Is it any wonder then that I caution intending travellers to think well before they rue, to get to know the difficulties that may beset them and the best means of overcoming them? For, truly, the man who attempts, single-handed, to dare the dangers of the desert must take his courage in both hands and be prepared to take his chance.'

He was now cycling through European-inhabited Australia, and from Adelaide to Melbourne he simply plugged away, until he finally reached the outskirts of Sydney. On 9 May 1908, having spent 113 days cycling across Australia, Frank arrived at Sydney Town Hall where he was met by his mother and his brother Clive, and feted by officials from New South Wales' premier cycling organisation, the League of Wheelmen. 'On his arrival Birtles was welcomed by Messrs. Allan McDougal and Alick McNicoll (vice presidents of the League of Wheelmen). There was also a host of cyclists present to pay their tribute to the plucky rider on the completion of his arduous task,' reported the *Sydney Morning Herald*. Frank was presented with a brand-new Davies-Franklin bicycle with a plaque fixed to the frame commemorating his ride.

After a momentary delay, during which the overlander was besieged with enquiries as to his trip, an adjournment was made to the premises of the Griffith Brothers Tea Rooms, where they 'gave Birtles a hearty reception and congratulated him on his meritorious performance of riding from the Indian Ocean to the Pacific Ocean'. McDougal launched into a stirring speech, pronouncing Frank's ride as 'being one of the most important that had been performed anywhere'. McDougal then went just that bit further. He was of the opinion that 'The time was not far distant when the military authorities would recognise the great services that were possible to be conducted by wheelmen in case war broke out.' Frank was glowing. That he was being feted by the vice-president of Sydney's League of Wheelmen as a pioneer cyclist to whom the military authorities might turn in case of war was unimaginable praise. But it made sense; Frank fitted the bill precisely – the vital Boer War scout, hardy bushman, intrepid cyclist. It started him thinking. He had a role to play in Australia's development – he'd head out to be the eyes and ears for the Australian people.

To officially complete his ride from ocean to ocean, Frank cycled down to Bondi Beach. The journey was over, and he was now back in the real world, the 'civilised' world. Yet for Frank, visiting Australia's most famous beach was somewhat of an anticlimax, as far removed from the imposing, grand expanses of the outback as he could imagine. He didn't fit in here. Bustling city life seemed all so pointless when compared to adventure in the big-sky country. Here, the majestic Pacific Ocean, once the domain of explorers like Cook and Tasman, was merely a backdrop for a colourless, working-class suburb. Bondi, with its ponderous, whining trams trundling in and out of the terminus, the coarse yell of the rabbit-oh, and the heap of rabbits lifeless on the back of his lumbering wagon. Where rent-collectors knocked on the doors of the dull identical bungalows lining Curlewis Street with their grey paling fences squaring off tiny backyards.

It was where skew-whiff clothes props were plonked alongside tiny outside wash-houses, where grim housewives tended enormous boiling coppers scalding nightshirts clean. People led depressing lives. Blokes staggered home from the Royal having long finished their shift at the shunting yards at Eveleigh or the docks at Woolloomooloo, or one of the breweries in the city. Families – arguing mums and dads with tribes of howling ungrateful kids – whose sole experience of Australia was this miserable place. This was not the world for Francis Birtles. He was not going to die one of the mob.

As he said, he possessed 'the desire to do and dare something outside the humdrum limits of city life'. Simply to survive a bicycle ride across the desolate and merciless expanse that was Australia in 1906 would surely be enough to put anyone off attempting a reprise of such a high-risk adventure. But for Frank the alternative of 'settling down' was unthinkable. In hindsight, his first ride across the continent could be viewed as irresponsible, dangerous and in some ways just plain insane. But somehow or other Frank survived, and got away with it.

4

Branching Out

On his arrival in Sydney, Frank had received a taste of something that would set him on the path for undertaking even riskier missions for the next 20 years: fame. Suddenly everyone wanted to know him. In one long bicycle ride, he'd travelled more than 6,000 kilometres, and from being a bloody fool to becoming a hero. Certainly what he'd achieved had seen him championed by the hordes of fellow Australian cyclists who greeted him on the outskirts of Sydney; he was feted by politicians, and had now become the hot topic for conversation among the wider public.

Frank was developing a feel for the adulation the great explorers must have received in accomplishing some arduous feat. He'd tasted fame and he liked it. How did you do it, Frank? What was it like out there, Frank? What are you planning to do next, Frank? Everyone wanted to know. They wanted to know . . . Surely Frank, with his boundless enthusiasm, his keen observational eye, his ability to write and draw, his fascination with photography and his love of the lonely lands, could tell a decent story. He could unlock the secrets of the interior and bring them back for the public to see. He began to devise a sequel to his first great ride.

Frank returned to Fitzroy in Melbourne only to be bitterly reminded of how cruel life was in the slums. A police report read: 'Frank Birtles, cyclist, "Valinda", Westgarth-street, North Fitzroy, reports stolen from the Melbourne Bicycle Club, Collins-street, Melbourne, on the 11th inst., a Davies-Franklin bicycle, 21-inch frame, several transfers on it; "Lily and Forget-me-not" on enamel, nickel points, fluted forks, triple crown, Kelly reversible handle bars, sliding back stay, one-eighth inch roller chain, BSA parts, Brooks B 120 spring saddle, Dunlop handmade tires, name plate on top bar with "Presented to Francis Birtles in memory of his perilous ride into and across the Great Victorian Desert" on it. Value £25.' This was typical of life in the city. Every time you did anything of note someone would stick the shiv between your ribs.

The theft only strengthened Frank's resolve. Frank's heart and mind were still out in the never-never. There was something about Australia's dead heart that had truly captivated him – more so than the wilds of Africa ever did. Something mysterious out there excited him. No doubt some of the intrigue was due to the raw, stark and strange beauty of the wilderness, which appealed to his artist's eye. And its loneliness beguiled him.

But there was more to it for Frank. He could see white Australia's future out in this ancient land. All that incalculable space lying empty within the Australian interior, as yet untapped for agriculture, for industry, waiting for Australia's as yet unrealised burgeoning population – it all made sense.

That's what was needed out there: a new, growing population. A white population.

'Since the immigration movement, the Defence of Northern Australia, and the peopling of the Northern Territory became live questions,' he wrote, 'the thought had often occurred to me that it would be a good thing if someone would bring the matter down to a practical basis by exploring the districts under discussion, and finding out the possibilities of planting a white population in the northern lands that lay between us and those Asiatic hordes who might at any moment swarm across the Torres Straits and invade our unguarded shores.'

Around Australia this was the hot topic. Only three years earlier, the Japanese – caricatured in local political cartoons as dumpy, bespectacled opportunists ridiculously attired in polished top hats and tails – had proven themselves to be a formidable fighting force when they destroyed the Russian fleet at Port Arthur on the eastern coast of China. The annihilation of a European fleet by an upstart Asian naval force mortified Australians. Japan was shaping up as a worrisome presence in the Pacific. How could the minuscule white population dotted sporadically along the Australian coast hope to contend with an aggressive and malevolent Japanese navy on the warpath?

Frank Birtles was going to cycle out into the wilderness, work out how Australia should defend itself, and report back. That's what a Boer War scout did. Reconnoitre and report. He made it clear his self-proposed findings would be impartial, being '. . . neither retained by the Government nor refreshed by the Opposition, I set out as a freelance, paying my own expenses and looking for no reward beyond the satisfaction of enjoying myself in a somewhat unique fashion, and incidentally, of contributing a quota, from personal observation, towards the solving of the "White Australia equation".'

While such motivation might seem a bit on the extremist side in the 21st century, a white Australia was favoured enormously around the time of Federation. Australia's first Prime Minister, Edmund Barton, was a particularly enthusiastic supporter. Advertisements for soap powder at the time parodied Barton, depicting a caricature of him on the newly formed bench of the High Court, with the caption, 'The Highest Authorities Agree, Velvet Soap Washes Linen Snow White'. Race and colour were ready-made issues for galvanising a white British Australian public – a society demanding adequate defence. Frank was going to head north ostensibly to see first-hand the landing zones for foreign invaders.

Without realising it, Frank's bicycle expedition journey up through the wilds of northern Australia would be another part of an ever-expanding training ground for his later adventures. He'd recently had his baptism of fire through the desert, and now he was to extend his education by conquering the tropics. He'd experience an altogether different, forbidding adventure – Aboriginal tribes, wet seasons, Barcoo fever, bushfires, sharks, crocodiles, snakes – and along the way he'd encounter the motor car.

This new journey would pick up where the previous one finished. Starting in Sydney, he'd cycle up through Newcastle, Brisbane, Townsville, Cairns, Normanton, and Burketown, the Gulf of Carpentaria, across the Roper River, Port Darwin, then south to Alice Springs, Oodnadatta, Adelaide, Mount Gambier, Hamilton, Warrnambool, Melbourne, Albury and Sydney. A distance of almost 13,000 kilometres.

'Some encouraged, others commiserated, a few derided, many gave me what they called "a bit of good advice",' wrote Frank, 'and nearly every one called me affectionately, "old man". It was, "Look here, old man!" and, "I'll tell you what, old man!" until I began to feel quite patriarchal notwithstanding my twenty-five years.' Despite Frank's assurances that he was undertaking the journey at his own expense, this ride was in reality shaping up as his first true commercial travelling enterprise. Frank had made an arrangement with the NSW Bookstall Company to write a book of his adventures on his return. He also received a small stipend to gather information for the Government Map Compiler, which supplied him with an aneroid barometer.

Frank would test specific mountain heights along the way, a task he regarded as money for jam. He was also given a cyclometer for measuring the travelled distance between various points. Sydney cycle retailers Bennett & Wood presented him with a three-speed Royal Speedwell road-racing bike fitted with a front hub brake and Dunlop canvas-lined tyres. Photographic suppliers Harringtons gave him a 'postcard camera' – a Number 3 Ensign camera, and Ensign daylight-loading rolled films.

The new idea of film in rolls had an advantage over the use of cumbersome glass plates – which Frank nevertheless took with him – particularly when your entire world is carried on the saddle. 'When you are compelled to carry your house on your back like a snail, you soon learn the things you can do without,' wrote Frank, 'and so the cyclist setting out on a lengthy tour must reduce his wants to a minimum and exercise not a little ingenuity as to his packing powers.'

Frank's kit consisted of a bronze metal tank fitted underneath the bicycle's cross-member capable of holding 5 litres of water, a light waterproof sleeping bag lined with beaver fur, a Winchester lever-action rifle with 200 rounds of ammunition, his camera, with 200 exposures sealed and waterproofed, rolled film, waterproof canvas bags for flour, tea, sugar, etc., pocket compass, folding double billy can – one for cooking, one for tea – concentrate foods, Bovril, grapenuts, soup tablets, pea-sausage soup, chocolate, medicines, permanganate of potash, cayenne pepper, quinine, boracic acid, charts, the aneroid barometer, cyclometer and compass, matches in waterproof cases, wide felt hat, flannel singlet, woollen guernsey, woollen racing knickers, woollen cycling hose, and 'long topped boots to stay the legs and help keep sand and water out'. All up, the total weight of the outfit was 40 kilograms, of which the bike weighed 12 kilograms.

At three o'clock on the afternoon of 21 August 1907 Frank saddled up outside Bennett & Wood's shop in Market Street. Fellow cyclists and boater-hatted well-wishers had gathered to give him a rousing sendoff. 'I was snapshotted from every point of the compass . . .' he wrote. 'I was shaken by the hand by men I had never seen before, as well as by mine own familiar friends, until I began to wonder if these demonstrations were meant for me personally or merely intended to honour British pluck and endurance, of which I happened, for the moment, to be the representative.'

Frank might have tasted fame, but now he possessed it. Nevertheless, he had his reservations about the upcoming ride. 'I was not without confidence that I would be successful,' he wrote 'as my previous rides had put me in good form, but there remained that slight tremor from around the heart that footballers know just the moment before the kickoff.'

There was no shortage of kindred spirits mounted on bicycles ready to cycle with him to Parramatta on the outskirts of Sydney. 'Nowhere in my travels have I met with a finer spirit of camaraderie than amongst the cyclists of Australia,' Frank wrote. From Parramatta Frank turned north towards the Hawkesbury River, crossing it on the punt at Wiseman's Ferry to head along the steep gravel of the convict-built Great Northern Road.

The journey towards Queensland was fairly uneventful, yet a couple of times he came a cropper – once when the brake-line slipped while descending a mountain, and another time misjudging what he thought was a fairly insignificant creek crossing which turned out to be more like the Marianas Trench. 'If the authorities should ever introduce bicycle hurdle-racing I feel confident even after that short experience, I could qualify and win.'

He cycled across the border into Queensland and made for Ipswich, talking a 'shortcut' over the mountains. 'The road has not been used for 20 years and is consequently in a vile condition. Ruts or water courses rather 3 yards deep cross the road while boulders are the rule not the exception.' The further north he rode the warmer and more tropical the climate became. The foliage grew dense and became greener. There were stagnant lagoons and the dull sound of bullfrogs. And in the long grass, his greatest fear, snakes.

Frank described the discovery of an enormous snake lying across the track ahead that frightened the living daylights out of him. He found an equally enormous stick. 'I had never killed a snake before, but I knew the theory of the short, sharp stroke that breaks the back and I hastened to put it into practice accordingly. I am afraid, however, that anyone looking on would have come to the conclusion that I was an apprentice at the job, for I brought down that stick with a welt that would have floored an ox, at the same time emitting a blood-curdling yell that would have done credit to one of Fenimore Cooper's dusky chieftains. I struck him fair in the middle of the back and he doubled up and performed a wriggling somersault in the air, whilst I jumped back a dozen yards or so, nervously clutching my club lest he might require another bludgeon stroke to finish him. But, as he fell, so he lay, and on risking a nearer approach, I noticed that his head had evidently been crushed by a wagon-wheel and that he had been dead for days.'

Frank took on the role of what was popularly known as a 'sundowner' – a traveller who'd turn up unannounced at a homestead at sundown, just in time for a feed. Sometimes 'sundowners' were well-received by those living on remote properties, desperate for news from the outside world. But at other times, when settlers had hardly enough to feed themselves, these 'sundowners' were a pain in the neck.

'Curiously enough the attitude of the people one meets out back furnishes the greatest contrast of all,' Frank wrote. 'In some parts the visitor is welcomed with open arms and treated to the best of everything. In other parts he is looked upon as an intruder, treated with cold suspicion, refused food, and sometimes even the cup of cold water, notwithstanding the fact that he proffers payment for the things he asks.'

Frank pedalled further north, where not far from Gympie he suddenly found himself trapped in a bushfire. 'Red-hot cinders were everywhere, and I had not gone far before one stuck to my front tyre and burned it through. Still I drove on, but a few minutes later my back tyre burst and I was forced to dismount and review the situation. Turning back was hopeless, for there the path had been entirely swallowed up, and burning limbs were crackling and falling in all directions. As I pushed my machine in front of me the soles of my boots began to pick up, and hold, lumps of glowing charcoal, a thirst, that, at another time, would have been priceless, parched my tongue and I must admit I felt scared.' With two burst tyres, and his hair singed, Frank finally made it the last 80 kilometres to Gympie, the clattering of the steel rims on the main street generating tremendous attention. He stayed several days to recover.

If narrowly escaping a bushfire wasn't testing enough, Frank then encountered a vast blue-bush swamp – a scrubby, waterlogged depression that is more or less a wetlands drain – stretching for miles. Blue-bush swamps were generally regarded as virtually impossible to traverse, and Frank claimed this one was the worst he'd ever seen. The swamp had all the viscosity of quicksand. 'Before I had gone ten yards I sank knee-deep in white clay and water, and, on endeavouring to extricate myself, I found that in getting out of the bog, I had also got out of my boots, leaving them eighteen inches under the surface. With considerable difficulty I pushed my machine over to a blue bush near, and, laying it down, returned to fish out my buried boots.'

This was easier said than done, for the tighter he tugged, the deeper he sank until 'It seemed to me that it would be better to lose my boots than my body, for I was fast going down to perdition. At last with a final effort I managed to dredge the oozy deep and bring up my bluchers, filled to the brim with clay and water. It took me some little time to scoop out the filling, and then, for further safety, I tied the salvage round my neck and fairly floundered towards my bike.'

In order to retrieve the bicycle Frank decided to take the plunge. 'I went from bad to worse, until at last I went to jump up to my chin in slimy, lukewarm water, holding on to the handles with difficulty. I tiptoed along for a hundred yards or so with lips tightly closed and nose just above the bog, when, to my delight, I felt my feet on firmer ground.' Everything he owned was now soaking wet, including his camera, food and clothing. His legs were bleeding from the attacks of leeches and his feet cut open by sharp sticks. He covered the wounds with clay to keep the flies off, 'but the heat of the sun soon cracked the clay and I suffered from festering sores for weeks after'.

Clearly, his adventures, gruelling as they were, were never dull. One afternoon, he rounded a bend and chanced on what he thought was a litter of wild dingo pups. They were, however, dogs belonging to a group of Aboriginal women, who shrieked when Frank's bicycle startled the pups, something the cyclist suddenly realised he should never have done. Frank then hurtled through a band of Aboriginal men, who were evidently on a hunting expedition, as they were fully armed.

'Attracted by the howling of the pups and the screaming of their women folk they stood like statues, with spears poised and eyes ablaze, awaiting my oncoming. It did not take me long to grasp the situation, and, concluding that a flash past would be my best move. I put my head down and pedalled for all I was worth. The rush rather upset their calculations, for although fully a dozen spears were sent whizzing after me and the sound of their peculiar "singing" sent a few shivers down my spine I escaped unscathed.' But not entirely. One spear shot clean through the spokes of the front wheel, snapped and rebounded, smashing into Frank's arm. 'I was hardly aware of the stroke,' he wrote, 'but later on I had occasion to rub the place to make it well and to thank my stars that things were no worse. I rode fully fifty miles before I camped that night, and as a precautionary measure I lit no fire, but was content to have a cold tea.'

Frank eventually pedalled into Croydon on the Gulf of Carpentaria, arriving to witness the town smashed apart by a willy-willy – a tornado that appeared as if from nowhere. 'A tall, thin column of dirt sucked up like a waterspout at sea came careering down the centre of the street, playing pranks with every loose thing that it met on its way and causing considerable commotion among the terrified shopkeepers.

'It remained for some few minutes dancing a hornpipe in front of my hotel, at a cross street, as if undecided which way to go, all the while whirling like a dancing dervish, sucking up straw, paper, dust, and gaining in volume every minute. It was most fascinating to watch, but woe betide those who may be caught in the maelstrom. Down the street it went, forming a thin, yellow column a couple of hundred feet high and carrying everything before it. By this time the whole town was on the *qui vive* and crowding in its wake to watch its career.

'It went up another street at right angles and then made a straight dart for "Chinatown". I followed as quickly as I could and got on to an hotel verandah where I had an uninterrupted view. As it passed the back premises I got a fair idea of its power. It just seemed to touch a stable and up went the roof exposing two terrified horses inside. The great sheets of iron, gyrating and whirling, were sucked up like paper, threatening death or destruction to anything they might meet. With a roar like a furnace the column swept on towards the miserable Chinese tenements on the outskirts of the town. No-one there seemed to be aware of the approaching fury, for not a soul was about. Suddenly roof after roof went up in the air, the alarmed Chinese flew hither and thither distractedly, believing their last hour had come. They were too far off for us to hear their screams, but I was told that they were heartrending. In less time than it takes to tell, the "willy willy" had completely devastated the place and passed on to the bush, leaving a trail of wreck and ruin behind it.'

Finally, Darwin was close – he could smell it. 'I was within a few miles of my northern destination, and the fresh, salt air from the ocean seemed to put new life into me. Four miles out a party of cyclists met me and escorted me into Palmerston, or Port Darwin. It is a town of alternatives in more ways than one. On our arrival we were welcomed by the other members of the club and after "several washing-the-dust-downs", we disbanded for dinner.'

Frank's few palate-cleansers with the locals is unusual. He hardly ever drank – and certainly not beer. He just didn't like it much. Not that he was a complete teetotaller. Frank appreciated a decent wine, especially a German riesling, and later in life occasionally mentioned trying moonshine, but in Darwin – sometimes rated the beer drinking capital of the world – he might have had no option.

Frank, the bicycle-mounted national affairs commentator, began his investigation of the defence of northern Australia, warning, 'The state of affairs, as far as the invasion is concerned, should cause our statesmen to look around for a remedy and, if necessary, appoint a commission to inquire into the problems connected with white settlement in the tropics. The peopling of the far north is really one of our most pressing national questions, and we may well wake up to the fact that it is a question beset with many and peculiar difficulties.

'Leaving Port Darwin accompanied by some local sports, who came out a few miles just to see me off the premises, as it were, I set out for the journey down through the heart of Australia to Adelaide. Owing to my recent illness I found that ten miles a day was quite enough travelling in the hot sun, and it just began to be borne in on me that I had hardly the fitness of the proverbial fiddle.

'At Tennant Creek I was most hospitably received. I had a good "clean up", which was a longed-for luxury, and a splendid meal of beef and vegetables, after which I had a look at the garden. The vegetables were growing as well as ever I had seen them anywhere, and I came to the conclusion that even the desert will grow anything when water is obtainable.' Yet viable agriculture wasn't the only surprise in the desert.

'Snakes, death adders, and centipedes were plentiful around these parts. Whenever an opening offered I killed what I could. I had learned a lot since my first adventure in the snake line and could now execute commissions with promptitude and despatch. The biggest snake I bagged was a nine-footer, which I met near Murrundi and which I snuffed out with half a railway sleeper. I "snapped" him as soon as I got him to remain steady.

'It is remarkable that every snake I encountered made for the bicycle. Perhaps the glitter and silent running appealed to them.'

Sixty kilometres south of Tennant Creek, Frank stumbled on something extraordinary sitting in the long grass. A motor car, of all things. Out here? It was indeed a large machine, bogged firmly to the axles. The ground had dried around it like cement. The car looked as if it had been abandoned for some time. Its paintwork had dulled and it was showing signs of rust. The radiator had a badge depicting a lion and a crown with the words 'Talbot – London'. Toolboxes fitted to the running boards had been broken open and clearly everything in it had been pinched. Birds had made nests within the car. The seats had split along the seams and some of the horsehair stuffing was coming through. Who the hell would drive a car out into the dead heart? They needed their head read. Frank remounted and continued pedalling south.

'Most of the "creeks" in this part have no water in them. Barrow Creek is one of that kind, and is mentioned here because some years ago it was the scene of a terrible tragedy, a number of post officials having been foully murdered by hostile blacks. The graves of the unfortunate men may be seen about a hundred yards away from the telegraph station. The "hands" on an overland telegraph station generally consist of the telegraph master, an operator, and one or two line repairers.

'These men lead a life of lonely monotony; the work is not hard, but the dullness is terribly so. Most of them become students of nature and know their surroundings like a book. As a class they know more about our native tribes than any "learned" body of savants to be found in Australia, and a more kindly lot of men does not exist. They were of infinite assistance to me, for they gave me most valuable information about the route, advising me what to avoid and what to avail myself of, besides wiring down from station to station that I was on the way, with the happy result that on reaching the next stage I was an expected and welcome guest.

'When a "break" occurs, packhorses are brought in, food and water supplies strapped on, and in a few hours "the flying gang" is well under way. [Indeed, occasionally when outback travellers found themselves in dire situations they would cut the line to be rescued by the gangers.] It often happens that the repairers have to inspect scores of miles of line before the damage is located, and they may be away from headquarters for weeks at a time. The telegraph line does not run straight, as many people imagine, but follows along the top of the ridges as far as possible, in order to avoid the boggy country, which in the wet season is practically impassable.'

Frank pressed further south; the meeting with Dutton, Aunger and Allchurch had jolted him into realising the methods of outback travel were now rapidly changing. The car would soon outstrip the bicycle which had been outstripping the old-time ways of transportation.

'There are approximately a thousand camels carrying goods up, most of them driven by Afghans and, in some cases, owned by them as well. These Afghans are allowed to carry firearms and have their revolvers stuck conspicuously in their belts. Relying on their arms they treat the natives badly, and more than once the white people have had to interfere to stop trouble . . .

'At Charlotte Waters I was out on to the gibber country; big, open, stony plains stretched away as far as the eye could see, the "Stony Desert" of the early explorers. The general colour of the country is a blood-red, and the glitter of the sunlight on the stones is very trying to the eyes. At Oodnadatta I was once more into civilisation and on to the railway line. I passed across the southern end of Lake Eyre, with its white, gleaming expanse of salt. Here I gathered some petrified shells (one of the curiosities of this country) and inspected the natural artesian mineral waters. Some parts of the country are twenty-eight feet below sea level.

'But is there is little mystery about the road from Melbourne to Sydney, and, as many cyclists have traversed the route before, giving descriptions more or less graphic, it is sufficient for the purpose . . . to say that I duly covered the ground that was necessary to complete my record round and arrived in Sydney.

'I had thus covered a distance of eight thousand three hundred miles and been 13 months on the trip.'

•

In Sydney, Frank finished writing his manuscript and sent it to the publishers, the resultant book titled *Lonely Lands; Through the Heart of Australia*. He started earning a living writing articles for newspapers and periodicals. Yet Birtles had by now become well and truly addicted to travel and the 'hard life', and before long he was cycling alone out into the 'camel country' of western Queensland.

Later, as public interest in Francis Birtles grew, in 1911 the Gaumont Film Company sent Frank with cine-cameraman Robert Primmer on a bicycle-driven cinematographic mission from Sydney to Darwin, carrying a whopping and unwieldy 35mm Gaumont cinecamera and tripod, 50,000 feet of film, a Kodak box camera, and a Hawkeye stereoscopic camera.

Primmer, the cinematographer, taught Frank how to use the cinematograph and moving pictures suddenly opened up a world of possibilities for visually-oriented Frank. The film they shot included dramatised action between white settlers and Aborigines. Frank was even given permission – 'at his own risk' – to film from a platform fixed to the front of a steam locomotive as it ran along the Darwin to Pine Creek line. This was the 1911 equivalent of Imax.

While in Darwin, Frank picked up a blue-heeler pup he named Dinkum, which would become the first in a long line of canine companions he took with him wherever he travelled in Australia.

Frank still had a burning desire to complete his circumnavigation of the continent by bicycle – on 13 May 1911 he farewelled Primmer in Darwin and pedalled with Dinkum to follow the west coast – into 'unknown territory' that took him through Broome to return to Fremantle. He was back at his familiar starting place to once again cross the continental divide and he and Dinkum tore across it to Adelaide, beating his own record. He cycled eighteen hours per day, reducing his time to 20 days, 12 hours, 35 minutes. It was a typical Frank Birtles ride – long and gruelling – and not without drama. On the way, he drank from a poisoned waterhole, making him violently ill for two days. 'Instead of a dingo they caught an overlanding cyclist, though fortunately without any permanent effects,' Frank commented wryly in an interview.

His arrival at Martin Place in Sydney was nothing short of sensational. He was a natural sporting hero. The Gaumont Film he'd made with Primmer, *Across Australia with Francis Birtles, the Intrepid Overlander*, opened in both Sydney and Melbourne to huge audiences. Frank was onto something. 'It is surprising,' he said in an interview, 'that while other countries have been ransacked for cinematograph subjects, the interior of Australia has scarcely been touched.' He'd fix that.

5

Ferguson and Brush 1912

For the everyday turn-of-the-century Australian, understanding the motor car was a quantum leap from understanding the bicycle. Certainly the bicycle had given men and women an excellent introduction to basic mechanics: a pedal turning a sprocket which turned a chain, which turned another sprocket, which turned a wheel – it was all easy to understand. Furthermore, you could watch it all happening – it was simple to comprehend the cause and effect of pedalling a bicycle.

But the internal combustion engine required an altogether different level of mechanical appreciation. Other than hand-cranking a car to start it, there was no overtly physical requirement from the operator; propulsion didn't come from personal exertion. What made a motor car move was simply a mystery contained under the bonnet. Propulsion was created by burning a liquid fuel inside cylinders bored within a cast iron engine, this ignition creating rapid, small explosions which then forced pistons contained within the cylinders to move up and down. These moving pistons were bolted to a crankshaft, which then turned a driveshaft connected to a differential, which turned the axles, which turned the rear wheels. For those accustomed to bicycles it was a lot to comprehend.

In 1908, two months after Birtles, Dutton, Aunger and Allchurch had boiled the billy north of Alice Springs on the lonely overland telegraph track, an American inventor from Michigan named Henry Ford unveiled a motor car with the rather unimaginative title of 'Model T'. Ford's car arrived unannounced in the British, European and American automotive market.

For its time the Model T was extraordinary in almost every way – four-cylindered, well-made, powerful, simple, robust, reliable, easy to drive and, above all, affordable. That made it absolutely nothing like the motor car as the world knew it. The Model T caused automotive manufacturers around the globe to squirm in their seats, forcing them to rethink almost every aspect of their business: quality control, pricing, speed of manufacture; and just how on earth they were going to combat this juggernaut of world-dominating Americana.

In 1912, realising that the Model T was gaining an enormously strong foothold in Australia – particularly in the bush – the Sydney office of the little-known Canada Cycle & Motor Company put forward an audacious and eyebrow-raising plan to push their own little car into the limelight. They were the agents for the American-built Brush Runabout – an attractive yet rudimentary two-seater car powered by a ten-horsepower motor with one cylinder containing one piston. In America it sold for just $475.

It was, in a word, basic. No windscreen, no doors, four flimsy mudguards and two running boards. The machine was tiny, to say the least – a driver and passenger sitting side by side looked uncomfortable. The motor had one spark plug from which one wire connected to a magneto, which generated an electrical spark to ignite the fuel, and from there another wire hooked up to the ignition switch. If something went wrong with this wire while the car was running, you couldn't turn the thing off.

Like all petrol-driven cars of the era, the little Brush required starting with a crank handle, an overly physical black art that (thanks to the modern electric starter motor) has mercifully faded with the passage of time. Simply starting a car could be a dangerous exercise when the crank handle could suddenly fly back in the opposite direction to which it was being turned, potentially breaking thumbs and wrists.

The ingenious Brush Car Company was well aware of the potential of this idiosyncrasy to ruin motorists' piano-playing careers, and designed the engine to rotate in a counterclockwise direction, meaning that if the handle suddenly took on a life of its own it would pull away from the cranker's hand. Once started, the little Brush, with its one piston flying up and down, would shake like a wet dog, shuddering and juddering, its mudguards quivering, its hinged bonnet shivering. Owners would regularly have to tighten things up and strap things down after a simple drive.

The car had coil springs on each corner, and the rear wheels were driven by what were fundamentally two oversized bicycle chains. Its quirkiest feature was that it had wooden axles made from American hickory, and a timber chassis, which capped off an altogether awkward picture of a motor car you'd have reservations about travelling to the corner shop in. If it had just a bit more power, it could possibly match a modern ride-on lawnmower.

The Brush company had a motto – 'Brush – it sweeps all before it'. Some wag invented another catchcry for the little Brush – 'Wooden axles, wooden chassis, wooden go.' Nevertheless, the Canada Cycle & Motor Company was prepared to send its own very capable Sydney-based mechanic, Syd Ferguson, on an extraordinary mission – to drive a Brush car 4,000 kilometres across Australia, from Perth to Sydney. This would be the first latitudinal crossing of Australia by motor car, and a phenomenal publicity coup for Brush Cars if Ferguson pulled it off. It would also be nothing short of a miracle.

Harry Dutton and Murray Aunger's south–north journey from Adelaide to Darwin in 1908 was one thing, but this west–east proposition was considered completely out of the question for a motorised expedition. The problems seemed countless and insurmountable. For the best part of the drive between the Indian Ocean and the Pacific Ocean, there was no road whatsoever. No water, no communications – and the none-too-small issue of the reputedly impassable 600 kilometres of drifting sand between Norseman and Eucla on the edge of the Great Australian Bight. No motor car – let alone a diminutive, ridiculous contraption like the Brush – could hope to get through that.

Nevertheless, Syd Ferguson was charged with somehow making this extraordinary mission succeed. There was no argument that Ferguson was an expert and resourceful mechanic and a first-rate pioneer motorist, yet the Canada Cycle & Motor Company was insistent that he take a competent navigator for the expedition. As far as they were concerned, there was of course only one person capable of the task – the bloke who'd travelled by bicycle that very route, that very year.

By 1912, Birtles claimed to have cycled across the continent six times within the previous six years, clocking up more than 110,000 kilometres. He was also becoming something of an early 20th century Australian celebrity and entertainer. He had even lugged heavy still and cinematograph cameras and ancillary equipment with him on his bicycle travels to photograph and film outback sights ordinary Australians never thought they'd see.

Frank was actually turning a quid from his adventures. He was now regaling theatre audiences with his tales from the outback, showing magic lantern slides and genuine moving pictures he'd filmed way out in the never-never. Posters depicted a photograph of the young Francis Birtles adorned with a Kitchener-esque moustache.

BIRTLES IN BRUNSWICK

Come and hear him at the LYRIC. 'No moving picture has ever made such an instantaneous hit on Australians. It will open your eyes. Under great expense, the management has engaged The Great Overlander who will relate his thrilling experiences in the wilds of Australia. Across Australia. Are Pictures Educational? See and HEAR for Yourselves. Prices as Usual.

His most recent motion picture, *Across Australia with Francis Birtles, The Intrepid Overlander*, ran for 10 days and 10 nights – a record for 1912. With it went a good deal of old-time pantomime. Crowds were amazed by these silent, flickering films which were accompanied by a repertoire of sounds – running water created by a revolving drum with a few pebbles thrown inside; sheets of sandpaper rubbed together to make the sound of a steam locomotive.

But he wasn't all show. Earlier that year, he brought Martin Place in Sydney to a standstill, where he was swamped by boater- and bowler-hat-wearing crowds congratulating him on the completion of his circumnavigation of Australia by bicycle.

He'd cycled out of Fremantle on New Year's Day and pedalled flat out from the Indian Ocean to the Pacific, reducing his own Fremantle–Melbourne–Sydney record to 31 days, 2 hours. He was one of only a handful of people who had ever circumnavigated the continent. And by 1912, he'd ridden around it twice. There was no-one on earth who better knew the places where the Canada Cycle & Motor Company wanted to send their little Brush car.

In so many ways, the inclusion of Birtles made sound commercial sense. The Canada Cycle & Motor Company made and sold – and still does to this day – bicycles. And as the Australian agent for Brush Cars, having the nation's most prominent cyclist adapting to the new ways of the automobile was a pleasant promotional opportunity. After all, the transition from manufacturing bicycles to cars was particularly common – Peugeot, De Dion-Bouton, Humber, Singer, Opel – all made and sold bicycles before building automobiles. Furthermore, the Canada Cycle & Motor Company promised they would actually pay Frank for his invaluable skills. Payment for adventure – Frank's star was on the rise.

During his recent cycling exploits, Birtles had become fully aware of the ever-increasing presence of motor cars on outback roads. The car's influence in Australia had started to take hold, particularly with the growing popularity of the Model T.

Frank knew nothing about the automobile. Even in 1912, motoring was an experience well out of the reach of the everyday Australian – particularly for an itinerant cyclist who hardly ever had two bob to rub together. Yet here was a once-in-a-lifetime opportunity for Birtles to leap from the saddle of a diamond-frame bicycle onto the running board of a whole new medium for adventure.

The Birtles–Ferguson relationship wasn't great from the start, with Syd Ferguson not convinced of the worth of including the famous cyclist in the expedition.

In Sydney, the Brush was roped up and hoisted aboard a steamer bound for Fremantle. Before undertaking the long haul west across the Great Southern Ocean, the ship stopped briefly in Melbourne, where Ferguson picked up a mascot for the expedition, a smooth-haired terrier he named Rex. Rex was an enthusiastic pup with one ear pointing up, the other down, and a patch of black over one eye. In the weeks that followed, Rex would become a great friend, particularly for Syd Ferguson when the two motorists' bonhomie started to fray.

On arrival in Western Australia, the car was unloaded onto the Fremantle dock and the serious work of preparing the Brush for the epic drive began. The tiny car was piled high, loaded up so that it almost disappeared under a mountain of gear, well beyond the realms of whatever maximum weight the manufacturers might have recommended. They'd have been hyperventilating at the thought of what Ferguson and Birtles were doing. The car itself weighed only 600 kilograms, yet it had 407 kilograms of equipment roped and strapped onto its mudguards and timber-framed bodywork.

'We had a mass of kit; petrol and oil for a thousand miles,' Birtles wrote, 'tools, spare parts, axes, shovels, bedding, food and, strapped on behind, as a sort of lifeboat in case of desperate need, was the trusty old bike. A seasoned traveller hesitates to throw away dirty water before he has clean.'

Frank was still wary about the ways of the automobile – if it all went wrong he could always cycle his way out of a catastrophe.

In the same way that Dutton and Aunger utilised the cameleers who regularly crisscrossed the outback, the expedition's co-sponsors, the Vacuum Oil Company and Dunlop Rubber, set down depots of fuel and tyres at various points along the way. The expedition's success and the pair's survival depended on Frank's navigational ability to locate these sites with his hand-held compass. The pressure was on – this expedition wasn't just Francis Birtles alone in the outback of his own volition. The whole voyage was to prove a vertical learning curve for Frank.

On the crisp, clear, sunny day of 16 March 1912, the trio set off from Perth with a slight breeze from the Indian Ocean at their backs, cruising eastward at a top speed of 30 km/h. Any faster and the radiator would boil. Rex found a happy position, sitting on a blanket roll on the running board. A length of sapling was tied from the front mudguard to the rear as a safety rail so the little dog didn't fall off. The three were embarking on a tremendous undertaking and they were well prepared. Yet, for all the gear they had lashed onto the little Brush, Ferguson and Birtles were heading 4,000 kilometres east wearing the only clothes they had.

It didn't take long before the pair had reached the outskirts of Perth. They were saying goodbye to 20th century civilisation to drive headlong into one of the world's most desolate and primitive landscapes. They were two insignificant figures and their dog, sitting on top of a fragile, sputtering contraption on the lonely track to the old goldmining town of Coolgardie, 560 kilometres east.

Here was the plan: once they'd reached Coolgardie, they would turn south-east 165 kilometres for Norseman, head directly across the Nullarbor Plain following the edge of the Great Australian Bight 750 kilometres to Eucla, then to Port Augusta in South Australia, then Broken Hill, then across western New South Wales, and over the Blue Mountains to arrive in Sydney. It sounded simple. Yet none of this had ever been attempted in a motor car before and they knew that for almost the whole journey they would hardly see anyone. They were on their own.

With all signs of civilisation gone, they were now pushing their way through overhanging scrub and other obstructions. Frank would climb out of the car to hack a path through some of the more overgrown sections, while Syd carefully negotiated the car through.

They arrived at what was more or less a cliff-top, overlooking a vast salt lake stretching to the horizon. Its sheer size was emphasised by a line of spindly white-anted timber telegraph poles below, which disappeared into the distance towards Kalgoorlie. The drop from the cliff-top to its base was severe. Somehow they needed to get the car down the cliff face and onto the lake in one piece. And once on the lake, what would happen to the car?

Birtles had ridden – and then carried – bicycles across salt lakes plenty of times before, but he wasn't sure it would work with a motor car.

They had no option but to get the car over the edge. The plan was to repack all the gear on the car to one side in the hope that would stop it overturning during the descent. Ferguson would roll the Brush forward, holding in the clutch but with the gearbox idling in reverse. Once it had dropped over the edge, he would lock the brakes and release the clutch, the wheels spinning backwards hopefully slowing the car down, and, with the brake on, skid calmly to the bottom.

The actual attempt didn't quite go to plan. Once tipped over the edge, the car rocketed uncontrollably down the hillside before finally bouncing onto the salt lake's surface, the spinning wheels busting through the crust, showering Ferguson and Birtles with a slurry of mud and salt before it sank to the axles.

'It had a crust on the surface that looked like concrete,' wrote Birtles. 'We had to off-load and carry our boxes (to hard ground) for over a mile. We cut scrub and packed it under the car, but the wheels, with their chain drive, revolved merrily.'

They came up with the idea of placing ropes around the extended hubs on the back wheels and then tying the other ends to a telegraph pole 50 metres away. When the car was placed in first gear and the wheels turned, the ropes would wind around the hubs, winching the car forward. 'The engine was set at top speed – there was a great whirring sound – two fountains of slush were thrown high in the air by the back wheels and the telegraph pole almost came up by the roots.' Probably not too many telegraph messages received between Kalgoorlie and Perth that day.

The pair pressed on, hauling the car out only for it to sink again. 'For five hours in the intense heat,' wrote Birtles, 'worried by salt dust and pestered by flies, we kept at it until, late in the afternoon, we succeeded in getting clear. Our water supply was giving out, and what little remained had to be kept for the radiator. We camped at the waterhole – but not to rest.'

Daily, thick swarms of bush flies would arrive just after the appearance of the sun and reach an infuriating crescendo lasting until sunset. They had the potential to send a man mad: 'The flies were unbearable; [they] got into our eyes, our ears, and down our necks; got into our tea, and insisted on forming part of our meal.'

The following day, it drizzled with rain. Boggy salt lake after salt lake lay ahead. If they were to keep going, they needed some clever, alternative thinking. Ferguson and Birtles decided to head for the recently built railway line linking Perth to Kalgoorlie, put the car on top of the railway tracks so that the wheels straddled the narrow-gauge rails, and jolt along over the wooden sleepers as far as they could go.

It might have been quicker going, but the railway was horrendously punishing on the little car – and dangerous. In the light rain, the slippery, mud-encrusted wheels would slide as if they'd been smeared with butter and would unexpectedly become jammed between unevenly spaced sleepers, bringing the Brush to an immediate, crashing halt, the car then needing to be jacked up and jostled around to free the wheel.

On one occasion they came close to what would have been the certain demise of the whole enterprise. In places, the railway line ran across long bridges that crossed vast saltpans. 'The mud and slime on our tyres made the car slip and bounce, each time

coming perilously close to going off the edge of the bridge. At one place a front wheel slipped down between two far-apart sleepers; we were jacking up and pushing for an hour before we got on our way again.'

At Coolgardie, they turned towards Norseman and made good time following the tracks of old camel-wagoneers, in the process inadvertently breaking the speed record for the Cobb & Co. mail run.

They called into one cattle station along the way where everyone turned out amazed to see a cloud of dust in which a motor car arrived. You can only imagine what a spectacle it must have made in remote Western Australia in 1912 to a bull-dust-covered station worker, battered bush hat, a long matted moustache, bowyangs tied around his moleskins just below the knees. Cars have always had the capacity to fascinate blokes in any location, from any era. 'So this is a motor car? By the living snakes – you're a mad couple of coves bringing it out here. But, by geez, I'd love to have a ride – you know – just to see how it goes . . .'

Just for fun, Ferguson and Birtles gave a few station hands a ride as they headed south-east. The motor car was something the locals out here had never seen before, let alone had the opportunity to ride on. 'They'd come along part of the way,' recalled Birtles. 'Some were so enthusiastic that they forgot about having to walk back; awakening to the fact with suddenness and alarm.' Not a welcome realisation on a property probably the size of Belgium.

Ahead of them now was a journey across 1,000 kilometres of limestone plateau: the Nullarbor Plain. The going was dangerous and slow. They were following the telegraph repairers' buggy tracks through thick scrub when they discovered, concealed in the long grass between the wheel ruts, huge numbers of sump-busting stumps. Birtles reckoned even 10 km/h was unsafe. If the car holed the sump out, here he would be waving farewell from the bicycle's saddle.

The going became increasingly rough. Thick, hard vegetation eventually smashed the brass headlamps to pieces and when they finally reached the sandhills, '. . . this open country caused us many an hour of digging out,' Birtles wrote. 'Cutting bushes to lay down and miles of walking in order to find out means of dodging such hills as the "Bullocky's" and other sand-ridges with boggy salt lakes between.' There was no fun in this. And the punishment on the car was beginning to take its toll. The steering arm became so bent Birtles had to start a small fire to make a forge to heat the steel so that it could be hammered back into shape.

The reality of just how vulnerable they were was beginning to set in. After some time, they realised packs of dingoes had been following their tyre tracks. At dusk the dingoes would prowl the perimeter of the camp, their howling through the desert night preventing anyone from sleeping. Rex the terrier was chained up, frantic to get at them. Ferguson and Birtles knew that if he'd been let loose the dingoes would have ripped the little dog to pieces.

The car, the miles and time moved at glacial pace. The long, monotonous days – sitting shoulder against shoulder as the Brush shuddered along, the racket of its one piston thumping up and down, the car crawling and bouncing over stones and tree roots, Ferguson constantly weaving it around stumps and rocks – raised boredom to new heights.

By now the novelty of motoring had well and truly worn off, giving rise to a degree of angst and suspicion between the two. Syd and Frank's relationship was deteriorating and had become 'prickly'. In this partnership it was Frank, as the passenger, who had to climb out of the car to open and close gates, who hacked away at scrub with a tomahawk, who cleared away rocks, who laid down the matting strips across the sand for Syd to drive over. No doubt there was an inadvertent dynamic of driver/servant brewing.

Ferguson was never entirely convinced of Birtles' navigational skills. Frank just sat there silently, occasionally waving his hand in a particular direction for Ferguson to follow. Somehow they'd missed some of the fuel depots laid down for the journey – they still had enough supplies to continue but couldn't afford to miss any more.

For days the pair motored along with no hint of conversation. At one point Ferguson couldn't stand it any longer. He hauled the car up and turned to Birtles: 'Do you know where we are? I don't want to be driving for fun.' Without a word, Birtles climbed out of the car and took six paces in front. He removed his pocket compass, looked at it and turned to Ferguson. 'We'll go two degrees to the left.' Ferguson just shook his head and put the car back into gear.

Frank was the consummate loner. He wasn't into conversation. He liked his own company and, besides, he was only riding shotgun on this expedition. This was really Syd Ferguson's voyage. Previously, people had been feting Birtles for his own record-breaking adventures. At any time he could easily unstrap his bicycle and take off, be shot of the whole motoring thing and continue doing what he knew best: cycling. This silent threat had occurred to Ferguson too. He was acutely aware of the bicycle lashed to the back of the car as Birtles' 'lifeboat' and was worried Frank might decide to cut him adrift in the desert. After all, he'd already cycled across it earlier that year – and survived.

For Ferguson, the thought of waking up one morning to find Birtles gone was terrifying. If this journey was to succeed, it needed both of them. Ferguson had no desire to die in the desert alone. One evening, while Birtles wasn't looking, Ferguson wandered around to the bicycle tied to the rear of the car. He removed the crank-pin which held the pedals on. He put it into his waistcoat pocket.

Birtles wasn't going anywhere.

Nullarbor is Latin for 'no trees'. It was an understatement – they might as well have been on the moon. Day after day, the little car soldiered on, just a speck on this never-ending plain. Then, in the stupor of this endless drive, Ferguson suddenly jumped, switching the car's ignition off after an excruciatingly loud, grinding rattle came from the engine. The pair looked at each other. It didn't sound good. Ferguson lifted the hinged bonnet.

The Brush had worn out a big-end bearing, which was now a collection of fractured shards, lying at the bottom of the sump. 'Our big end had turned into lots of little ends,' Ferguson recalled years later. Ordinarily this would be catastrophic, but Ferguson had an idea. He explained to Frank that he needed to cut up his bicycle to use some of the tubular frame to replace the collapsed bearing. This was nothing short of sacrilege to Frank. 'He (Frank) did a week's talking in a few minutes,' Ferguson recalled, 'but I pointed out we'd have to cut up his bike or starve to death. That moved him. I dismantled the bike and used parts to make the back stays to make an oil dipper for the main bearings.'

With a few strokes of the hacksaw, Birtles' lifeboat was gone. As painful for Frank as the sacrifice of his pushbike would have been, he was learning on the job the black arts of automotive mechanics. In particular, bush mechanics – discovering there were all sorts of ingenious ways to keep a car alive in the outback. In the days that followed, the little Brush began to disintegrate even further, but somehow Ferguson and Birtles kept the car going. At one point a wooden axle broke and, by using the cut-up shaft of a screwdriver, Ferguson was able to pin it back together.

Heading further eastward, they had passed through Broken Hill when the Brush began to list seriously to one side. Suddenly the car collapsed – the timber chassis rail had cracked right through. Ferguson had spotted a bloke sawing wood a few kilometres back and returned to approach him to fashion a chassis rail out of a length of eucalypt.

The little car arrived at the only true mountain they had encountered on the entire journey; Mount Victoria, on the western side of Sydney's Blue Mountains. They found the convict-built road closed, and had to crawl up a walking track instead. To their amazement, at the top they found snow. Looking east, they could see 'over the plains around Penrith and . . . in the distance the smoke haze of Sydney.' They had all but traversed the breadth of the Australian continent.

Word reached the Sydney office of the Canada Cycle & Motor Company that Ferguson and Birtles had been sighted on the outskirts of Sydney, and they scrambled to assemble as many Brush cars as possible to escort them into the city. They were as shocked as anyone, Ferguson recalling 'The promoters of the stunt were going to keep quiet about it because they thought we wouldn't make it . . .'

The *Sydney Morning Herald* reported on 15 April 1912: 'Those who received the motorists at the top of Taverner's Hill [on Parramatta Road], saw between the two bronzed and weather-beaten occupants of the car a terrier dog, which bristled with canine excitement, and appeared to be more interested in the motor cars and spectators at this point of the journey than the two overlanders. This is Birtles' sixth overland trip – five times on a bicycle, once in a motor car and now his ambition is to fly across Australia on an aeroplane.' (Frank had successfully made the jump from the horse to the bicycle to the motor car and was now ready to take to the skies.) '. . . it was a wonderful achievement that such a small piece of mechanism could have successfully negotiated the journey.'

The 'mechanism' survived the journey, but Birtles and Ferguson's relationship did not. On arrival at the Sydney GPO at Martin Place, Ferguson brought the little car to a stop as a growing, enthusiastic crowd cheered their success. It was a strange parting between the two men who had spent 28 days and four hours in a car crossing the continent. Ferguson recalled the Brush car's arrival: 'I got out of ours, said goodbye to Birtles, who didn't reply as I remember, and ran ahead to meet my sister.'

There was a celebratory function in the offices of the Canada Cycle & Motor Company, but other than that it was probably the last time they spoke to each other. Nevertheless, theirs was an absolutely extraordinary accomplishment. A motor car had driven across Australia and broken the isolation of the west from the rest of the nation. It was Saturday, 13 April 1912.

In Monday's newspapers, Ferguson and Birtles were to be feted as heroes. Their achievement would become the most fashionable topic discussed in the well-to-do circles of Melbourne, Sydney, Adelaide and Perth for years to come. Theirs was a triumph of 20th century technology over the insurmountably cruel forces of nature.

Yet their victory was to be eclipsed. The very next day, another challenge between technology and nature would steal their limelight. On a black ocean on the other side of the world, the bridge on RMS *Titanic* received a call from one of the ship's six lookouts, Frederick Fleet. There was an iceberg on the horizon.

6

The Ford Years

The journey across Australia in the single-cylinder Brush had been Frank Birtles' brief motoring apprenticeship, and he could have had no greater tutor than Syd Ferguson. Not that Frank saw fit to acknowledge it. Time eventually remoulded Syd Ferguson's drive across Australia into a Francis Birtles triumph. In his memoirs, written in 1935, Frank described the Brush car as his own. 'I had a car. In those days it was a very good car,' he wrote.

That Birtles was actually employed as Ferguson's navigator and sat in the passenger seat the whole way from Fremantle to Sydney didn't quite measure up to the motoring lore that eventually grew around Frank. Birtles painted Syd Ferguson more or less as a sidekick who was described quaintly as 'skilled in the queer ways of early time motors'. Thirty-seven years after the 1912 crossing, Syd Ferguson was interviewed on a radio program in Sydney, where he recalled the transcontinental adventure.

While trying to remain gracious, he remembered Birtles as being a puzzling figure. 'It's a funny thing – he was on the trip with me for the whole twenty-eight and a half days and I learned nothing about him,' Ferguson pondered.

'Perhaps he was the mechanic?' asked the interviewer.

'I was the mechanic,' Ferguson replied.

'The driver, then.'

'I was the driver – all the way.'

'Perhaps he was the relief driver or relief mechanic.'

'He couldn't have been that. When the trip was over, Mr Birtles knew as much about mechanics or driving as when he started – and that was nothing.'

Almost everyone who met Frank Birtles went away scratching their heads. He was an extraordinarily difficult person to read. Even the remarkable Syd Ferguson failed to appreciate that every second of the 28-day motorised journey across Australia was being downloaded into Birtles' overactive brain – filtered, processed and filed away for use at a later date. Within months of the 1912 transcontinental crossing, Ferguson and the Brush were ancient history as far as Birtles was concerned. His attentions had moved on.

Birtles was now discovering just how useful the motor car could be for long-distance travel. It could do things no bicycle ever could. And it generated publicity better than any form of transport he'd seen. Keen to expand on what he'd just learned, Frank and his brother Clive drove from Sydney along the eastern seaboard to Rockhampton in Queensland and up into the Gulf of Carpentaria on what was more or less a holiday in an American-made Flanders tourer.

'Motor tramps, we styled ourselves,' wrote Birtles. Clive was in fact a motor mechanic and a particularly accomplished driver. With Clive's patience, the journey north unravelled for Frank the mysteries of the motor car: how to drive it and how to keep it going. He understood you could never simply be a motorist. You needed to be several things at once – a driver, a mechanic, an auto-electrician, a tyre changer, a bog-digger and, at times, a pedestrian.

The short-lived Flanders motor car was very much like a Model T Ford. The car's designer, Walter Flanders, had worked for Henry Ford in preparing the Model T for production and decided to set up his own company. The journey north from Sydney was largely uneventful – except for the odd flood here and there – but Frank, the cyclist, was learning just how quickly a four-cylinder car like the Flanders could cover ground.

They charged effortlessly up the coastline, making astonishing time through small town after small town, but here Frank had cottoned onto something. People actually didn't travel. Outside of major cities, a journey anywhere for most people was almost impossible. Horse and buggy was really only for short distances. Horses tired easily and required drinking water in places where there simply wasn't any. There was, of course, rail in some places, yet lines were limited and confounding once you reached a state border, with conflicting gauges from state to state creating a nightmare. There were those born in country New South Wales who would never see Sydney in their entire lifetimes, those who lived in the outback who would never see the sea, and those who lived on the coast who would never see the outback.

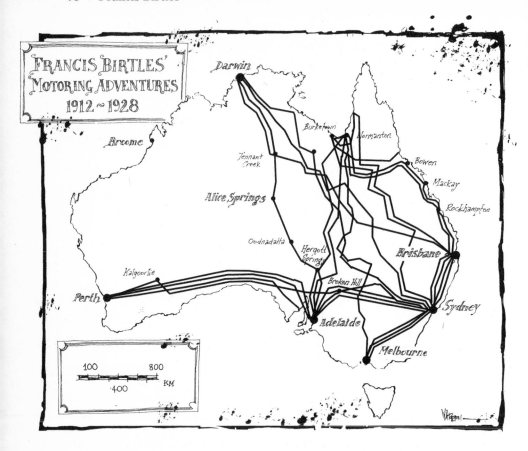

Now, with the combination of the phenomenal distance-busting motor car and a cinecamera, Frank could do all this for them. He could bring Australia – the real Australia – to Australians. He was now truly finding his niche as Australia's intrepid, outback adventurer. Through his films, photographs and articles he was bringing to Australia's largely urbanised population a glimpse of the outback. What he needed was an automotive partner – a bit of quid pro quo whereby a car manufacturer could use Francis Birtles the intrepid overlander, and he could use their cars.

Frank was now becoming a household name, and he was quick to capitalise on it. He found an excellent patron in Ford

Motors, which kicked off an extremely successful publicity campaign using Frank as their adventuresome spokesman. It seemed a marriage made in heaven – the ubiquitous and robust Model T, the first car truly suited to Australian conditions, put to the test by the only bloke who really knew the outback, Francis Birtles. If anyone was going to prove a Ford's reliability, it'd be him – why, his life depended on a Ford.

In August 1913, the New South Wales importers of Ford cars sent Frank and a brand-new Model T by ship from Sydney to Townsville, with Frank taking possession of the car at Charters Towers. He would drive the Ford north-west to Burketown on the Gulf of Carpentaria and then head south 5,600 kilometres alone by way of Cloncurry, Hughenden, Tambo, Barcaldine and Boggabri to Sydney and on to arrive at Port Phillip Bay in Victoria. In 1913, this was a serious drive.

Ford's advertising campaign was particularly well executed – a kind of well-thought-out, public-friendly version of the Brush journey. Ford promotional booklets published on the completion of the journey would encourage readers – potential Ford customers – to experience Frank's exciting adventures with a Model T across Australia. The publication would start with a neatly scrubbed-up Birtles and a new Model T, and by journey's end they'd see the mud-spattered, well-travelled car and the well-worn driver happy and none the worse for wear.

In 1913, this was the nearest thing to a road movie. For its time, the idea was inspired. Although they never met, Francis Birtles and Henry Ford would have probably got along like a house on fire. Both were quick-witted, irascible, ingenious, determined, difficult and stubborn – they even looked somewhat alike. Motoring proponents like Birtles were made for Henry Ford – and Ford's Model T was made for Birtles.

The Model T was the first car truly suitable for the world's underdeveloped roads, and Australia possessed some of the most underdeveloped road systems in the world. The car ticked all the boxes as the pre-war predecessor to the modern off-road vehicle. (Prior to World War II, few Australians would have heard of four-wheel-drive – with very few exceptions, motor cars came with the rear wheels driven only – like the Model T.) It had fundamental design qualities that catered for poor roads: a wheel at each corner; little or no overhanging bodywork, enabling good angles of approach and departure; low gearing; and high ground clearance. To a large extent, the Model T opened up much of Australia, not only through adventuring and expeditions, but because it was a car anyone could drive.

By modern standards, the Model T goes against what we understand the fundamentals of operating a modern car to be – a key start, accelerator pedal, gear lever, clutch. It doesn't have any of these features. Yet if you took someone who had no experience or preconceptions as to how to start and drive a car and gave them a Model T they'd very soon get the hang of it.

Starting the car was almost a religious ritual. First, pull the handbrake lever back completely – which aside from securing the car also puts the gearbox into neutral. On the right side of the steering column is the throttle lever, something like an indicator switch (there's no accelerator pedal, so this is what you use to accelerate), which you 'open' by sliding it to somewhere about the fifth or sixth notch. Then push the advance lever on the left side of the steering column upwards – which retards the ignition spark, preventing the engine from 'kickback', where the engine might fire and the crank handle suddenly fly backwards, in the process breaking your thumb. Move around to the front of the car and pull the end of the choke wire protruding through the radiator.

Turn the crank handle a few times to ensure a piston is at 'top-dead-centre'. Move back around to the dashboard and switch the ignition on. Walk back to the car's front, cup your palm and place your hand on the crank handle with your thumb out of the way in case there is a kickback – and with all your might give the crank handle a determined spin. As the engine fires up, release the choke, race around to the driver's side of the car, move the ignition lever down a few notches and adjust the throttle lever. See? Easy. Sometimes.

The gearbox was ingenious, more or less a Jurassic-era semi-automatic planetary transmission, with a high and low speed, requiring no clutch pedal. Changing gears also worked differently from in today's cars, with a foot pedal that engaged one of the two forward gears. Another pedal would engage reverse and a third pedal operated a transmission brake. And value for money (at one point it was selling for as little as £160) – it was a knockout.

At the journey's outset, Frank posed alongside a gleaming, brand-new Model T tourer for a publicity photograph taken in Charters Towers' main street. He was awkwardly posed in an extraordinary white tropical suit, with white shoes and wearing a white Chesapeake cap. The outfit was a kind of visual shorthand, underscoring for the readers that he was actually in the tropics, an important message for anyone viewing the photographs. He looked somewhat ridiculous. It went against the Frank Birtles rough-and-ready image everyone was familiar with. Frank was many things – but never a fashion plate.

Frank's lairy tropical outfit might have been a set-up by Ford, but interestingly, something else in the photograph certainly wasn't. Fitted to the car's running board is Birtles' trusty bicycle – just in case. He might have been a recent convert to the motor car but he hadn't been confirmed.

It was a fairly leisurely three-week drive to cover the distance, Frank regularly telegraphing Ford agents and making personal appearances at local dealerships, delighting Ford management. Promotional photographs taken along the way depicted Frank and the Ford in remote locations in dramatic poses – at an outback homestead, Frank swigging from a water bag while standing in front of his mechanical companion. It was as if the car had replaced the horse – which in fact it almost had.

Slick, neatly presented promotional booklets were produced: 'Across Australia in a Ford by Francis Birtles' described Frank's travels with a no-nonsense diary-style narrative of his adventures, illustrated with some dramatic photographs of Frank and the Ford. And to make sure every reader got the point, wherever an image of the Model T appeared, a photo retoucher had labelled the car FORD in large letters on the windscreen, on the radiator – or wherever it could fit.

This had been Frank's first foray into solo, long-distance motoring – and the Model T helped him through it. He experienced no troubles, increasing his confidence when dealing with a motor car alone in the outback. Until around 1920 Frank became Ford's key proponent in Australia and, more often than not, Frank's magazine articles were accompanied by a photo showing a Model T climbing the banks of a boggy creek, negotiating rocky ground or being dug out of a dry sandy creek bed. Wherever the Model T was, it was where a car, by all rights, shouldn't be. An article about Frank and his exploits in the wilds of Australia was even published in Ford's own in-house magazine in the United States.

It is not known precisely how many Model T adventures Frank undertook, as not all were reliably recorded. He did set off on a solo trip from Adelaide and drove across Sturt's Stony Desert to film the route undertaken by Charles Sturt – this had only ever been traversed by camel train – and he later motored out into the red centre to investigate a personal theory about possible locations for a transcontinental railway.

In an age long before specialised, off-the-shelf, off-road accessories, Frank was making his own. He described stripping down one Model T and, removing 'the bodywork, running boards and mudguards, I made a light platform on the chassis with detachable flooring boards, for use (underneath the wheels – like sand channels) in a bog or heavy sand'. Six empty benzine cases were placed on the boards, used as storage units for petrol tins, oil and 150 litres of water. He fitted the car with oversize tyres, stocked up with flour, tea and sugar, threw in his rifle to secure fresh meat and he was off.

All of this was excellent publicity for Ford in Australia. Yet Frank's improving sponsorship deals and the ensuing publicity might have been more than he could deal with. A flaw in Frank's personality began to emerge, one that in years to come would ultimately bite him. He was developing a tendency to overstep the mark with sponsors, becoming overly presumptuous as to what his entitlements were. Maybe it was the long, lonely hours on the road, thinking, always thinking, that gave him this skewed sense of his importance.

There is a story that has circulated about Frank since those days, where he once arrived from the Gulf driving a limping, mud-spattered, bush-bashed Model T into the garage of an outback Ford agency. The car had barely made it; the engine was clearly on its last legs. Frank demanded to see the manager, telling him he needed a new engine immediately. Bemused, the manager told him the cost of such an operation, whereby Frank, in high dudgeon, gave the manager a free character analysis, letting him know that Francis Birtles had been Ford's great ambassador in the Australian outback and the very least Ford could do was give him a free engine. The manager didn't agree. Frank stormed out.

The following day, a cow cocky wandered in to the dealership scratching his head. He told the manager that a most puzzling thing had happened. That morning he went to start his Model T – the one he'd bought from the dealership only a few weeks before – and he couldn't get the thing to go. Frustrated after many turns of the crank handle, he lifted the bonnet to find the most clapped-out Ford engine he'd ever seen, sitting on the chassis and disconnected from the gearbox. By now Frank was well on the road, happily motoring along with a new Ford engine.

It is one of those Frank Birtles yarns that's been told in pubs and around camp fires for a century, but in fact, on 5 January 1917, Frank and his brother Clive were charged with having stolen a 'Ford Motor engine and carburettor', the property of a John Norman McIntyre, and were bailed to appear in Burketown Court. On 17 May that year, Frank and Clive were exonerated. However, it showed that Frank was prepared to bend the rules – something he'd ultimately live to regret.

•

Frank possessed an exceptional talent – swearing. He was famous for it. A journalist once described Frank's eyebrow-raising ribald turn of phrase as 'Birtles-ese'. And he didn't swear the way you might suspect people would swear a century ago.

Frank had an excellent handle on every variety of word that began with a B or an F or a C. Years in the merchant navy, the army and the Transvaal constabulary had given him an astonishingly colourful vocabulary. But that's how blokes from the bush spoke. They swore to the point where only 10 per cent of a sentence was actually message. A passenger with him on an expedition recounted that Frank could 'swear beyond the limits of ordinary profanity', launching into a long, bawdy song, 'Heaven only knows where he learnt it, but it dates back to the long past days of the bullock teams. It has 219 verses and a chorus. Very little of it, except the chorus, is printable . . .'

Frank's most trusted travelling companions were his dogs. Over the years he had a variety of dogs as companions. They tended to be bulldogs or cattle dogs, and even a German Shepherd. All had great Australian names – Dinkum, Chance-it, Wowser, Yeo, Yowie. All had different personalities, and on occasion would seemingly disapprove of something Frank had done. They'd guard the car and campsite, or protect him against snakes or prowling dingoes at night. They'd launch off a moving car to tackle a kangaroo or charge after a water buffalo.

Frank loved them. The hard-bitten, hard-swearing bushman would suddenly dissolve into the sort of goo-gooing babble one might murmur when tickling a newborn baby under the chin. In time, his dogs became almost as famous as Frank, often photographed for the newspapers sitting proudly in one of Frank's cars, wearing enormous driving goggles. The public adored them and Frank even more so. He dedicated his 1935 book *Battle Fronts of Outback* to 'Dinkum – A blue Australian cattle dog, my sole companion on many a tough track in the great outback wilds of Australia'.

7

With Hurley into Australia's Unknown

Only weeks before World War I broke out in 1914, Francis Birtles emerged from the sweltering snake- and crocodile-infested backblocks of the Gulf of Carpentaria behind the wheel of a disintegrating Model T Ford that had been given the unsurprising name of Lizzie.

With a boiling radiator, and the carcass of a shot kangaroo draped across the bonnet ready as dog meat for Wowser, the Model T shuddered along what was presumably the main street of the corrugated iron frontier town of Burketown. In the passenger's seat was an up-and-coming photographer and cinecameraman called Frank Hurley, who only the year before had returned from an expedition to the Antarctic with the already legendary Australian polar explorer Douglas Mawson.

Hurley had recently made a name for himself with his own documentary from the Mawson expedition, titled *Home of the*

Blizzard, a strikingly unusual film for its time in that it didn't depict the predictable stoic and heroic posturing of explorers planting flags in the ice. Rather, Hurley's footage concentrated on the unimaginable beauty and breathtakingly bizarre landscapes contained within the Antarctic continent.

The film, and his extraordinary stills photography, had suddenly made Hurley international hot property. Wiry-haired, ambitious and every bit as hungry for recognition as Birtles, Hurley agreed to accompany him on a 5,000 kilometre drive to the gulf to film a feature documentary for Australasian Films Ltd, which would ultimately be called *Into Australia's Unknown*. For Hurley, the already famous Francis Birtles was an inspiration – he was carving out a business from raw adventure, and Hurley was keen to learn from him how to do it.

The two Franks had an uproarious time while filming on the road, Hurley telling newspaper reporters of the worry of 'alligators' when washing developed films in the river. 'It gave me a creepy feeling to watch those great brutes sneaking along the bottom preparatory to making a sudden rush out on the bank to grab something. One day we shot an alligator 15 feet long and while I went away to boil the billy another came out of the water and dragged the corpse of its brother to the river's edge. I think it intended to have a feast.'

Photographs of the expedition suggest it was something of an overenthusiastic hunting trip, resulting in an astonishing variety of recently deceased wildlife propped up around the Model T for the camera. Red kangaroos, bush turkeys, wallabies – all fair game in 1914. Guns were an essential tool for any outback expedition and, when required, Frank would select a weapon from his travelling arsenal the way a golfer selects clubs from his golf bag. He's recorded as taking with him rifles including .22 calibre, .32/20, .303 and .44, and most likely would have packed a shotgun, as they were cheap and particularly useful out in the scrub.

Earlier that year, Birtles had used some footage of a corroboree he had shot previously to convince Australasian Films to send him back up to the gulf and supply him with a new Model T tourer. It worked. As always, Frank then went to work on this brand-new car with a hacksaw and a hand-drill, constructing a rear platform on which they could mount a cinecamera. Even though the pairing of Birtles and Hurley had been orchestrated by the film company, Hurley's vision of the Antarctic was very much aligned with Birtles' vision of the outback. Neither wanted to present a gaudy Brighton-Pier-postcard contrivance of their worlds to an audience.

Birtles had now spent years attempting to educate an Anglocentric public, whose idea of natural beauty was a bed of geraniums at Kew Gardens, about the dramatic wonders of the Australian interior. And when Hurley attempted to portray the calamity of modern warfare in World War I by producing composite photographs involving the superimposition of various images of aircraft and exploding artillery shells over no-man's-land, it demonstrated one thing – both Hurley and Birtles were storytellers.

A film that was the product of a union of Frank Birtles and Frank Hurley could be a masterstroke – Birtles' unassailable outback experience and knowledge combined with Hurley's masterful, imaginative camerawork showing the panache and pluck of rip-roaring adventure in Australia. As far as Birtles was concerned, for Australians real adventures were to be had

right here in their own backyard and yet they had absolutely no idea. A Birtles and Hurley team could reveal to Australians the wonders of their own country – educate them.

But whatever Birtles supposed might happen, Hurley had bigger fish to fry. Filming with Birtles out in the never-never for Australasian Films was probably a decent earner and not bad for publicity in the local cinema market, but Frank Hurley was angling for further polar exploration. Hurley was supposed to be assisting Mawson with the pre-publication of a book with the same title as the film, *Home of the Blizzard*, when he suddenly announced he would be disappearing up into the Gulf country with Francis Birtles. Mawson, in London, was particularly angry. Frustrated, he wrote to Hurley, announcing, 'Altogether the book will suffer considerably by your rushing into the interior of Australia . . . It has annoyed me extremely.'

There was however, a third strand to Hurley's agenda. Birtles and Mawson were both vaguely aware that Hurley was hedging his bets with a third adventurer – the British polar explorer Sir Ernest Shackleton, who had seen Hurley's cinematic work and was particularly keen for him to accompany his expedition to the Antarctic aboard the *Endurance*. Hurley had in fact been keeping Mawson at bay while Shackleton was courting him – and he was possibly stringing Frank Birtles along, too.

The tin-sided telegraph office in Burketown had never been busier, with Hurley cabling and receiving messages with both Mawson and Shackleton in London. While motoring with Frank around the gulf, Hurley was anticipating what Shackleton's next move might be, and on their return approach to Burketown, he found out in a most dramatic fashion.

As the Model T rattled into the town's outskirts, an Aborigine came sprinting out of the scrub holding a telegram high in the air. 'There emerged from the undergrowth a semi-clad Aborigine,' Hurley recalled, 'holding in his hands a short, cleft stick, in the end of which a letter was clamped . . . "Boss, Jacky bring 'em big white fella talk along you." I took the proffered letter . . . It was from Sir Ernest Shackleton. As I read it, I could only express myself in spasmodic ejaculations.'

Shackleton urged Hurley to join his expedition in Buenos Aires in five weeks' time, to which Hurley instantly agreed. He claimed that he and Birtles 'danced for joy'; however, it's unlikely that Frank would have been completely over the moon. Of the two, he was in fact the better known, and to watch Hurley receive an invitation to accompany Sir Ernest Shackleton on a British Antarctic expedition would have been like a knife through the heart. Birtles and Hurley hurried back to Sydney in the Model T, Hurley recalling, 'I hastened day and night to Sydney and arrived to find a steamer leaving for South America in a few days.'

Into Australia's Unknown was a tremendous success and Hurley's face featured prominently in the newspaper advertisements.

The story of the Shackleton expedition was to become one of the greatest survival epics of all time, as the crew helplessly watched their ship, the *Endurance*, destroyed by pack ice. The reason the story of their survival is so well known today is due in no small part to Hurley's extraordinarily dramatic and timeless photographs.

Hurley's reputation went from strength to strength as he jumped from one adventure to another, photographing and filming diverse and dangerous subjects from Papuan tribes to world wars. If you ask any photographer in Australia today, they'll probably know of Frank Hurley but may never have heard of Frank Birtles.

And there's a simple reason: Hurley was a photographer who loved adventure; Birtles was an adventurer who loved photography.

8

The War

When Australia declared war on Germany in 1914, Frank was quick to respond; but straight-out enlistment wasn't for him. Frank wrote to the Commonwealth government as early as November 1914 to offer his services. However for Frank to volunteer, the War Office needed to understand it would be on his terms.

He wrote to Commander Petheridge, the Secretary of Defence:

> Sir, I would like to study practical military aviation and am prepared to volunteer in connection with same. I have a good knowledge of motor mechanics [and] after journeying around and across Australia 16 times I know local conditions and landmarks which I hope will be of value to the intelligence department.
>
> Would you please use your influence and give me an opportunity to join the Flying Corps. I would also like to

mention I am well-versed in map drawing and photography and active service in scouting.

Yours Sincerely,
Francis Birtles

In the skies – that's where Frank predicted the future of warfare would be. As it transpired, Birtles was quite a visionary when it came to military aviation. (In the years following the war he continually proposed ideas for aerodromes and seaplane bases for Australia's defence.)

Within a few weeks, Commander Petheridge responded, acknowledging Frank's request and after some careful consideration posted a formal reply. 'No.' Frank was notified there weren't any vacancies at the flying school at Point Cook; however, they did enclose a pamphlet and told him he would be contacted should a vacancy arise.

Frank made his feelings about the Great War known. He was in fact a veteran of an earlier war. He knew what battle looked like.

When troops from Australia sailed to South Africa to fight the Boers in 1899 Francis Birtles had been an apprentice seaman in the merchant navy serving on the dangerous run from Melbourne to Perth and across the Indian Ocean to South Africa. It's probable Frank spent at least one trans-Indian Ocean crossing to South Africa ferrying troops from the Australian colonies. The six colonies sent their own military forces to a war that on the face of it was a Dutch farmers' rebellion. Over the next two and a half years this armed, overly religious and determined farming community would cost Britain 200 million pounds, draw in 448,435 British imperial forces and leave 22,000 of them dead.

Frank clearly had enough of life in the merchant navy – the sea was something over which he had no influence and he was never comfortable in situations where he didn't have his hands on the controls. He'd had quite a few close scrapes during his nautical adventures so it's little wonder he was keen to hit terra firma and enlist with the Australian militia in South Africa, especially with Australia contributing sizeable mounted infantry units to the campaign, two of which were termed the 'Bushmen' contingent and the 'Imperial Bushmen'.

Shortly after Australia began committing troops, Frank's ship anchored in Cape Town Harbour where the crew was immediately advised they were prohibited from coming ashore. The threat of crew members jumping ship to join up was a serious concern to ship owners – only those with specific duties in ship maintenance and re-supply were allowed to set foot on the docks. The *Merchant Shipping Act* of 1854 had in store seriously harsh penalties for those wanting to jump ship – '12 weeks' imprisonment, with or without hard labour, and forfeiture of wages and effects on board'.

It didn't matter – Frank had made up his mind. He had no intention of staying onboard. 'I had to resort to strategy,' he recalled. He was ready to jump.

The khaki pith-helmeted guards chatting among themselves at the wharf entry didn't bat an eyelid when a soot-covered ship-worker struggled past with a bucket of coal-ash in each hand. Frank had shimmied down the side of his ship in his overalls and made it ashore with his best clothes concealed at the bottom of the buckets, which had then been covered with cinders. 'I toiled across to the ash-heap giving my best impersonation of a hard-working lawful-minded member of the mercantile marine. I emptied the buckets, grabbed my clothes, and ran.'

He didn't muck around. Frank set about climbing Table Mountain – the spectacular sandstone plateau that overshadows the entire colony at more than a thousand metres above sea level – and found a cave at a point called Devil's Peak.

From this vast natural amphitheatre he was able to monitor the movements to and from his own ship moored in the harbour far below. He had a little food and by drinking from a puddle of rainwater at the cave's mouth he was set for a few days at least.

It was now a waiting game. From high on the mountain summit he waited for the ship to leave – and after three days it finally sailed. Frank made his way down from the mountain and attempted to join up with Australian forces. Yet he was rejected, perhaps because he had not quite reached the minimum enlistment age of twenty, or perhaps it was because he was already indentured to the merchant navy.

It didn't matter; there was no shortage of contingents in which to enlist. Cape Town was awash with khaki-uniformed pith-helmeted and slouch-hatted regiments and units from the four corners of the British Empire.

He was able to enlist with the South African Cape Colonial Forces as part of an Irregular Mounted Infantry unit. The Cape Colonial Forces were more or less South Africa's defence force, guarding railways and communication lines while the British army was at the front dealing with incursions from the Boers into the Cape Colony. Frank was in his element.

'The marching measure, sung half-sarcastically but with an underlying note of great weariness came bawling from a four abreast squad of the ranks of a mobile section of mounted rifle-men, and I was one of them.' Sitting on his horse, Frank was typical of the Cape Colonial mounted troopers – fitted out in his khaki uniform, wearing a slouch hat with a diagonally striped puggaree, a long-barrelled Lee Enfield rifle slung over his shoulder, the butt carried in a leather rifle bucket.

His time in the mounted infantry opened up a new world for him: learning how to survive in the rough, to read the landscape, observing changes in vegetation, learning to ride, learning to shoot, learning to live off the land. This was what he loved – as he put it 'the hard life'.

It was here that Frank began learning his amazing bush craft skills. Yet for all the wild experience on the veldt – this was war.

Frank wrote of a typically long, slow and miserable ride back from a sortie, the two-mile long column of men on horseback wearing 'those big khaki waterproofs that were issued to the Cape Forces. They had stout collars worn turned up to protect our freezing ears and the lower half of our unshaven faces. Blinking with the dust of an all-night trek, and stiff with saddle weariness, knee to knee we rode along . . . The air that we breathed as we rode on mile after mile, was polluted with the odour of week-old, jackal-torn carcasses of horses which had met with cruel lingering deaths in a disastrous running skirmish several days before. Some of their former veldt riders were now sleeping peacefully beneath scattered earth mounds. Our men gave passing salute . . .'

But in 1914, Frank Birtles didn't enlist to head off to the Great War. He gave no explanations as to why he didn't join up – he had turned 33 just after the war broke out, so he'd have still been eligible. Instead, he went bush to make films.

While the campaign on the Gallipoli Peninsula was spiralling to its grave during 1915 one of Frank's outback photographs was published in a Sydney magazine. It was a beautifully composed picture of an Australian stockman mounted on a stock-horse standing shoulder-deep in long grass – cattle are just visible in the distant background. The bushman looks relaxed in the saddle – his bedroll haphazardly roped across his back – and he's clearly just lit his pipe.

Yet there's something edgy and alert about this stockman – despite his calm overall appearance, his shoulders are broad, his hands hold the reins as if he's ready to ride, his legs are ramrod straight, pushing the stirrups well forward. With his bush hat and moleskins there is something soldierly about him, as if he could be out on the veldt in South Africa.

A long caption underneath gives a sense of what the portrait is about: 'This is a photograph taken by Francis Birtles, the famous overlander, in the far north. It's a glimpse of the real outback. The stockman is lean, sinewy, and he and his horse are one. He has the wonderful vision that is developed in men who ride within wide horizons. He would look anything but imposing beside the broad-faced blonde Uhlan of the Kaiser's army, but he would lose the German in all that makes a soldier. He would not relish work in the trenches. His strong point is to scour the country fearlessly and swiftly, and would live up to the reputation given him by General Sir Ian Hamilton – "The best scout in the world". If need be he would die in sustaining that reputation. He is a "sport" who plays "the game" fairly, and his sense of duty to his country has been fully demonstrated by the splendid fashion he and his mates all over the Commonwealth have responded to the call for volunteers to assist the Mother country in her hour of trial.'

The photograph and its accompanying text give a feel for Frank's frustration with the war in Europe. His war was fighting the Boer in the open. War is supposed to be fought under big skies and on the veldt – on horseback where everyone is a 'sport' in 'the game'. If you scratch an Australian soldier there's a bushman raring to go who is now wasting his valuable time in some stupid trench. Didn't people understand? What's wrong with everyone? General Hamilton said it: 'Australians are the best scouts in the world'. So get out there and get on with it.

9

In the Track of
Burke and Wills

While the Anzacs were scrambling ashore on a sliver of beach
in some remote part of western Turkey, Frank and his brother
Clive were negotiating the rough country out near Coopers
Creek in south-western Queensland. They were rattling along
a camel track in Lizzie, the Model T that Frank had driven a
year earlier with Frank Hurley, which by now was quite possibly
on its second or third engine.

The pair were in the process of making a feature film with
the title *Across Australia in the Track of Burke and Wills*. This
was a particularly clever concept for the time – the film would
attempt to answer questions and clear up misconceptions about
this nineteenth century mystery of the explorers' demise, by
tackling it from a twentieth century perspective.

The idea was to follow Burke and Wills' ill-fated tracks into
the dead heart and up into the Gulf country to try to make

sense for the film's audience of what had happened during the expedition 54 years before. To some degree the film was a form of investigative journalism – and ultimately their investigation discovered more than they hoped for.

Clive Birtles wrote to his girlfriend Olive in Geelong, revealing their discovery: 'Two days travelling brought us over the South Australian border after which we headed north west and plowed through sand hills and gibber stones onto the famous "Coopers Creek".' Coopers Creek is a series of deep water holes connected by a dry, sometimes sandy, sometimes rocky watercourse.

'On a slight bank beside a shallow pool we found traces of the Burke and Wills expedition. A tree carved deeply with the word "Dig" and the date. An old stockade remains. This stockade was erected to keep the natives off. Further up-stream we came across the tree at the foot of which Burke died. The lettering on this tree is badly eaten by ants and we could not decipher it.'

Clive's letter then revealed an extraordinary discovery. 'We got a lot of strange history about the Burke and Wills expedition, from the old blacks, one old fellow named "Wompie" having lived with King [the only survivor] during his stay with the blacks here.'

Frank was able to find first-hand information about Burke and Wills' demise – incredibly from those who'd actually seen the party perish fifty years earlier. He filmed three Innamincka Aboriginal elders who'd looked after King back in 1862, recalling they had fed him with seedcakes made from the nardoo plant. That Frank had found and was filming the very Aborigines who'd nursed the only surviving member of the Burke and Wills expedition was astonishing. He wanted them to show him how

Birtles traced every mile of Burke and Wills' expedition in the Model T, filming and writing the whole way. And Frank was only too quick to remind 20th-century Australians that the never-never is just as lethal as it was then. 'It will be remembered,' he said, 'that King, in his evidence before the Inquiry Commission, stated that the horses and camels of the expedition knocked up [died] in the sun-cracked level country which is subjected to the overflow of the Georgina River. It is terrible country. I nearly perished through running out of water. For 36 hours I battled without a drop of water and just managed to reach the river.'

When the film opened at Christmas time in 1916, it was a sensation and received rave reviews.

Francis Birtles had captured on film a piece of Australian history – eyewitnesses to the nation's most famous exploration tragedy.

10

Frank and Clive

'Gone to the Wilds, Recalcitrant Cadet Taking Travel Pictures'
ran the headline for the *Sydney Morning Herald* article dated 8
October 1912. 'Melbourne, Monday. In the Northcote Court
today Lieut. Fargher, area officer, proceeded against Clive Irwin
David Birtles, for failing to attend for a medical examination.
Lieut. Fargher stated that the case had been adjourned previously to give defendant a chance of attending for examination,
but he had failed to keep two appointments made for him,
and his father had written to say he had gone with his brother,
Francis Birtles, on a picture-taking tour through Northern
Australia.'

Forget army medical examinations – Frank Birtles had far
more important work for his mechanically-minded brother Clive.
From 1912 through to 1919 they would spend month after
month way up in the never-never, Clive behind the wheel and
Frank cranking a cinematograph camera – and with 20-year-old
Clive pining for his girlfriend back in Geelong.

The public's fascination with long, arduous, outback motorised expeditions was being gradually eclipsed by reliability trials, which in turn transformed into the craze for speed record breaking. Once people realised the motor car could reliably deliver them to a destination, the logical question that followed was just how fast could they get there? With an eye on this, in 1917 Frank and Clive were preparing to attempt a speed trial from Brisbane to Sydney, driving a Maxwell tourer. With the Birtles brothers behind the wheel – Clive as the appointed driver and Frank navigating – it was guaranteed to be a hair-raising ride. In order to give an authoritative air to the proceedings, the *Brisbane Courier* newspaper appointed an official timekeeper to travel with them, an irascible 27-year-old reporter, Malcolm Henry Ellis.

Ordinarily it would be hard to imagine a young city newspaper correspondent fitting in with a pair of wild and reckless bush motorists like Frank and Clive, but Malcolm Ellis was different from the typical journalists of his era. He loved the bush and he loved motoring. Born near Dirranbandi in south-west Queensland, Ellis had derived a love of adventure from his Irish-born storekeeper father, and a marked desire for learning and an appreciation of British culture from his English-born mother. Like Frank Birtles, Malcolm Ellis was egocentric, both of them possessing forceful personalities and vitriolic tempers. He was well-read and opinionated – incapable of seeing anything from any perspective other than his own. Like Birtles, he was fascinated with the motor car. Yet neither Birtles nor Ellis would have had the faintest idea that their meeting on this journey would develop into a bizarre motoring partnership that in exactly ten years' time would bring the pair to the brink of death on the other side of the world.

The drive from Brisbane to Sydney was indeed a hair-raiser, the three motorists hanging onto the Maxwell tourer for dear life as they took off, farewelled by Brisbane's mayor. Clive put the car through its paces, eventually cracking the 1917 speed record in 29 hours and 10 minutes. Mind you, the Birtles brothers and Malcolm Ellis were all very nearly killed on the hairpin descent approaching Wiseman's Ferry on the Hawkesbury River. 'The horn was kept going continually, but at one point the party went round a corner to find a very sedate-looking tramp planted squarely in the middle of the road,' Ellis reported for the newspaper. 'He apparently was not going to move for a car or anything else, and as there were deep ruts on the roadway on one side, the tramp in the middle, and a precipice on the other side, the position was very precarious. There was no time to slow down, and so Mr. C. Birtles, who was driving, passed on the outer side and for a minute or two it looked as if the whole concern was going over the cliff, as the car kept jumping in and out of the ruts, and once or twice came within six inches of the edge.'

Frank and Clive – the record breakers – were now a pair of expert motorists, roaring about the countryside, a motoring team as thick as thieves. They shipped the rented Maxwell aboard the SS *Zealandia* to Western Australia in 1917 for an assault on the record for the fastest transcontinental crossing from Fremantle to Sydney. However, before long they experienced serious differential trouble, the car giving grief while attempting to traverse the Yardea sandhills in South Australia. Makeshift repairs allowed them to crawl to the Streaky Bay lighthouse on the Eyre Peninsula, where they caught a ferry to Adelaide.

With no money, and at the mercy of a shipping strike, Frank and Clive devised a plan to return to Fremantle by placing an advertisement in the Adelaide newspapers asking for paying passengers to travel with them across the desert. The pair managed to get hold of two more Maxwell cars, and with fourteen passengers in three cars (the third driver unknown), set off in convoy for Perth. In the years that followed, the two brothers would undertake more long-distance adventures together, but in time, as Frank's fame and reputation grew, the famous overlander would demand any traveller accompanying him on an expedition sign an exclusivity agreement not to write, photograph or publish any details or accounts of the journey. And eventually this included Clive.

•

Frank was only too happy to present himself to the public as the outback-wandering adventurer, motoring through the never-never, living with the Aborigines, pressing through hard luck but, as always with Frank, there was another reason why he would disappear into the Australian unknown for months on end: he was convinced that one day, he'd strike gold. Although he often joked about the idea of discovering a nugget or reef, he genuinely harboured the desire to find the mother lode.

Perhaps this was partly because money had always been a problem for Frank, and the older he grew, the more problematic it became. In truth, he had no real qualifications, no regular income – or real job for that matter – and in the early 20th century there was no History Channel to which he could sell his documentaries. So the most promising route to riches was to use his outback skills to go prospecting. Frank had acquired a fairly reasonable geological knowledge, particularly when it came to knowing what to look for in the search for alluvial deposits. The last time he'd been up to Cape York he'd ventured into an unprospected region and had taken a few samples of what he thought was 'flour gold', extremely fine traces of gold he found in iron-capped quartz. To his astonishment, the analyses came back very well indeed.

With what little money he had, Frank bought some fossicking equipment, loaded up the Model T, and sat Dinkum, his cattle dog, on the passenger's seat, ready to head back north to claim his gold reef. Frank was going to strike it rich.

Sadly, it wasn't to be. What he did strike was the first onslaught of trouble near the scene of Burke and Wills' demise at Cooper Creek in south-western Queensland. For three days, Frank attempted to drive the Model T through a blustering sandstorm that racked the car, Dinkum and himself mercilessly, until one morning the wind suddenly dropped and he found himself motoring through a kind of fog made up of fine, grey dust. It was disorientating – a silent and eerie world in which it was almost impossible to see through a strange, bleak murkiness. There was no contrast – no sun and no shadow.

To cope with the soft, powdery sand, Frank deflated the tyres to 20 pounds per square inch and continued on, the Model T struggling over sandhills that were growing increasingly steep. He was attacking the dunes in second gear and then using the car's momentum down the other side, from dune-crest to dune-crest. Having almost reached the top of a dune, the car began to misfire and water began to spurt from the radiator cap. He'd blown a head gasket.

Frank's problem was that he had only one spare head gasket. At the top of the sand dune he removed the car's bonnet and unbolted the cylinder head, prising it off the engine block to reveal the cylinder bores and pistons – the engine's vital organs. With the head off, an engine is especially vulnerable. It's as if the car is having open-heart surgery – everything must be kept as clean and as uncontaminated as possible. Frank drained the water-contaminated oil from the sump and replaced it with engine oil from a square gallon tin. As he attempted to massage smooth the damaged copper head gasket, the wind started again in earnest, skimming sand from the dune caps over the engine.

'A giant sand hill to the windward nearly smothered me,' Birtles wrote. 'The fall of sand threatened to bury the wheels.' Frank hastily placed the gasket on the engine block and then clamped the cast iron cylinder head on top. He could feel the grind of grit between the parts – this couldn't be good. With the sandstorm's intensity increasing, he replaced the bonnet and refilled the radiator with precious water from the water bag. Frank flicked the ignition switch on and went back around to the front of the car to crank start it. He pulled the handle up ready for the downward swing. Throw. Nothing. He tried again, but the car wouldn't start. He rigged up a windbreak with a couple of blankets and tried to start the car, over and over again.

Frank poked his head under the folding bonnet. The magneto – the electrical heart of the car – was full of fine sand. Frank checked the magneto's ignition points by removing the ignition cover. He discovered they were jammed with grit and

then found he couldn't fit the parts back together. No luck.
With the storm escalating, Frank decided to batten down. He
ripped out as many saltbushes as he could find and placed
them on the windward side of the car to prevent it from being
buried. Frank braced himself on the other side, settling in for
a long and painful wait. 'I had food and water so I rigged up
a cheesecloth shelter from the myriad of flies and ants.'

That evening, the wind died down and Frank set to work. Under an electric spotlight he cleaned and put back together the ignition parts, eventually cranking the engine to start. In the black desert night, blue electrical currents ran like small streams of lightning along the car's wiring. 'I rubbed Dinkum's coat. It crackled and sparkled. Feeling my own hair I found it was in the same condition.'

Frank waited until midnight, when the cold night air had cooled the sand, making a harder surface to drive on. With the headlights illuminating the sand dunes ahead, one after the other, the Model T's tyres were finally running on the smooth hard surface of a salt pan. He was finally out of the rough stuff, so he pulled up for a brief kip.

At dawn, Frank was ready to get cracking again, swinging the crank handle to start the car for the day's running. As he rotated the crank he could hear the swish of water in the sump. He'd blown the head gasket again. As the sun rose higher, the flies came back, swarming around Frank's head by the thousands. He lit two small, smoky fires in an effort to keep the flies away while he began unbolting the cylinder head again. The gasket didn't look too bad, so Frank pulled a bottle of shellac from his tool bag and smeared the gasket surface and the top of the engine block with the resin, using it as gasket sealer. The sticky surfaces were instantly smothered in big black flies, stuck fast in the shellac, buzzing, their wings and bodies unable to move. Frank dropped the head gasket on top of the whole lot and tightened it up.

Amazingly, the car started and Frank pushed on, but before long he was back driving in sand, causing a greater load on the car, and could hear the engine shutting down. He didn't care – the sun was now blazing hot and the car limped along on three cylinders until he pulled up in some sort of shade under a spindly, stunted tree. Frank removed the cylinder head again to discover the gasket had blown to pieces – destroyed beyond any salvation.

With no spare gasket, Frank set about cutting a makeshift one out of the Model T's canvas folding roof. He figured it might just seal if he smeared it with enough axle grease. He tightened the head back on. Bang! It blew before the car reached 100 yards. Dinkum raced around the back of the Model T, snapping at the wheels to get it to move. Frank hadn't given up either. With his pocketknife he began to cut a head gasket from his leather suitcase, strapped to the back of the Ford. It too failed. By now, all the close-fitting machined surfaces on the head and block were filthy, and the leather gasket just couldn't seat properly.

Frank and Dinkum camped for two days. In that time Frank attempted to patch up with brass shims the ruin that was the original gasket and, astonishingly, managed to get the car going. The gasket held – for the time being.

They motored out onto the gibber plains, where smooth, glossy, blood-red stones the size of footballs reflected the searing heat from the desert sun like mirrors. It was nothing short of an inferno – the scorching, furnace-hot ironstone soil beneath the Model T's wheels was lifting the tyre repair patches on the inner tubes, Frank not only having to try and fix them but also having to use the hand-pump to reinflate the tyres. Within the next two days, the head gasket blew a further eleven times. Running out of options, Frank cut up his old Fibrolite suitcase to have another try at making a head gasket. He soaked it in hot oil and then smeared the suitcase gasket and the surfaces of the head and block with apple jam as sealer. When it was all screwed down, Frank poured the last of his water into the radiator, 'keeping back only sufficient for a quart pot of tea'.

Very carefully, Frank nursed the car forwards as best he could – it would be another 50 kilometres until the next waterhole – every now and then stopping to retension the head bolts and over-oil the engine, hoping a carbon build-up would seal any weak spots. He kept the car moving steadily in second (top) gear. Frank was just realising the terrain seemed to be becoming even more drought-affected, when suddenly the wind whipped up again. To compound matters, the car bogged itself, just as the sandstorm took control. While he was digging the car out, a clump of shadowy figures emerged through the dusty fog.

A straggle of emaciated cows and calves wandered by – their bellies were bloated, yet they had damp mud on their legs: water. Frank extricated the car and followed the cattle track through the dust for a few kilometres before he was suddenly overcome with the stench of dead animals. He'd found the waterhole – clogged with dozens of dead and dying cattle, 'a green slime on the coats of some. Dingoes had been eating them alive. Eyes, picked out by the crows, were flyblown. I waded into the muddy water and filled the tins.'

Frank managed to keep the Model T with its suitcase-gasket going for a further 3,000 kilometres, driving as carefully as he could without having to change gear. He was now in open-forest country, the wheels were churning up ash, and Frank could smell the acrid trace of a bushfire growing stronger with every yard.

He'd caught up with a bushfire lit by Aborigines – a few kilometres away, a paperbark swamp was fully ablaze, giving off a tremendous pall of smoke, and a thick wall of blue-black cloud rose from the flames, filling the sky.

Then the wind changed. The flames shifted from the swamp and tore across the tussocky plains towards the Model T. There was nowhere to go, as Frank was following the edge of a dry creek-bed, which then began to veer in the direction of the flames. He decided to turn around, and as he did so saw the radiator cap spurt water. There followed a loud, disturbing grind from the engine. He immediately switched the engine off and leaped out to grab his shovel to beat down any approaching flames.

In time, the fire burned itself out and Frank returned to the car to investigate what had happened with the engine. The head gasket had blown so badly that water filled the number one cylinder, and on the compression stroke blew the piston to pieces. For now, the car was dead. Frank had spare pistons packed in his kit, but as the wet season was about to break, where the car was sitting would be very soon under water. Somehow he needed to drag the car to higher ground.

Frank was approached by two Aborigines, who agreed to help him carry his stores into the hills. They showed him where to find water and said they'd return – they were attending an initiation ceremony. 'I was delayed two weeks waiting for the blacks . . . the atmosphere, day and night, was of great humidity. The storms were coming.' Eventually the Aborigines returned, laughing and yelling – they'd burned a path through the scrub through which they'd pull the car. 'They said they were "strong fellah" and pulled the car for several kilometres to higher ground. They found it heavier dragging than they expected,' wrote Frank. As the storms broke, they took Frank, carrying his supplies, to his new 'wet-season home' – a cave in a mountainside – a week's walk away.

'For three months I was forced to remain in the hills. The low-lying country was interspersed with swamps and grasses. It was impossible to do anything about the car.' Frank was invited to accompany his new companions on a crocodile hunting expedition where 'the waters of the creek were deep, clear, and calm. Crocodile "roads" were to be seen leading up the steep grassy banks. Floating islands of grass made the passage at times very difficult. Beneath these the old-men crocodiles often made their daytime camp.'

Frank arrived to find a hunting party was already well underway. Suddenly an Aborigine called from a canoe, picking up a bamboo spear with a rope fastened to the head and swiftly drove it through the body of an enormous saltwater crocodile. 'Up to the surface the crocodile came in a tangle of foam and grasses. It bellowed deafeningly, snapped its jaws and struck terrific blows with its tail; then it tore along the surface of the water with its head up, dragging the canoe after it,' Frank wrote. 'It looked like a launch . . . An aboriginal charged at the monster with a long pole . . . six feet of it went down its gullet. The crocodile threw itself over and over in its struggles and threw itself on its back. More natives rushed in and hung onto the animal's tail. One swung a tomahawk and severed one side of the jawbone. Another furiously hacked away at the body base of the tail – hacked savagely until the hangers-on dragged it apart from the living beast.'

That night 'huge chunks of crocodile were put into underground ovens; an enormous haggis made under hot ashes, and the camp dogs feasted royally. There was a great feast in the Aboriginal camp.'

Frank stayed with the tribe for some time until eventually the floodwaters subsided. One day two Aborigines from an outback station arrived with mail – spare parts, including two new head gaskets. Frank made his way back to the car, now sitting in grass 3 metres high. The magneto was shorted, battery flat and everything rusted. It took him two weeks to get the car going, all the while living on 'sand palm tops and black bream'.

'My gold-mining venture did not prove successful and after a short while I headed back across the continent, travelling on three cylinders. There was no compression in number one, water and grit having cut out the white metal connecting-rod bearings. It took me six months to travel two thousand miles, then one day, while going down a steep grade in desert country, the gasket blew again. Water jammed on the compression stroke and a big piece blew out of the wall of number three cylinder. In a howling sandstorm, I walked to the railway. I camped there and after a few weeks of waiting, managed to get hold of an old Model T Ford engine. I bolted this to the chassis and threw the other engine away. This carried me back to Melbourne.'

11

Francis Birtles
Film Enterprises

World War I had unveiled a new and unexpected warrior-hero – the aviator. The arrival of pilots and airmen was a kind of psychological godsend, giving the wider public some sort of respite from the grim realities of war. Men in flying machines weren't mired in the madness of what was taking place on the ground – they were well above it. Their battles weren't considered murderous, and were given the sporting, playful euphemism of 'dogfights'.

Aviators offered a glimmer of humanity in all the incomprehensible madness – the open skies, the soft-edged clouds, the heavens where a one-on-one duel was played out in another world, disconnected from the barbed-wire entanglements at the Somme and Passchendaele below.

There was a romance about flyers. They were different – somehow elite. That German air ace Manfred von Richthofen – the Red Baron, shot down by the Australian 24th Machine

Gun Company – should be buried with full military honours by No. 3 Squadron Australian Flying Corps gives a sobering idea of the esteem in which wartime aviators were held. Members of the Australian Flying Corps came with modern and evocative ranks – Flight Sergeants, Pilot Officers, Flight Lieutenants, Squadron Leaders, Wing Commanders.

Frank had been particularly keen on aviation from the outset. On various occasions, he had announced his intention to take up flying, even as early as 1912, only nine years after the Wright brothers kicked the whole world of aviation off. At the outbreak of the war he had offered his services to the Australian Flying Corps, and in 1917 he talked of procuring a French Caudron biplane so that he could take cinefilm from the air. The first flight from England to Australia by Ross and Keith Smith saw Frank pick up on aviation fever, completing his film *On the Track of Ross Smith*.

It wasn't until February 1920 that Frank began his serious foray into flying. Frank and a Lieutenant Nigel D. Love flew from Sydney to Cootamundra within three hours in an Avro aircraft. 'The Avro Company [said the Sydney correspondent of the *Advertiser*] arranged the flight as one of a series which will demonstrate aircraft communication for distances under 300 miles to be safe and speedy. The aeroplane is to tour the Riverina for a fortnight before returning to Sydney. Mr. Birtles is taking moving pictures of the flights.'

Certainly flight raised a whole range of unexplored possibilities for cinema, but for Frank, entry into the world of aviation meant something more. Just as the long-distance motorist had eclipsed the overlanding cyclist, the aviator could well overtake the motorist. He didn't want to be left behind.

Aerial photography was quite a phenomenon for cinema-goers and it propelled Frank further into the public eye. He was shaping himself up as an aviation star. Advertisements in newspapers contained line drawings of the remarkable Francis Birtles smiling from the cockpit of an aircraft, clutching his cinematograph camera and tripod: 'I always carry "Aspro" tablets on my across Australia journeys.' Birtles was only too keen to talk of his foray into the prestigious world of aviators as being a matter of course. 'It's only another phase of the moving madness,' said Birtles in a newspaper interview. Readers delighted in looking up to see Mr Birtles flying over Melbourne, taking moving pictures. 'Mr Francis Birtles has again broken all world records, having flown from Cape York, around Australia in three minutes. It was however, around the map of Australia formed by 10,000 Victorian schoolchildren on the Melbourne Cricket Ground yesterday during the children's demonstration which Mr. Birtles was cinematographing.'

Although not a pilot – he would no doubt have taken the controls whenever he could – Frank enrolled in an aviation navigation course. During 1920, he had the use of an ex-Australian Flying Corps Maurice Farman biplane, a rather unconventional French trainer powered by a Renault 80 horsepower engine facing backwards. 'Francis Birtles, the Australian explorer, in his Maurice Farman aeroplane, had a mishap among the Dandenong Ranges today. Running short of benzine, he made a forced landing at Upper Ferntree Gully. He rose again, and in attempting to land at Sassafras his machine suffered a mishap through running into a wire fence, which caused it to stand on its nose. No-one was injured but damage was done to the machine.' And certainly no damage to his reputation.

Frank's fame grew with every story he wrote, every photograph he sold, every movie he'd made – largely thanks to improvements in technology. In print, the world had changed: the ability to reproduce photographs, the quality of stock for magazines, the quick turnaround in publishing and more accessible styles of writing brought new readers. But it was the gradual acceptance of motion pictures as an information source that was becomimg a valuable, and as yet little explored path.

The cinema had recently been considered worthless and brain-addling and derided by those in professional theatre as being a cheap and tawdry form of entertainment. But that was what the masses loved. Not *The Mikado* – they wanted laughs, amazement, thrills. But suddenly, all this stopped. The worldwide influenza pandemic of 1918–1920 which killed between 50 and 130 million people, saw picture theatres identified as prime locations for contracting the disease. Cinemas began to close. Like film makers everywhere, Frank was doing it tough.

Out of the blue, Frank was approached by an entrepreneurial cinema man, Arthur Tinsdale of United Theatres and Films, who saw great potential for a partnership in producing motion pictures for Australian audiences. Tinsdale had big plans for Frank. He believed Frank had what it took to be internationally famous as the intrepid Australian explorer who diced with death at every turn. Furthermore, the company would be called 'Francis Birtles Film Enterprises'. Frank was instantly besotted with the idea. His own motion picture company under his own name. Here was his chance.

Yet Frank had a serious issue – he didn't have the capital like the wealthy Tinsdale to put forward into their 50–50 partnership. That didn't matter – Frank already had a repertoire

of motion pictures he'd made. *Through the Australian Wilds,
Across Australia, On the Track of Burke and Wills* and *On the
Track of Sir Ross Smith*. If he put them into the company as
collateral, then they would hit the ground running with their
own ready-to-go inventory. Tinsdale even suggested he would
buy one of Frank's films, *Through the Australian Wilds*, from
him for 70 pounds, while Frank would retain ownership of the
other three. That sounded more than fair to Frank. He didn't
have to put a penny in, but he had just made 70 quid and,
thanks to Tinsdale, was about to become rich.

The company set up offices in Melbourne and Adelaide and
began cranking up publicity. Advertisements calling for share
subscribers started appearing in newspapers around the country,
announcing a once-in-a-lifetime opportunity to get in on 'Francis
Birtles Film Enterprises – Its Future in Australia of Interest
to Investors', and leaving no doubt as to who was leading the
charge. 'Australia's most popular explorer is at the head of this
enterprise. His associates are well known and experienced cinema
men. The company controls adequate supplies of raw material
and already has many fine finished productions, only a few of
which have been shown to the public. Mr Birtles himself has
secured splendid aerial pictures from his plane and will shortly
fly into the interior for new studies.'

The spiel went on to explain this was a form of national
cultural 'payback' to overseas film makers. 'The Australian
public wants good "Aussie" productions. British and European
Theatres will take all they can get. Investors should apply for
shares early. It is impossible to take up shares after a successful
company has completed its organization.' Other ads claimed the
company had received '. . . letters from the largest film houses

in London' clamouring for Francis Birtles films, and 'There is no other man in Australia who knows more about this grand continent of ours than Francis Birtles. His own efforts have made him famous, Australian film will make him rich. Will you be carried on to prosperity with him?' For the subscription of £1 per share in Francis Birtles Film Enterprises, you'd be a mug for not taking part 'in this splendid money making venture'. As money started rolling in during the following weeks, Frank saw and heard less of Tinsdale, who was presumably busy negotiating deals in Sydney.

One morning in early September, Frank arrived at the film company's Melbourne office in Elizabeth Street to discover Tinsdale's office bare. Bookwork, cheque books, cash, everything – gone. He asked one of the film editors where Tinsdale was and she replied he'd caught the train to the Adelaide bureau. He turned the office upside down only to confirm his greatest fear – all the negatives and copies of his four films were missing too.

Frank's world had suddenly turned inside out – all his motion picture work stolen. In a panic, he ran to the post office and sent a telegram to Tinsdale in Adelaide. Frank was blunt. 'Where are my films? Unless telegraph reply immediately, will take drastic action.' Birtles received no reply. In the days following, Francis learned the company had been placed in the hands of the receivers, who now had his films under lock and key.

As Frank soon found out, Arthur Charles Tinsdale had form. For years he'd been making appearances in courts all over the country. Tinsdale had been involved in predicaments not unlike this one before, setting up motion picture companies such as the Austral Photo Play Company and the Seddon Citizens Picture

Company, taking share subscriptions, employing people for work, taking out rental leases – and then doing a runner with whatever he could pack in his suitcase. He'd been charged over the years with a variety of misdemeanours, including breach of contract, absconding, operating a company prior to registration, and failing to appear. When victims did catch up with him in court, the one-time music hall actor and 'silvery tenor', as he was known, would obfuscate proceedings, befuddling everyone from the magistrate down with his determined recollections of misconstrued handshake arrangements, and as a result the case would be thrown out. But not this time. Frank was going to make sure this 'swindler' – as he called Tinsdale – would get his comeuppance.

12

The Strange Case of Roy Fry

There are times when your life can abruptly shift 90 degrees without warning, where your whole world changes irrevocably, simply through some minor chance happening – an unforeseen event or an unexpected meeting.

In hindsight, if only you'd arrived somewhere 10 minutes earlier or 10 minutes later, your life might have gone down a completely different path. If only . . .

Such was the case for 21-year-old Roy Fry, a law clerk from the Brisbane legal firm of McNab & McNab, who during the winter of 1920 decided to spend his annual fortnight's holiday in Melbourne. Fry arrived at Spencer Street Station having undergone the tiresome luggage hauling and train-swapping rigmarole of switching railway gauges from state to state – from the narrow-gauge railway line in Queensland to the standard-gauge line through New South Wales and the broad-gauge line of Victoria. Simply travelling down the eastern seaboard in a straight line was an ordeal.

Francis Birtles: Australia's greatest overlander. An overlanding cyclist carried his entire world on a bicycle – Frank's Winchester rifle can be seen strapped to the bedroll.

Prepared for any contingency: Frank's bike laden with kit, including a billy for tea. Strong black tea was used to disguise the taste of fetid water.

The grave of a thirst victim. The bicycle took riders into the dead heart and further away from reliable water supplies.

Francis Birtles on the overland telegraph track, north of Alice Springs, in 1908. Heading south from Darwin, he had run headlong into Harry Dutton, Murray Aunger and Ernest Allchurch making the first transcontinental crossing of Australia by motor car.

Syd Ferguson and Rex the terrier, aboard the one-cylinder Brush, making the first latitudinal crossing of Australia by motor car in 1912. Ferguson drove the entire distance from Fremantle to Sydney – and had reservations about his navigator Frank Birtles.

BIRTLES in BRUNSWICK
TO-NIGHT

COME AND HEAR
HIM AT THE

LYRIC

SYDNEY ROAD,
BRUNSWICK.'

No
Moving Picture
has ever
made such an
instantaneous
hit on
Australians.

It will
Open Your Eyes

MR. FRANCIS BIRTLES

Under Great
Expense, the
Management has
engaged
**The Great
Overlander**
who will relate
his
THRILLING
EXPERIENCES in
the wilds of
Australia.

Across Australia

In Addition to our Superb Programme.

Are Pictures Educational?   See and **HEAR** for Yourselves

PRICES AS USUAL

Renwick, Pride, Nuttall, 25-29 Tattersall Place, Melb.

Frank's outback films were immensely popular with cinema-
mad Australians. In an age before talking pictures, Frank's
commentary supplied the accompanying sound every night.

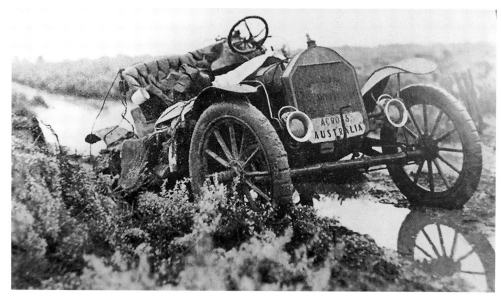

The Brush car – bogged again. Salt pans and bluebush swamp weren't
the only curse for pioneer motorists. Sharp tree stumps had the potential
to puncture a motor car's sump, drain the oil and destroy the engine.

In a Ford promotional photo, Frank Birtles takes a swig of
water while standing alongside his trusty Model T, suggesting
the car had replaced the horse in the outback.

The car, in this case Frank's Model T, combined with rail made
travelling to remote parts of Australia more possible.

To boldly go where no car had gone before: decades before the four-wheel drive,
the Model T was king of the bush. Note Frank's bicycle strapped to the side.

Aborigines knew when Francis Birtles was approaching, simply by the sound of the Model T's engine. 'Motorcar Frank', they called him.

Frank Birtles' photo of a stockman captured the popular image of the classic Australian horseman.

Frank's brother, Clive, and bulldog, Wowser. Frank had a succession of dogs through his overlanding career – the public marvelled at photographs like these.

Frank would set up makeshift darkrooms to develop motion-picture footage, occasionally dodging crocodiles when washing the negatives in Arnhem Land's rivers.

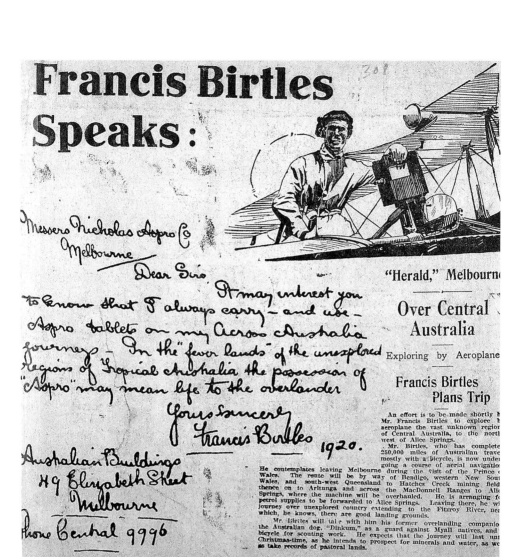

Frank in 1920: the beret-wearing, aerial cinematographer advertising headache tablets. Product endorsement was just one of the ways he'd earn a quid.

Not knowing his way around Melbourne, Fry pushed through the heavy glass doors of a cafeteria to escape the miserable weather. Waitresses bustled from table to table. His eyes scanned the room for a place to sit down, when he recognised the face of a weather-beaten, suntanned man sitting alone in a booth. Fry knew who he was – the famous Francis Birtles – the explorer, the cyclist, the adventurer – the Overlander.

Fry had read of Frank's adventures over the years, and now here he was – Australia's greatest adventurer, the King of Arnhem Land himself. Fry asked Frank if he minded if he sat down at the table and introduced himself. Fry was in awe of Frank – all that he'd accomplished, where he'd travelled, the things he'd seen and written about and photographed and filmed. Only recently he'd been reading articles about his new film company and how it was going to take on the Americans in Australia.

Frank seemed bitter, disillusioned with his achievements. He talked of how he'd had enough of overlanding and was thinking of giving the whole game away. He began to unburden himself to Fry about the fiasco with Tinsdale. Clearly it had devastated him.

The film company that bore his name had been placed into liquidation and the receivers now had possession of his four films. All that work from years ago, some made with his brother Clive way out in the never-never, finding the Aborigines who'd seen Burke and Wills, how he'd put his life on the line just to crank a reel of footage – all this now taken away from him and locked away in some bean-counter's safe.

Fry hung off every word, and in the course of conversation gave Frank some much-needed encouragement, urging him not to give up. There were ways in which the legal system could be employed to set things right. Frank nodded – he was going to use the long arm of the law to hunt down Tinsdale. He wanted his films back, or he wanted decent compensation.

He felt better. In some ways Frank had met a kindred spirit in Fry – someone who revelled in the sort of high adventure he had based his entire life around. Perhaps 39-year-old Birtles saw something of himself in this young fellow – he was fit, intelligent and exuded the same inquisitiveness and exuberance in experiencing adventure, a desire so few people genuinely understood. In hindsight it would have been better if at the end of their conversation they'd just shaken hands and said farewell.

Unknowingly, Fry was wandering into an era of what would become a crucial turning point in Frank's life. Fry didn't return to his job in Brisbane – he decided to stay in Melbourne, unaware he was slowly being dragged into the vortex of Francis Birtles' disintegrating world.

In the wake of what had happened with Tinsdale – and perhaps with Fry's enthusiastic encouragement – Birtles decided to have one last determined shot at the film-making business, and wrote directly to Prime Minister William Morris Hughes requesting a federal government grant for the funding of a documentary. Frank envisaged creating a film for the Department of Immigration depicting the wonders of Australia – its natural splendour and its thriving industry. Birtles threw almost every-thing he could think of into the proposal.

'Sir, I have the honour to inform you that it is my intention to make an overland journey across Australia, for the purpose of obtaining not less than 10,000 feet of Australian travelogue, educational, historical and industrial cinematograph films.'

Frank's proposal was comprehensive: 'four experts and artists would accompany me including Lieut. Borella VC.' The letter went on attempting to cover every conceivable filmic aspect of Australian life '. . . scenes around Melbourne and its industries, through Ballarat, Mildura, Broken Hill, Burke and Wills' depots . . . scenes along explorers' routes . . . nature studies of reptiles, birds . . . views along the two proposed North–South Railway lines (Katherine–Oodnadatta and Katherine–Queensland). Buffalo, wild bull and wild pig hunting, crocodile . . .', and finally Birtles arrived at the pointy bit. 'To enable me to successfully carry out the expedition, I respectfully request that you will approach your Government with a view to subsidising the expedition to the extent of £1,500.'

Fifteen hundred pounds was a big ask but, as far as Frank was concerned, his travelogue had all the ingredients for a government-funded smash hit – depictions of civilised metropolitan Australia, a bit of history, some Burke and Wills, a bit of industry, the outback, wildlife and Victoria Cross winner Albert Borella thrown in for some gravitas, and genuine star quality.

Enclosed with Frank's proposal to the prime minister was a letter addressed to his secretary by way of introduction, requesting his application for funding be placed before the prime minister as soon as possible. For all the bravado of the proposal, the letter gives a remarkable insight into Frank's state of mind at this time. 'On the completion of this expedition,' Frank wrote, 'I intend to terminate my Australian overlanding, having travelled a quarter of a million miles during the last 20 years.'

Frank's handwritten proposal and accompanying letter arrived on the prime ministerial secretary's desk on 27 October 1920, where surprisingly it was received with considerable interest.

Under normal circumstances, an unsolicited request for a government grant would be filed away with the other countless proposals for funding – except one line in the three-page application caught the eye of the prime minister's secretary, Malcolm Shepherd: '. . . views along the two proposed North–South Railway lines (Katherine–Oodnadatta and Katherine–Queensland) . . .'

Shepherd, a close confidant of the prime minister, wrote a note at the bottom of Birtles' letter and passed it to a subordinate – 'Mr Fuller, would you look into this?' Frank's letter couldn't have arrived at a more opportune time. Birtles wasn't to know but at that very moment the prime minister was in the position of trying to appease three Australian states, namely South Australia, Western Australia and Queensland, regarding a proposed survey of a transcontinental railway connecting Adelaide to Darwin. At that time, the railway was considered paramount in helping to unite a disparate nation.

Rail would then have linked four of Australia's great ports – north, south, east and west – and in the process turn central Australia into a transport hub. On paper it seemed an obvious idea, but just how feasible was it? The very idea of running steam locomotives across a continent that was largely waterless was mind-boggling. Yet the vast majority of Australians had absolutely no idea what lay in the heart of Australia and would have no understanding of why such a project would be so expensive.

Hughes was in the process of assembling several committees of experts who would venture out into central Australia to study and survey the regions for the proposed railway line. These experts were the usual suspects – engineers, surveyors, and so forth – but perhaps the inclusion of someone like Frank

Birtles would be of benefit. With his extraordinary outback knowledge and his ability to film and photograph, what Birtles was proposing gave an alternative and exciting public edge to what would otherwise be a typical lacklustre government fact-finding mission.

Secretary Shepherd and his staff entered into a discussion with Frank about the idea of conducting a survey alongside the other appointed parties and returning with film footage, photographs and a personal report outlining his appraisal of the regions suggested for the railway. He would be paid for his services, of course, and the government would supply a car . . . Birtles couldn't believe it. At last, the Prime Minister's Office – no less – was asking Francis Birtles, the famous overlander, to help in solving the nation's problems and assist in devising Australia's future.

Frank's head was now brimming with countless ideas: all those months – years – spent cycling and motoring alone through Australia's lonely lands – thinking, perpetually thinking. He knew just how to help the prime minister, just what to suggest, and more.

Excited, Frank told Roy of the prospect and urged him to accompany him. Plans had changed and Borella VC and Major Scarlett had now pulled out of the original idea, so here was a great opportunity for a young man keen for excitement. 'Being of an adventurous nature, I was greatly pleased with this opportunity,' Fry later wrote. 'Frank was at that time a very well-known explorer and overlander, having ridden a push bicycle criss-crossing Australia many times, and I, being only 21 at the time, felt I could trust this hard, tough, sun-baked man who was

20 years my senior, and who, I felt, could handle any emergency which was sure to occur once we left the beaten tracks.'

Roy was in awe of Frank. As far as he was concerned, Frank was a genuine 20th century star, and now here was young Fry, a 21-year-old swept up in an adventure with the famous Francis Birtles on behalf of the prime minister. 'I had often read his articles in various Australian Magazines, but it never occurred to me that one day I would be his companion on his greatest exploit.'

The deal was done. A contract was negotiated with the Prime Minister's Office whereby Frank was to be paid the astonishing amount of £1,000 in four instalments – £500 before leaving Melbourne, £100 on arrival at Alice Springs, £200 at Katherine and £200 at Camooweal. The government agreed to purchase, at the cost of £925, a new American Hudson Super Six tourer – with whatever spares would be required – and loan the car to Frank for the duration of the expedition.

The proviso was that Frank pay for fuel and the car's maintenance. A thousand quid! With this, he could buy the latest – and very best – in photographic equipment. What a kit he could put together! Still cameras, cinecameras, glass plates, paintable emulsion, rolled film, developing chemicals, trays, thermometers, tripods, magnesium flares. And best of all, a Hudson Super Six – the car alone was worth more than four times a yearly wage! This was the type of car Frank could only dream of: six cylinders; a self-starter; big, strong, robust, comfortable. It was more than perfect for carrying the equipment needed for such a photographic expedition.

On top of that, all Frank had to do was pay for fuel out of what change was left over. As for young Roy Fry, he didn't need to be paid. His input would be purely honorary, of course. What he was receiving was the inestimable privilege of an adventure with the great Frank Birtles. And furthermore, the government didn't need to know he had a helper with him. After all – it was Frank the government had commissioned.

Birtles put together a comprehensive list for spare parts for the journey and presented it to Kellow-Falkiner, the Melbourne agents for Hudson cars. In 1920, Hudson cars were considered one of America's most prestigious marques and the straight 'super six' engine one of the finest in the world. In Frank's case, he needed a car that was really to double as a truck in that it had to carry the occupants, their provisions, the weight of the extra fuel required and the extremely heavy photographic equipment, comfortably and quickly.

The formalities between Birtles and the government were now drawing to a close, and Frank had the timing of his first payment and delivery of the car worked out to the minute. If all went according to plan, he would sign his contract on 22 November, receive payment of £500 the next day and then pick up the keys to the Hudson from Kellow-Falkiner the day after. Everything needed to run like clockwork.

Then, all of a sudden, Frank announced he would be marrying a girl half his age on 27 November – the day after he picked up the car. According to Fry, 'Frank was in love' with 23-year-old Frances Knight from Prahran, Victoria, describing her as 'a beautiful girl', the daughter of a piano tuner from Woollahra in Sydney. Perhaps Frank was genuinely 'in love' with his bride-to-be. However, his actions during the next few months suggest something entirely different. Unlike his brother Clive, who pined for his sweetheart Olive during the months he spent with Frank out in the never-never, Frank never mentioned an interest in a woman. His life had tipped from one hairy-chested episode into another – the merchant navy, the army, the constabulary, his outback adventures . . . by all accounts, he rarely seemed to come into contact with women. His conversational repertoire was generally limited to topics such as side-valve cylinder heads and water buffaloes. A friend once remarked that 'women simply bored him'.

Exactly when and how Frank met and proposed to Frances and arranged the marriage is unclear, only that the ceremony was to be swift and the nuptials even swifter.

Francis and Frances were to be married at St Paul's Cathedral in Melbourne. Out of the blue, Birtles asked his new-found mate Roy Fry to be best man. On 27 November, Mr and Mrs Francis Birtles strolled down the steps of St Paul's, from where the newlyweds set off for Sydney on their honeymoon in the government-loaned Hudson Super Six.

It was a cosy honeymoon, to say the least. The honeymooners' car also contained Roy, Frances's sister and Frank's mate Major Scarlett. The five motored along the Princes Highway, and they eventually stopped in the Sydney beachside suburb of Bondi, where Frank set to work preparing the Hudson for the outback trip. Three and a half weeks after his wedding and two days before Christmas, Frank said farewell to his new bride and headed off towards the Blue Mountains with Roy in the passenger's seat, bound for central Australia.

On 25 January 1921, little more than a month after Birtles and Fry had taken off for the outback in the Hudson Super Six, Prime Minister Hughes finally announced the commissioning of his three reports for the railway. The first report would be by '. . . a committee of men with first-hand knowledge of the western district of Queensland and the Northern Territory who would report on the proposed alternative route which would link up the western ends of the Queensland railways and reach the Northern Territory via Camooweal. Senators will be permitted to accompany this committee on its inspection.' The second report was to look at the Queensland route, and the committee would commence their work about May or June when the rainy season was over. Hughes drew a long breath. His next announcement had already been a controversial subject for discussion among members of parliament. The third report would be 'furnished by Mr Francis Birtles on the character of the country between Oodnadatta and Katherine River. He will travel by motorcycle northwards on one side of the telegraph line and on the other side when returning and explore the country some miles east and west of the line.'

Curiously, Hughes talked of Birtles travelling by motorcycle when the prime minister himself had personally signed off on the expensive Hudson Super Six more than two months earlier. In fact, Birtles had picked up the keys to the Hudson two months before – to the day. It suggests perhaps Hughes might not have been receiving the best advice. Or maybe he was downplaying the cost of bringing Birtles onboard – a brand-new taxpayer-funded Hudson Super Six for such an unpredictable adventurer might be difficult to justify.

The prime minister then came to the crunch. He knew the announcement of a government-funded Birtles expedition was going to be a hot topic for debate, and so he attempted to bluff it out. 'There has been some criticism of Mr Birtles' appointment,' Hughes continued, 'but he has travelled over

150,000 miles over Australia on a "push" bicycle. When his critics know as much about Australia as he knows, I will listen to them.' In the attempt to short-circuit opposition to Birtles' inclusion, Hughes had inadvertently fired a flare illuminating his appointment to the nation.

Those who had a genuine understanding of geotechnical engineering, railway construction and agriculture were disappointed that the federal government was funding this 'adventurer' to submit a report on what would influence one of the greatest engineering feats Australia had ever undertaken. Some of Hughes' Cabinet were outraged. They knew nothing whatsoever of the decision to finance a Birtles expedition for such an important undertaking until after the deal had been signed.

The following day, Hughes received a vitriolic letter from Mr David Lindsay of Sydney, Fellow of the Royal Geographic Society, who was appalled with the appointment.

Sir,

In yesterday's Sydney Morning Herald regarding the North South Railway you are reported to have said 'The third report will be furnished by Mr Francis Birtles' . . . Will you pardon me for drawing to your attention the fact that your NT Lands Department in Melbourne can, within a week, furnish you with fairly full reports on the whole of the Country 100 to 200 miles on either side of the Overland Telegraph Line between the points you mention, compiled from reports and plans made by professional men of recognised ability . . . and very recent reports by Mr Day and myself and others – information and reports impossible for Mr Birtles to obtain from a motorcycle journey. Anyone who has been in that country will tell you that it is quite impossible for motorcycling.

Once Mr Birtles leaves the road track he will find it impossible to ride his machine over the sand hills then through the Ranges and Mulga Scrubs and spinifex covered sand plains and hills. God help Birtles when he gets into the melon hole Hedgewood Country or into ashy downs. As to Mr Birtles knowledge, without detracting from his gameness in pushing a bicycle over bush tracks, I have yet to learn that he has the necessary qualifications for reporting on Country. Has he ever been engaged to report on Country? Will anyone take any notice of his reports? Every man to his own job. Mr Birtles' engagement is a serious reflection on the professional men both in and out of the Service. I humbly think I am qualified to criticise Mr Birtles, as I have 'seen as much of Australia as he has.'

I have the honour to be, Sir,
Your obedient servant,
David Lindsay, F.R.G.S.

It was too late for Hughes to do anything about it now – Frank and Roy were hurtling along in the Hudson Super Six, way out in the never-never.

On 21 April, the battered Hudson pulled up at the corrugated iron depot store at Daly Waters. Frank climbed out and called over a mechanic, asking for the car and all the spare fuel tins to be refuelled with benzine. The car, its auxiliary fuel tanks and spare fuel tins were completely filled with petrol from the hand-pump at a whopping cost of £16. Frank waved his hand and instructed the mechanic to simply send the bill to the Prime Minister's Department. Frank was here on official business and they'd fix it up.

The proprietor was confused, and slightly suspicious. You can't just turn up and take sixteen quid of fuel and not pay, prime minister or not. He telegraphed Frederic Urquhart, the hard-headed Northern Territory Administrator in Darwin, to see if he knew anything about this. The Prime Minister's Office in Melbourne received an urgent telegram from Urquhart that Birtles had arrived at Daly Waters and was asking for petrol, the account to be forwarded to the federal government for payment. Was this correct?

A straightforward reply from the Prime Minister's Office stated that under the terms of the contract Birtles was to supply all the petrol and if he took some on board, he'd have to pay for it. The Administrator replied to the Daly Waters depot agreeing to bear the cost of the refuelling provided the amount of £16 and 16 shillings was deducted by the Prime Minister's Office from Birtles' next £200 payment and reimbursed. All very strange – Birtles knew perfectly well what the arrangement was. He had plenty of money. Why couldn't he pay?

In the weeks that followed, letters from far-flung outposts in the Northern Territory requesting payment began to arrive at the Prime Minister's Office – for 'motor covers' (tyres), for work carried out on Birtles' car, for one-off machined parts, nuts and bolts.

In the Prime Minister's Office in Melbourne, alarm bells started to ring. Frank and Roy were experiencing some pretty rough conditions. Unseasonal flooding had seen Birtles crossing swollen rivers by covering the Hudson's engine with canvas sheeting, removing the fanbelt and rigging up a snorkel arrangement on the carburettor intake so that the car could drive through submerged.

Due to the floods, obtaining food and fuel supplies had become problematic, and at one point they were forced to use kerosene when they were short of petrol. The car itself was faring badly. Its radiator was cemented hard with spinifex grass seeds and Birtles' punishing driving techniques had seen him telegraphing for the shipment of extra tyres and even a new cylinder head due to the kerosene burning out exhaust valves, indicating the sort of brutal treatment the car was receiving.

The magnificent four-month-old Hudson was now a rolling wreck. It had scraped trees and posts and stumps, and its body panels had been belted more or less back into shape in a blacksmith's shop in Katherine. It had been waterlogged in filthy outback floodwaters, the engine had been run on the wrong fuel, and in an attempt to improve upon the car's design, Frank had thrown away the lower half of the hinged bonnet and removed the entire exhaust system. He hated exhausts – he believed exhaust systems drained horsepower. The car was ear-splittingly loud and would spit flames from the exhaust ports even when idling.

Yet in the big picture this didn't really matter. The prestige the government would receive when showing Frank's film footage to the public would far outweigh the costs of a car. Frank and Roy were on the eve of having completed their filming and for their return they intended to follow the Queensland border south.

'The prettiness of the country surrounding Warlock Ponds is not altogether in keeping with the reputation of the country,' wrote Fry, 'as it is said that a "hoodoo" or curse has been placed upon the area owing to the prevalence of accidents or sickness to white men. Mrs Gunn, the author of *We of the Never Never*, lost her husband at the old Elsey Station, as his lonely grave bears witness. About 3 miles away, on the Longreach plain, Sir Ross Smith was forced to land owing to engine trouble. I have also met men who could tell of an accident to themselves or what they had witnessed. Then our own tragic accident later compelled me to admit that it seemed more than coincidence.'

Driving through long, dry grass the car hit a stump and exploded. With 80 gallons (300 litres) of petrol aboard, the Hudson became an instantaneous fireball.

'There was a roar and up shot a sheet of blinding orange coloured flame,' Frank recalled. 'Then with clothing ablaze I leaped out, and throwing myself on the ground, rolled over and over through the grass.' One after another the square fuel tins lashed to the car's blazing bodywork blew apart, sending burning pieces of the car in all directions. Dazed and burned, Frank suddenly realised Roy was missing.

'The grass around the car was alight. Even as I turned in search of Roy a huddled-up figure lurched out of the flames. He fell and then staggered to his feet. The car was now hidden by fire. The flames roared up to a height of 40 feet. Eighty gallons of petrol were ablaze and a strong side-wind was making intense heat . . . flames seared my face.' Frank watched as the Hudson blazed uncontrollably, burning flat to the ground, a wild column of black smoke billowing out at each continuing explosion.

Frank later wrote: 'The awful truth dawned on me. We had lost everything we possessed; the car and almost £2,000 of cameras, clothing, photos, cinema films and money in notes. The mental distress was as bad as the physical.' All of Frank's camera equipment and all the footage he'd shot for the expedition was now engulfed in flame, yard upon yard of nitro-cellulose negative burning like gunpowder-laced fuse.

Frank dragged Fry into long green grass to put out the flames. Roy looked up to see long strips of skin and flesh hanging from his fingertips. He had taken in a mouthful or two of the flames, and his tongue had swollen up to the roof of his mouth – his nostrils were burnt inside and he could not breathe through his nose. 'Frank kept telling me there was nothing wrong with my hair or face, but, although I could not use my hands, I could feel the tingling of the nerves in my face, while my hair felt dreadfully short.'

Frank took stock of Fry's predicament. Roy had been horrifically burned, and without urgent attention he was going to die.

They had driven through a camp of Aborigines about 10 kilometres earlier, and so set off on foot to try to get there. Frank clutched a waterbag, giving Roy, who was now delirious, a sip every few minutes. Their clothes almost completely burnt off, the pair staggered through the spinifex in search of help. 'The sharp pointed spear grass stuck into our burnt flesh, and the sharp rocks cut my mate's injured feet.' By evening they had stumbled through a swamp and in the dark reached the Aboriginal camp, collapsing by the fire. Stunned, the Aborigines immediately sent a runner to Mataranka for help.

'There followed a night of agony,' Birtles recalled. 'On the hard ground, we lay in bitterly cold wind. Our wounds could not endure the touch of our clothing. It seemed to be a never-ending night. Shivering, we crept nearer to the warmth of the camp fires, but raw flesh and tortured nerves could not endure the warmth. A jabbering of voices and the blackfellow came into the circle of light, a bottle of salad oil in his hand – medical aid from the Chinese cook in Mataranka. This blackfellow – his name I do not know – had travelled thirty-four miles during the night.'

Birtles was told the station hands who'd been out mustering were on their way and would reach them by midday. The

Aborigines tore up a calico tent fly in which they wrapped Fry and Birtles, placing them in the shade of a tree to wait for the rescue party. 'Parched I asked for water and drank greedily out of the cool water bag. My throat was dry and my tongue swollen. Both of us by now had big baggy blisters on our faces. Our eyebrows and eyelashes were gone.'

At midday, several station hands arrived with a dray pulled by five horses. The Aborigines made a mattress out of grass and placed a sheet of calico over the top, onto which Roy and Frank were lowered. The horse team set off on the slow and painful drive to the nearest hospital, 70 kilometres away. 'The heat of the day gave way to a chilly night. Continual clop-clop of the horses' hooves, cracks of a whip, "gee-ups" of the driver . . . heaves and bumps as the wheels struck ant-beds in the darkness.'

The following day they arrived at the Inland Mission Hospital at the Marranboy Tinfields, halfway between the accident site and Katherine, where they were lifted out and injected with morphine. The following morning, a nurse came to peel the bandages off. 'A graceful woman garbed in pink came soft-footed over to where I lay. Then, while her beautiful voice sounded nearby, the throbbing flesh of my arms was slowly torn off from shoulder to finger tips.'

In Melbourne, telegrams began arriving at the Prime Minister's Office suggesting that Birtles had been involved in an accident. No-one was exactly sure where and how, but as further messages arrived the story gained momentum. A rumour began circulating among the public that Birtles had been killed.

The Prime Minister's Office went into panic. What had happened? Word came through about the fire and that Birtles was alive but that his companion Roy Fry was in a critical condition.

Roy Fry? Who was he? – asked the Prime Minister's Office. They knew nothing about any companion on this journey. The agreement about the expedition had been with Francis Edwin Birtles only.

Memorandums started circulating as the picture became clearer – and the picture wasn't good. In a nutshell it was this: Francis Birtles – the contentious choice for this survey – and a mysterious, and hitherto unknown, 21-year-old Roy Fry, were both terribly burned in a car accident, and were lying in a hospital in the middle of the Northern Territory, with no clothing, no money and no way of extricating themselves. Not to mention that a £1,000 government-purchased Hudson Super Six was now lying somewhere in the outback, burnt to the ground, with all the film shot for the survey destroyed.

On top of that, an unknown amount of cash recently picked up from the post office in Katherine was supposedly burned in the fire. The superintendent of the Government Stamping Battery at Maranboy was sent out to give an initial appraisal as to what had happened at the accident site. His telegram to the Prime Minister's Office was unequivocal, laying the blame squarely with Birtles: 'Inspection – Fire due to carrying drum of benzine under chassis coupled with absence of exhaust is direct cause of fire. Business cannot be classed as accidental but pure indifference.'

In the weeks that followed, Frank was recuperating remarkably well, but not so Roy, who was still in a critical condition. It was only thanks to the amazing and diligent work of two nursing sisters, Doris Dunlop and Jean Hird, that he eventually began to scrape through.

The Prime Minister's Office decided to send an investigation team to the Northern Territory to ascertain what had actually happened. From Darwin they made their way to the accident site near Mataranka. where they found the remains of the Hudson. After careful inspection they filed their report. 'On examining the car it was found that Birtles had removed the silencer, exhaust pipe and exhaust manifold from the side of the engine . . . these are used for conveying the exploded charge from the engine into the air, thus acting as a safeguard. He had also removed the bottom leaf of the bonnet on the same side as the engine. There was nothing therefore to prevent the exploded charge from coming into contact with the dry grass alongside the tracks. The car had struck a stump about 9 inches high very forcibly with the rear wheel and no doubt this caused one or more of the petrol tins to burst.'

Once back in Melbourne, Frank wasn't prepared to give up. The government closing its doors to him only pushed him further into desperation. Money aside, Frank had seen his golden opportunity for fame and recognition burn to the ground with the Hudson out on Elsey Station, yet he was still campaigning, hoping to recover the situation. He wrote to Prime Minister Hughes explaining that he hadn't finished his report and intended to keep going – at his own expense.

At present my right arm is semi-paralysed. To complete the task I am now on my way to central Australia, per aeroplane and account of same will feature in this report. I am endeavouring to carry out this work at my own expense and intend to keep at it until an outcome is finally decided upon.

I am Sir, Your Obedient Servant, Francis Birtles

With whatever money Frank was bringing in from various magazine-article submissions, he managed to commission aviator Flight Lieutenant Frank Briggs to fly him from Melbourne to Alice Springs via Adelaide for an aerial survey for the proposed railway line. (In typical Frank Birtles style, this flight in a de Havilland 4 biplane would be another 'first' – becoming the first aerial crossing of the Simpson Desert, Lake Eyre, the MacDonnell Ranges and the first aircraft to land in Alice Springs.) Billy Hughes had been attending the Imperial Conference in London while the Birtles–Fry debacle had begun to unravel in Australia, and the government was becoming nervous as to where it would all end. They learned that Frank had chartered an aircraft from Melbourne and would attempt to ambush the prime minister on his arrival in Adelaide.

Prior to Hughes' return to Australia, a Cabinet minister sent him an urgent letter warning him of the situation he was returning to.

My Dear Prime Minister,

There is a small matter which I particularly wish to bring under your notice before you return to Melbourne. It is reported here that Francis Birtles is flying over to meet you in Adelaide, and in all probability will submit some proposition to you in connection with his exploratory work and tour in Central Australia. When I was in the Northern Territory I happened to be within a few miles of where he met with the accident, and made the necessary arrangements for his comfort while recovering from the injuries received in the explosion of the car.

The general opinion of Birtles among the settlers and graziers is not very good. It surprised me that he had gained for himself an unenviable character. His cheques are flying all around the Northern Territory, and in nine cases out of 10 are dishonoured. Only the other day the Department received telegraph advice from a settler in Central Australia who stated that the Commonwealth Bank had dishonoured a cheque drawn by Birtles. I sincerely trust that before you commit yourself to any proposal, you will give Cabinet and myself an opportunity of putting the matter before you. With kind regards to yourself and hoping to see you on Wednesday.

Clearly tipped off by disgruntled members of Hughes' cabinet, the Melbourne *Age* was critical of Birtles – *the cyclist* – asking for even more money in addition to the already ludicrous fee the prime minister had agreed upon. 'This, it was presumed, included a report with such recommendations as a cyclist could be expected to make regarding the route of a railway. That there should be additional expense however was apparently not contemplated by the Prime Minister, and was certainly not expected by other ministers, some of whom knew nothing about the appointment until all the conditions had been agreed upon . . . any further outlay in this connection would obviously amount to a wanton waste of public funds.'

Things went from bad to worse. Birtles' trail of ad hoc promissory notes and IOUs from all over the Northern Territory was now winding its way to the federal government in Melbourne.

It seemed that the prime minister's personal envoy in the wilds of the Australian outback was looking like a potential felon, and politically this was shaping up as a nightmare.

Roy Fry, meanwhile, was in a shocking state. Penniless and incapacitated, he had returned to his parents' home in Brisbane to convalesce. As part of a government expedition in which he had received no payment, Fry was hoping to mount a case for some sort of compensation. He'd written to Frank for help on several occasions but had received no reply. Frank had gone to ground. In desperation, he wrote to Senator H. S. Foll of the Public Works Committee, who had already lent a sympathetic ear.

Fry was desperate: 'Only you would recognize the hard and strenuous battle I put up with for months previous to the accident and considering the way Birtles has let me down, you can imagine my feelings at ever meeting him.' Foll followed up the case with the prime minister, stating he had visited Fry, who was 'in a very bad state of health indeed as a result of the severe burning, fever and shock that he received when the Hudson car supplied by the Government to Mr Birtles was burnt'.

The Prime Minister's Office wasn't giving Roy Fry any assistance. In the initial agreement, there had been no provision about Birtles taking an offsider and – as tough as it must be – Fry was on his own. Then, a forgotten victim reappeared. Frances, Frank's wife, had called in at the Prime Minister's Office in Melbourne, seeking assistance. She had not seen her husband since he left her in Sydney two weeks after their marriage six months earlier. Since that time, she had only received a cheque for £10 from him. She wanted to know if the Prime Minister's Office had any idea of his whereabouts. This was turning into a serious problem for the Prime Minister's Office. Fed up with trying to locate him and having letters returned from the Dead Letter Office, they suggested all matters concerning Birtles should now be placed in the hands of the Crown Solicitor.

Birtles' final report submitted to government regarding the transcontinental railway was sketchy, erratic and smacked of poor research. In fairness, the whole enterprise had been extremely traumatic for Frank, but considering the grief Hughes and his government had been through in dealing with crises wherever he had been, Frank's report didn't hold much worth.

His report touched on the obvious issues regarding the procurement of timber railway sleepers, ballast and the positioning of water towers for steam locomotives. However, he invariably strayed off course, espousing his obsession with redeveloping the whole of the top end of Australia, devising strategies for the handling of troops in case of a foreign attack, the necessity of semi-military control in the north and even detailing how in New Guinea '. . . Asiatic labour is now developing pronounced Bolshevik co-operation.'

Having read Birtles' effort, the unimpressed Minister for Home and Territories, Alexander Poynton, sent the report back to his departmental secretary with the note:

Reports by Mr Birtles are returned herewith and I have carefully perused them. Mr Birtles has touched on matters which are quite irrelevant to the subject of the best route for the line to take, and I consider that his report will be of little assistance in the matter under consideration. It is a pity that he did not confine his remarks to the work which he was supposed to have done.

Poynton.

The government had washed its hands of Francis Birtles.

In October 1921, Frances petitioned for the marriage to be annulled. She too had had enough. From the day she married Frank, Frances simply watched his life explode and tear apart. Not that she could have been there to help him. Frank was mentioned in the petition as 'an explorer, sometimes known as an overlander'.

Frank's world had all but completely unravelled, yet in December 1921 it seemed his fortunes might just change. Shortly before Christmas he received a tip-off that Arthur Charles Tinsdale – *the swindler* who had stolen his three films – had been sighted in Western Australia, as far from Frank Birtles' reach as possible.

Justice was about to be served. Frank had done everything within the legal boundaries to ensure his films were recovered and Tinsdale brought before the court to pay. Frank sailed to Perth aboard the *Karoola* from Sydney to try and find him. Frank knew Tinsdale had some sort of family connection in Bunbury, West Australia, and on a hunch boarded the train from Perth to go and get him.

What happened next was best described by the *Sunday Times* of 1 January 1922: 'Not coming across Tinsdale in Bunbury, Birtles decided to return to Perth. While on the way back, as the train pulled up at one of the stations, Birtles thought it might be necessary to change trains, and in order to inquire the position he put his head out of the window of his carriage and, lo and behold, he discovered that in the next compartment or so there was someone else of an inquiring turn of mind! Who should it be but the man he sought – Tinsdale! Thereafter, Birtles took care not to lose sight of his quarry.'

The West Australian police arrested Tinsdale and charged him with stealing £5000 worth of cinema films and remanded him on bail until New South Wales detectives arrived from Sydney to extradite him. For Perth, this was a big trial – Francis Birtles, Australia's very own star, the overlander, the adventurer versus the vaudevillian, smoke-and-mirror theatre operator.

On 20 January, Tinsdale gave a masterful performance in court whereby the magistrate decided to refuse New South Wales police the opportunity of extraditing him to Sydney. No sooner had Tinsdale left the court than he was marched back in – Frank now charging him with perjury. For Perth, this case was really starting to heat up.

The following month the perjury case began, where Frank's legal team unveiled a secret weapon – a star witness. Alice Snell was a widow from Roleystone in Melbourne who had worked as a film cutter for Francis Birtles Film Enterprises during 1920.

Under examination she said she was still working for the company after it went into liquidation and had been still employed by Tinsdale. Snell understood Francis Birtles owned his films *Across Australia*, *On the Track of Burke and Wills* and *On the Track of Ross Smith*, with the exception of *Through the Australian Wilds* which Tinsdale had bought from the overlander for £70. Upon the company's liquidation the negatives for all four films were presumably placed in the hands of the receivers.

Snell told the court Tinsdale was desperate to flee Melbourne because he was 'frightened the shareholders in the company were waiting for him', and wasn't game to take the train to Adelaide in case he was recognised; so, feeling pity for him, she bought him a boat ticket in her own name. During that time Snell was puzzled when Tinsdale changed his story about Francis Birtles' films, now claiming he personally owned all of them.

Some weeks later, while conducting an inventory in the Adelaide office, Snell made an astonishing discovery – Tinsdale in fact had hidden the negatives for all four of Francis Birtles' films in a storeroom. They were never in the hands of the receivers. She continued, 'When word came through that Birtles was burned to death in the Northern Territory, Tinsdale remarked that if it was so he would be "well rid of him".'

The public gallery was shocked.

After the defence made its final plea the court adjourned until the next day.

The magistrate said 'he had to ask himself did the accused have reasonable grounds for the belief that he bought the films at the figure stated. He did not think a prima facie case had been established . . . He was of the opinion that a case had not been made out in which a jury could convict.'

Birtles was outraged. The charge of perjury was dismissed, Tinsdale was free and the films were officially his. Frank never trusted the legal system again. Yet from there on the local press in Perth kept an eye on the shonky Tinsdale – his name would often pop up in gossip columns simply stating 'Film "Jonah" Tinsdale in trouble again' without elaborating why. This would be boiled down to 'Tinsdale again!'

Some months after the court case finished a fierce blaze broke out at 2 a.m. at the Barrack Street boatsheds in Perth. The *Western Mail* reported the fire 'totted up damage amounting in all to 6000 pounds, while various insurance company managers slumbered, blissfully unaware that claims estimated to the extent of 1,700 pounds had materialised against them . . . Amongst the occupants of the building was Arthur Charles Tinsdale, who was stated to have lost a quantity of film and business, papers in the blaze. Detective-Sergeant Muller is making an exhaustive inquiry in the happening and its origin.'

Francis Birtles' four films, *Across Australia*, *Through Australian Wilds*, *On the Track of Burke and Wills* and *On the Track of Ross Smith*, were lost to Australia forever.

13

Everything Changes...

After all the amazing things he'd achieved – his bicycle rides, his motoring adventures, his writing, his photography, his films – Frank's world had slid off the rails. His name was now appearing in the newspapers for different reasons – under attack in editorials for his unsuitability for the railway survey, reports of his divorce, and the train-wreck of his court case against Tinsdale.

Frank had become a deft hand at using the outback as an escape hatch in an emergency. If someone was after him for an unpaid account or an IOU, Frank was invariably impossible to find. He could simply climb into a car and disappear for months. Frank was perpetually on the move, ricocheting between Melbourne and Sydney, Darwin and Borroloola, and Perth and Coopers Creek and Alice Springs – always quite a few steps ahead of his creditors.

Every now and then they'd catch up with him. In September 1924, Frank was brought before the court for not having paid the £60 fee for the annulment of his marriage to Frances back in 1921. He'd physically threatened the issuing officers who'd returned to serve his summons with the police in tow, telling them, 'You can tell the court to go to hell, with my compliments.' He'd told the officer serving the summons, 'You won't get anything out of me. I am going to the Northern Territory and will stay there.'

And that's what he did.

•

Aborigines featured prominently in Frank Birtles' life. He sometimes went bush to live with them 'as a white native', as a relative of Frank's put it. They fascinated him and he fascinated them, yet this mutual admiration took many years to develop. His lengthy and numerous experiences in the outback helped him break away from ingrained white perceptions of the Australian Aborigines. But it took some time. Colonial Australia had different views.

In 1888, seven years after Frank Birtles was born, Australia celebrated the centenary of the arrival of the First Fleet and the raising of the British flag at Sydney Cove. It was a congratulatory salutation of just how far the colony had come since it had kicked off as a terminus for Britain's most unwanted. Convicts and their keepers had arrived in a land the size of continental Europe that was, as far as King George III was concerned, empty. The local inhabitants who had wandered the continent for tens of thousands of years didn't count.

On 3 March 1888, in what would have been an uncomfortable observation for many, the *Bulletin* published a provocative cartoon drawn by Phil May depicting a grotesque side of colonial

Australia. A city-dwelling Aboriginal mother holds her baby, around which a crowd of awkward white Australians jostle to gawk at them, as though they were some kind of circus attraction. The caption beneath reads: 'A curiosity in her own country'.

May's drawing of the mother and child is delicate and realistic; the contrast of her skin against the white background is the visual focus. Even the inclusion of a gawping Chinese figure among the white population – unusual in that the *Bulletin* was conducting an anti-Chinese campaign at the time – gives the Aborigines an even further remoteness from society. White Australia didn't think much of the Chinese, yet in the cartoon, they were more onside than Aborigines.

Most colonial Australians would have been outraged by May's cartoon's assertion that for Aborigines, this was their 'own country'. And initially, Francis Birtles was no exception; he grew up, like the majority of British Australians, with the firm belief Australia was a white man's country, where in everyday life Aborigines were talked about and written up as 'negroes' and 'niggers'. Most white city dwellers were generally ambivalent about Indigenous Australians, as they hardly ever saw them. Many lived in camps on the city's fringes, or on reserves. Yet others maintained varied opinions. Some viewed the plight of Aborigines with a sort of anthropological pity, as they were undoubtedly a dying race. Some viewed them as intellectually inferior and often lazy – with a bit of 'encouragement', they constituted a ready-made labour resource for a superior white society. And some regarded them as vermin to be eradicated: murder and massacres were far more prevalent out in the Australian wilds than anyone would have ever imagined – or admitted.

Frank's early writing mentions Aborigines more or less as an occupational hazard when overlanding, much in the way you might encounter a bushfire or a brown snake. He'd hear from bullock drivers, cow cockies, swagmen and other itinerants wandering up and down the track who'd pass on the latest news on where to avoid 'hostile blacks'. Some of the early overlanding cyclists, who were more likely to carry a firearm than a compass, would think nothing of taking 'pot shots' at Aborigines they'd encounter.

There are examples of Frank's early writing espousing his theories on Aborigines, and where they could be used as a source of labour. As far as he was concerned, his outback travels gave him first-hand experience and authority to comment on what was happening out there in the Australian interior. Frank's opinions were formulated from what he saw, and were further developed during weeks of solitude as he slogged his way along a bush track out in the never-never. He'd arrive with firm ideas as to what Australia should do with its vast, empty interior – and this sometimes included his theories on Aborigines.

But the more he travelled around the continent, the less mysterious its interior – including its Indigenous inhabitants – became. His theories changed. He thoroughly enjoyed their company and was grateful for their acceptance of him. He was allowed special privileges in attending sacred ceremonies – and he took them seriously.

When he'd head bush, they'd show him places to fish, areas to hunt, what to eat, how to cook – at the sound of a car engine in the distance they knew who was arriving – 'Motorcar Frank', as they called him. Birtles took extraordinary and exquisite photographs of Aborigines in their own environment, yet refrained from putting them in situations to present them as caricatures. In 1929, Frank made the first Australian film to have an all indigenous cast, *Coorab and the Island of Ghosts*. The National Library of Australia says of the film, 'Not only was it the first Australian film in which no white man appeared but, despite the paternalism apparent in the intertitles, there is a lack of stereotyping of blacks when compared to their portrayal in features films up to that time.'

Today more than 4,000 of his negatives are held at the Australian Institute of Aboriginal and Torres Strait Islander Studies in Canberra (AIATSIS), and in 2007 were included as part of a $10.2 million conservation program. They are now catalogued as the Francis Birtles Collection.

In the 1920s and 1930s, Frank was vocal about the appalling treatment Aborigines were receiving out in the bush, concerned they were succumbing to white man's diseases and no-one was doing anything about it. He was often furious with government and would let fly at those he felt were exploiting their vulnerability.

In 1932, Frank returned from Arnhem Land furious. The atrocities he'd witnessed there against Aborigines beggared belief. He prepared an address for the Racial Hygiene Society in Brisbane, and he was going in hard. The *Brisbane Worker* reported, 'That aboriginal women were bought and sold, and Aborigines murdered and assaulted by the police and other white people in the Northern Territory, is alleged by Francis Birtles, the well-known explorer, in a statement which he is preparing for the Racial Hygiene Society.'

Frank certainly had strong claims alleging 'prominent men' were involved in a drug ring where opium, methylated spirits and overproof rum were used to enslave Aboriginal labour. 'The inhuman treatment of the natives in the North has put civilisation back 100 years to the early days of Australia,' continued Frank, and he was pulling no punches, giving the city reader no doubt that there were whites living beyond the scrutiny of 'civilisation' who were sordid, corrupt and malevolent.

'The native is regarded as an animal,' Frank declared. 'Any newcomer who ventures to protest is ostracised. It is not too much to say that certain people there would not hesitate to do away with anyone who exposed them. Once I was wrongly informed that there was a waterhole on a route, and I nearly perished as a result.' Frank said he was prepared to back this up with the names of persons and the places. 'A police constable [whom Frank had driven] . . . to one of the stations viciously manhandled a native, who, battered and bleeding, was left chained to a post. The native had been thrashed to endurance point at a station for "cheeking the boss".

'Murder of the blacks is quite common, and the police had been implicated. Few blacks receive any payment for work done, being kept under control by drugs and liquor. [Frank said he saw] . . . natives coming from six months' work at a buffalo camp – which entails solid toil from 4 a.m. to 11 p.m. each day – with a sack of flour each as payment. Lubras are brought down from Arnhem Land, principally by half-castes, and disposed of in the settlements for opium. Opium and disease contracted from polyglot lugger crews are gradually wiping out the blacks. They are beaten if they absent themselves from their work or for tribal ceremonies, and cut off by their tribes if they do not.'

Frank had pulled the pin on a hand grenade, and it had the northerners up in arms. An unfortunate editorial in the

Northern Miner strengthened Frank's case, protesting: 'Few if any Territorians can get sufficient booze for themselves without supplying aboriginals, and that many a better man than Jacky has been thrashed for giving cheek and that Mr. Birtles is fortunate if he has never had that experience himself. The facts are that the Territory niggers are utterly spoiled and that anyone misguided enough to lay a hand on one of them finds in the morning that Jacky has eloped, taking with him the new and costly "tchirt" and "trousis" (sic – shirt and trousers) he gave him the day before.' It continued, 'This latest effort of Birtles to remain in the limelight will not help the aboriginals but it will provide a fine opportunity for some impossible American or Central European to tell the Council of the League of Nations what fiends Australians really are, on the authority of their own most famous living explorer!'

Frank's claim was given further impetus when a photograph was published in the London *Daily Herald* depicting Aborigines in chains purportedly being sold as slaves to Japanese pearlers.

•

Frank Birtles had only recently returned from the wilds with additional footage for his latest feature film, which would ultimately be titled *Francis Birtles in Australia's Lonely Lands*. The documentary was fundamentally the same sort of idea he had back before the accident with Roy Fry – the notion being he would construct a cinematic extravaganza of Australiana and sell it to the Commonwealth Immigration Office for propaganda purposes.

Just as in the old days, Birtles himself was billed as the key attraction, who would appear on stage to discuss his latest feature. However, Frank's music-hall-style film and chat show soon closed due to poor ticket sales. As far as audiences were concerned, Frank's outback adventures were old-time and outdated. By 1924, Australians' interests had moved on from Humptydoo to Hollywood. Why would you want to see weather-beaten Frank Birtles introduce another outback film when you could see Douglas Fairbanks in *The Thief of Baghdad*?

In many ways, Frank had become his own worst enemy. Probably more than anyone else, Frank Birtles was responsible for the public's waning interest in the mysteries of the outback during the twenties. The more he wrote, photographed and filmed, the more the wonder of the Australian wilderness diminished, to the point where his stories were beginning to sound the same. Readers grew tired of his close scrapes – running out of petrol in the desert or putting a bullet through an attacking 'alligator's' skull. Frank had shown film-goers Aborigines in the far-flung environs of the Northern Territory – and, somewhat disappointingly, it turned out they weren't the pack of treacherous caricature savages audiences were probably expecting.

Certainly the more motorists like Birtles tamed the outback, the less intrigue it seemed to have. The promise of discovery that had once captured the imagination of 19th century explorers like Stuart and Burke and Wills had vanished. It was as if the romance and mystery that once lay within Australia's dead heart had been laid bare by this ever-increasing band of transcontinental motorists; rifled through and discarded. There was nothing new out there any more. Now all that was left for an adventurer to do was to rip backwards and forwards across the country, shaving hours off the travelling time on each trip. The public's new-found obsession with the motor car and how fast it could go had eclipsed derring-do tales of mysterious corroborees in the never-never, close shaves with saltwater crocodiles and all the wonders of the outback Birtles had to offer.

Try as he might, Frank was struggling to keep up with what was happening. Back in 1909, he wrote of those who had inspired his yearning to explore: 'The names of men like Drake, Raleigh, Cavendish and Cook come rapidly to our recollection . . .' He even attempted to rationalise his own motives for continually traipsing across the continent, suggesting in a typically Edwardian, romantic way, '. . . it would be hard to explain, excepting that the old roving spirit of my English forefathers may have reasserted itself after lying dormant for generations, and awakening the desire to do and dare something outside the humdrum of city life, urged me to blaze the trail'. However, in 1924 people weren't interested in the fine deeds of Drake, Cavendish and Cook – it was the Roaring Twenties. People didn't want to learn; they wanted to be entertained.

Frank would find this out the hard way.

14

Special Service Squadron

On 9 April 1924, after a solid week of wet weather, Sydney turned on one of those spectacular, clear, crisp mornings as only Sydney can. In brilliant sunshine, the fortress of sandstone cliffs rising from the Pacific Ocean to Vaucluse glowed gold in the morning light, heralding the arrival of the most sophisticated weapon the world had ever seen. The 44,000 ton Royal Navy Flagship HMS *Hood* steamed past the lighthouse at South Head and into Sydney Harbour, followed by the cruiser HMS *Repulse* and a convoy of five warships. This flotilla, officially the British Special Service Squadron, had travelled nearly 50,000 kilometres in eight months on a public relations offensive known as the 'Empire Cruise' – an around-the-world jaunt to promote not only the Royal Navy but the British Empire as a whole. In the years of political uncertainty that followed World War I, this tour was just what an increasingly nervous Australia was crying out for.

At 10 a.m., the harbour foreshores erupted with the roar from tens of thousands of well-wishers as the battle fleet steamed slowly past Cremorne Point and Middle Head, flag-draped steamers blasting whistles and foghorns, tiny sailing boats jostling their way among the crowded ferries and lighters heading out to greet them. Sydneysiders crowded every conceivable vantage point along the harbour shores, waving Australian flags, Union Jacks and naval ensigns as *Hood* headed up towards Fort Denison to slowly wheel around and drop anchor at Kirribilli.

Braced on deck and revelling in this once-in-a-lifetime spectacle was 34-year-old Malcolm Henry Ellis, chief political correspondent for the Sydney *Daily Telegraph*, there in his capacity as the 'Official Australian Press Representative for the Special Service Squadron's Australian Visit'. Since he'd joined the fleet in Tasmania, he had been looking forward to this day, writing from Hobart that 'the entry into Sydney Harbour should be the scenic event of a century'. Tall, somewhat long-faced, hot-headed and prone to stutter slightly, Ellis loved an official title (he was also at that time Special Commissioner for the Australian Meat Council), and whenever he found the opportunity, would exert his authority to anybody in earshot.

Onboard the majestic *Hood*, he cut an officious if rather dull figure in his pork-pie hat and grey flannel three-piece suit, particularly when standing alongside the Royal Navy sailors in their dress whites. Ellis was the perfect representative to cover – and unquestionably promote – Britain's show of naval might in Australia. His thundering opinion pieces in the *Daily Telegraph* left readers in no doubt that he was a fierce Australian loyalist, particularly when it came to writing about commerce and international trade. However, later appraisals of Malcolm Ellis described him as 'more of a King and Empire man'. Ellis had a paternalistic view of Britain's role, whereby Australia was an enthusiastic adolescent, eagerly assisting an ageing parent in maintaining a composed and just world.

That Australia, with a population of less than five million, had been prepared to sacrifice the lives of 60,000 young men during the four years of World War I affirmed the fledgling nation's allegiance to Britain and her empire.

As an active part of that empire, Australia needed looking after as well.

One of the many hobbyhorses from which Ellis would regularly editorialise was the defence of Australia – those very words becoming the title of his book, later published in 1933. There was no question that Ellis was an alarmist when it came to the nation's vulnerability as a far-flung outpost of Great Britain bobbing around in the South Pacific. As far as he was concerned, Australia, with its vast, unpopulated northern regions, was ripe for the taking should any malevolent neighbour wish to do so. As it transpired, Ellis's alarmist bell-ringing wasn't far off the mark.

There were justifiable fears for the north – three years earlier the Japanese navy had added six battleships to its fleet. As far as Ellis was concerned, the Royal Navy's arrival in Australia was just in time.

He had been dazzled by the Royal Navy's technological might during this tour – allowed access to HMS *Hood*'s phenomenal ship's wireless, Ellis became the first Australian to talk directly to someone in the United States by way of radio. In 1924, this was science fiction.

The *Hood* was a technological marvel, then six years old and the most beautiful of modern warships – a battle-cruiser – fast, agile, lethal, its deep Atlantic-grey livery contrasting with the lighter grey of Australia's naval fleet.

The Empire Cruise that had toured Africa, Canada, the United States, Asia and now Australia was part carnival, where the ships arrived and flung open their steel doors for the public to see; and part standover, reminding the dominions and colonies around the world they needed the protection provided by vessels like HMS *Hood*.

However, despite maintaining the iron-clad traditions of centuries of upstanding Royal Navy heritage, the Empire Cruise of 1924 – sometimes referred to as the 'Booze Cruise' – was distinctly and unusually American in style. It was seen as a mission of goodwill, and was surprisingly relaxed and informal.

On arriving at a 2,000-strong dance held at Sydney Town Hall, the squadron's commander, Vice-Admiral Sir Frederick Field, was given a standing ovation. Seizing the opportunity, the admiral responded by standing on a chair, putting his hands to his mouth like a megaphone and bellowing his appreciation. The crowd, putty in his hands, went wild. He spent the rest of the evening signing autographs on souvenir programs and serviettes like a Hollywood star.

After two exhilarating weeks the Special Service Squadron's stay in Sydney was drawing to a close. At a farewell dinner at Sydney's town hall, the vice-admiral thanked all those who had looked after the 4,500 British sailors who had swamped the city's streets during the past fortnight, curiously closing with a special mention of thanks to Sydney's Royal Automobile Club (RAC), which had organised a transport fleet to shuttle the tourists around the city.

'The provision of motor cars for the use of officers and men attending entertainments, and the willing and arduous service of their drivers were of inestimable benefit. The work of the RAC in this connection was beyond all praise.' The RAC had given sailors stranded in Sydney unprecedented mobility. Motor cars fascinated Ellis – he had a well-known passion for motoring, and one of his special interests was the British motor car and, more importantly, the British motor industry. Frustrated by the ever-increasing volume of American motor vehicles being imported into Australia, he had already bestowed upon himself another title as 'an unofficial propagandist for British cars'.

One morning, during a lull in the squadron's Sydney schedule, Ellis was wandering along the waterfront inspecting the RAC motor-pool when he spotted a motor car he was unfamiliar with. It was a scarlet soft-top, four-door tourer, parked neatly alongside the Rolls-Royce Silver Ghost that had been placed at Admiral Field's disposal. The car's wheels were heavy pressed steel – Sankey wheels as they were known – which gave the machine away as being distinctly English.

It seemed fairly austere and particularly solid – more robust than most of the English cars Australians had seen. Ellis moved in for a closer inspection. The polished silver radiator was unusual, sort of egg-shaped; the badge below the radiator cap depicted a blue lion and the word 'Bean'. Ellis had read of Bean cars but had never seen one before. He ran his hand along the bonnet . . . The whole machine seized his imagination. As far as he was concerned, this marvellous Bean motor car was British to the big-end bearings.

'There she lay alongside the Admiral's Rolls-Royce,' he gushed, '. . . a red fourteen horsepower, new model Bean, made in Dudley with Midland Country staunchness, of the famous Hadfields steels.' It transpired that this was the only Bean car in Australia. Further, it had just competed in – and won – the Australian Alpine Trial in the Snowy Mountains. Ellis learned the Bean company was setting up offices in Sydney and Melbourne, and that the car had been brought in for the Royal Navy fleet to use as part of a promotional exercise.

The cogs began to turn in Ellis's mind . . .

He was trying to think of a plan that could somehow incorporate all his diverse agendas: international trade, the defence of Australia, agriculture, motoring and the British Empire – the mind boggled at the possibilities. He wasn't to know his idea would eventually gather momentum, turning from a small plan into something beyond anyone's control.

Ellis decided there was only one person who could help him make this plan succeed – Frank Birtles.

15

All-British Expedition

Malcolm Ellis pushed his way through the crowd of riff-raff clogging the platform exit gate at the Eddy Avenue end of Central Railway Station. Ellis was frustrated at being jostled and eager to get on with his urgent mission. He was on his way to meet Francis Birtles to put forward a proposal for the pair to undertake a political fact-finding mission in Australia's outback.

Historian Manning Clark wrote of Ellis: 'He entered on the stage of public life in Sydney in the 1920s as a young man who was convinced that the Protestant religion and British political institutions were the recipe for men of heroic ingredients and that the Russian Revolution of 1917 was an international conspiracy to degrade and besmirch mankind.' Labour historian E. C. Fry described Ellis as 'one of nature's fascists'.

Australia in the 1920s was awash with broken men from World War I. Brave men who'd volunteered to fight when they were needed – not like the Bolshevik shirkers who were now threatening to undo their heroic legacy and destroy the nation they had so bravely fought for. Ellis had done his bit for empire during the war too – not in the army, mind you – he was unfit for service, having been blinded in one eye as a child. Ellis had another career, separate to journalism – a secret career.

During World War I he'd been engaged in 'special duties' as the Queensland representative of a short-lived federal intelligence bureau, the Commonwealth Directorate of War Propaganda, acting as a counter-revolutionary observer reporting on the threat of fifth-columnists and agent-provocateurs in Australia, a clandestine role he maintained well after the war. In short, Malcolm Henry Ellis had been a spy.

Ellis's covert government role had begun in 1917 – the year of the Russian Revolution. Anglo-Australians were horrified when a violent Bolshevik communist uprising in Russia – a nation allied with Britain and Australia, fighting a common enemy – saw the ruling monarchs imprisoned and the country's war effort shut down in the middle of the war. Indeed, it gave the cold horrors to every European empire still in existence, even filtering down to the pro-British outpost of Australia.

At the time, there were genuine fears that a similar uprising might occur locally, and industrial action from militant, Bolshevik sympathising trade unions hampering wartime production fuelled the paranoia. The federal government invoked the *War Precautions Act*, which enabled it to override the unions and quash disputes.

At the time, Queensland possessed the largest population of Russian immigrants in Australia, and an anti-Russian, anti-union paranoia combined with a high unemployment rate saw Brisbane spiralling towards civil unrest. Malcolm Ellis had been recruited by the Special Investigation Bureau in Brisbane to devise a report on the socialist-leaning Queensland State Labor Government of Premier T. J. Ryan for 'disloyalty'.

It was grubby stuff, with Ellis compiling dossiers on individual suspects – remarking in one report on a particular anti-conscriptionist: 'Looks a dangerous type of man. Had two illegitimate children by his wife before he married her. (I have seen the birth certificates).'

The *War Precautions Act* further inflamed tensions when it announced a ban on the flying of the red flag, the most clear-cut symbol of communism. Trade unionists were outraged. On 23 March 1919, one of several demonstrations against the *War Precautions Act* took place in Queen and William streets in Brisbane, where a crowd of around 7,000 gathered and speakers urged the crowd to take the law into their own hands. In Merivale Street, they ran headlong into a group of 60 mounted police armed with rifles and bayonets. In the ensuing clash, at least 100 rioters were bayoneted.

In the wash-up, Ellis testified under oath that the Russians involved in the riots were 'foaming at the mouth as they waved their red flags'.

•

Ellis stepped off at the tram stop halfway up Wentworth Avenue and crossed the road, pushing open the heavy glass door of the Griffiths Brothers Tea Rooms, where Frank sat spooning sugar into a cup of black tea.

Frank looked up, smiled and put out his hand. Ellis shook it with gusto, placed his hat on the table and sat down. It was great to see Frank again – a welcome relief to sit down with an old friend and a like-minded fellow – a rarity in this age of anarchy – well, almost.

It had been three years since the pair had seen each other, and Ellis was surprised at how his friend had aged. 'The lines were a little deeper on his weather-beaten face. His hands were a trifle more scarred. His grey eyes were a trifle older and his Viking hair a little less golden, but with his forty-odd years he was still as lithe as a youngster and straight as an arrow.' Ellis continued, 'Fever had marked him a little but, as ever since I saw him start off to ride a bicycle round Australia in the days of 1908 when that was really a feat, his countenance was lit by a questing eagerness to be gone upon adventure. I asked him how he had been faring, and he said that since he had seen me little had been happening. It was true that he had run out of rations in the Gulf country and had starved for three months. And then he had a row with a teamster who had cast aspersions on his mother and they had both taken a bit of time to convalesce.'

Ellis had kept in touch with Frank on and off since the crazy old days when he acted in another of his 'official' capacities as 'official timekeeper' during the Maxwell roadster drive on the Brisbane-to-Sydney speed run in 1917. They were men of similar minds – both loved adrenalin-pumping excitement, the thrill of danger and radical adventure. However, neither were backward in espousing their extreme – if conservative – political views.

Ellis ordered a pot of tea and wasted no time revisiting a vague proposal he and Birtles had occasionally discussed, of mounting a motorised expedition into the Australian interior. The last time they'd mentioned it was when Ellis discovered Birtles' dilapidated Oldsmobile parked in George Street guarded by Dinkum, his trusty cattle dog, 'surveying an astonished city through a pair of enormous black goggles, which gave him a surprisingly human air'. Frank eventually turned up, delighted to see Ellis, and brought up the whole idea of the great overland trip again. Since those days, Ellis had given the proposal further thought. What if this concept was massaged a little more, whereby every single component used in the expedition – knife, fork and spoon – would be of British or Australian manufacture.

'Everything,' Ellis wrote, 'accessories, benzine, tools, equipment – must have been made under the Union Jack or Australian Flag.' This would be Ellis's onslaught as he waded into a pro-British – perhaps even anti-American – motor industry campaign that would somehow help give beleaguered post-war Britain some economic stimulus from Australia. Ellis was out to prove the worth of fine, solid British engineering and manufacture to help thwart the tidal wave of American cars arriving in Australia.

Birtles' extensive experience of motoring in the Australian bush would have no doubt given him serious reservations about Ellis's 'all-British' idea. There was no question of Frank's patriotic allegiance to Britain, but he'd successfully battled through the scrub and across deserts in a variety of robust American-made cars, starting with the Brush, the short-lived Flanders, a couple of Maxwells, no end of Model T Fords, the Hudson Super Six, and most recently an Oldsmobile. In fact, previous discussions the pair had had as to what car they would use for such a journey had arrived at either Fords or Oldsmobiles 'as the most suitable for the type of country to be crossed'.

The problem was that most English cars simply weren't up to surviving Australian outback conditions. They were devised, designed and manufactured to putter around a country that could fit inside the Australian continent more than 30 times.

British engineers in some fog-bound factory in Birmingham weren't factoring in the track to Borroloola when drawing up the blueprints. For Ellis, this would have been an annoying triviality. He pressed on anyway, excitedly announcing to Frank how he'd finally found the ideal British motor car for their all-British expedition, brand-new to Australia – a Bean 14 four-cylinder tourer: strong, reliable, practical and a magnificent rolling example of modern British industry. 'In a word, what we needed was the impossible and I found it . . .' Ellis wrote.

And now, he was about to reveal his coup. Ellis had managed to persuade the manufacturer in Britain to let him take the car on a long expedition into the outback for publicity purposes. He had it all worked out. With the car already placed at his disposal, he had also convinced his employers at the *Daily Telegraph* to sponsor what he intended to be a political fact-finding expedition. They would drive from Sydney to Darwin and back – 'the longest overland continuous motor trek achieved within the Commonwealth'.

However, the journey was 'not to achieve a motoring feat', as Ellis put it, but to allow him, as 'Special Commissioner of a powerful group of Australian newspapers, headed by the Sydney *Daily Telegraph*, and of the Australian Meat Council, to investigate why after more than a century of European settlement, the Northern Territory had such an insignificant white population of less than 3,000'. All that land up there, and nobody using it. Surely it could be irrigated and made arable? Why was it, since first white settlement up in that Northern Territory in 1828 – almost 100 years ago – that there were so few whites living there today?

Even more importantly, Ellis, as counter-revolutionary special agent, was itching to see first-hand what was taking place on Port Darwin's industrial front. Despite the town's relative insignificance compared to Australia's other great ports, Darwin had reputedly become a festering breeding ground for militant Bolshevik-supporting trade unionists, with 'turbulent revolutionaries marching through the streets of a small scale Glasgow gone mad in the wilderness', as Ellis put it.

Then the inevitable, more serious question arose. What if some other – unfriendly – neighbour was thinking along the same lines? Ellis expounded an imperative to head to northern Australia to investigate 'the belief that its emptiness renders it an Achilles heel in respect of oriental invasion'. This would have convinced Frank – he'd written about these very subjects back in 1909 when he published his book *Lonely Lands*. Ellis would be delighted with Frank's participation, except he needed to advise him of one small detail. The Bean Car Company in England insisted on sending their own driver/mechanic to travel with them. It was to be an even more all-British expedition than either had bargained for. Two would be company, but three . . .

16

The Scarlet Runner

On a broad table, Birtles and Ellis began unfurling large survey maps to plan the long drive to Darwin and back. With innumerable cups of tea and lengthy discussions as to whether a particular well or bore would be in operation at certain times of the year, as to where river crossings should be made and fuel requirements from Point A to Point B, Ellis later recalled those times as 'happy days, those days when you might behold us, of a sunny April afternoon, remoulding the Government charts on my verandah . . .'

Ellis, the self-proclaimed 'expedition leader', could hardly wait to get his hands on the Bean motor car. Even before seeing the bright red Bean again, he had christened it the 'Scarlet Runner', due to its brilliant colour and also the fact a 'scarlet runner' is a species of bean. The name would stick for the duration of the expedition.

The Bean 14 was a conventional 1920s English car: a four-cylinder, side-valve-engined, four-door tourer. It had a four-speed 'crash' gearbox – no synchromesh requiring the fancy footwork of double-declutching (or double-shuffling) – and although it might seem odd today, the gear lever was situated on the right-hand side, between the driver's leg and the door. This wasn't too uncommon an arrangement for English cars of the period – Bentleys and Vauxhalls were other contemporary examples using this configuration. The Bean had dual ignition systems, both a distributor with coil and the traditional magneto – a belt-and-braces effort in case one or the other broke down – and both an electric starter motor and a crank handle for the same reason. The car was certainly sturdy and heavy, making it a particularly modest performer.

The Scarlet Runner had just arrived back in Australia after having been spirited away to New Zealand on attachment with the Special Service Squadron. With it came the Bean Car Company's own representative, John Simpson, a young English engineer who had been sent along as a walking, talking mobile workshop and to act as the car's chaperone and protector, making sure it came back in one piece. The Bean Car Company might have been prepared to loan the car to Ellis for the purpose of the expedition, but they were fully aware it might not return in quite the same condition as it started out. Frank Birtles' reputation for being reckless – if not brutal – with cars preceded him.

From the outset, Ellis and Birtles took a particular dislike to Simpson, or 'the Engineer', as Ellis disparagingly referred to him. Despite Ellis's championing of Britain and her Empire, the simple presence of this Pommy 'new chum' seemed to embody and exacerbate all his gripes about the failure of trade opportunities between Britain and Australia. Ellis saw the practical outcome of the expedition as demonstrating to British car manufacturers how their home-grown products performed in tough Australian conditions when driven by tough Australians.

From this gruelling outback test, manufacturers could learn of weaknesses in their designs and, in so doing, build a more suitable English car for Australia. As a result they could manufacture cars that would capture the Australian public's attention and eclipse American sales. The Bean Car Company saw it another way. They wanted their unquestionably robust car to return from the wilderness in a tidal wave of publicity to testify as to the suitability of Bean motor cars in Australia. It looked to Ellis and Birtles like Bean had posted some young know-it-all public-school boffin from Britain to show the colonials how to drive. What would this peacock from the Midlands know about motoring in the bush? Indignant, Ellis pointed out that, after all, Frank held 'nine of the ten great transcontinental driving records in Australia'.

Ellis and Birtles' first meeting with Simpson was frosty. Before the expedition had turned a wheel, arguments were unfolding between Simpson and Birtles as to how the expedition should be run. Simpson was aghast at what Birtles was intending to do with the car, piling it high and roping it down with heavy equipment. Simpson claimed it 'was murder to any car to cruelly load her up'.

Birtles responded by saying he had 'murdered many cars in his time and another more or less would not make much difference'.

It was true – in nine years Frank had destroyed nine cars. For him the motor car was simply a tool, swung as hard as any mattock, smashed as forcefully as any hammer. When he told Simpson of the time he'd broken a car clean in half up near the Calvert River in the Northern Territory, the appalled English engineer retorted that the car's destruction was only due to Frank's carelessness. For Simpson, who'd been placed as official guardian of the only Bean motor car in Australia, Birtles' actions were beyond the pale. Simpson didn't want Birtles anywhere near the steering wheel and approached Ellis expressing his concerns that 'Francis might be a great bushman but knew nothing whatever about motor cars'. He suggested Ellis 'might tactfully break the ground for a few lessons for Francis'.

This irked Ellis, whose opinion of Simpson was that he had 'an assumption that all roads were paved roads, and there was a tramcar and a traffic policeman always lurking somewhere handy'.

It was going to be an interesting journey.

At 10.45 a.m. on 4 June 1924 the Sydney–Darwin–Sydney expedition, with its three uneasy participants, was ready to roll. A crowd gathered around the Scarlet Runner outside the *Daily Telegraph*'s office in Pitt Street. The red Bean sat submerged beneath a sea of roped-down timber boxes filled with rations, tarpaulins, new green swag covers rolled and strapped to the mudguards, rifles, fuel tins, water bottles – all carefully interlocked in a Chinese puzzle by Birtles, who had been awake all night loading the car.

There was some degree of theatre with their departure, intended to project the earnestness of this worthy yet grand adventure. All three expeditioners were sporting pith helmets as if they were off in search of the source of the Nile. That nobody wore 19th century pith helmets in Australia in 1924 didn't matter – the expedition had the look and feel of some imperial sojourn into the dark continent or Abyssinia or the

Khyber Pass. Above the car's radiator cap a small Union Jack sat with a small Australian flag, 'a symbol of the fact we were an all-British outfit' as Ellis put it, and in the driver's seat sat Birtles wearing his South African campaign ribbons. With him were his two dogs – 'Dinkum, old and knowing and blue with one ear up and another one down, quite at ease' and 'Wowser, our bull-pup on a leash wondering what it was all about'.

In the offices of the *Daily Telegraph*, they toasted their farewell with 'a stirrup-cup' – the traditional parting libation before setting off on a foxhunt. It was a grand departure, with hundreds crowding around the car as Birtles engaged gear and nosed the radiator through the mob.

With Birtles at the wheel, the overloaded Scarlet Runner headed flat out along the Great Western Highway for the Blue Mountains, crossing the Great Dividing Range to arrive at Bathurst by 9 p.m., when it poured mercilessly. The following day the rains became even worse as the open car motored through Molong, Wellington and Dubbo before becoming bogged to the running boards just outside Narromine.

'It was all very miserable,' wrote Ellis. 'Already the Scarlet Runner was losing her pristine newness, though her blue lion badge shone untarnished on her radiator.'

Yet here it was, the pride and future of the British automotive industry in Australia stuck fast in a western New South Wales mire. Birtles was much the same, his ankles protruded from under the car, blue with cold. He was clawing great clods of mud from beneath the floor and chassis when he finally emerged.

Crossing the border from New South Wales to Queensland at Hungerford, Ellis commented to Simpson, whose turn it was behind the wheel, that he should follow Birtles' instructions about speed and driving on outback tracks, otherwise they'd soon have an accident. Simpson had the car up to nearly 50 km/h – way too fast for the loose red soil beneath the skinny Sankey wheels. Ellis commented later, 'It wasn't a road at all; it was just a place where the grass had been worn off.'

The dead-straight track took a sudden turn, raising the alarm for old hands like Birtles and Ellis – the only reason it would do so was to avoid some obstacle probably half hidden in the dust. Birtles and Ellis yelled simultaneously, 'Look out – there's a tyre twister!'

'Tyre twisters?' asked Simpson, turning over his shoulder. 'What are they?'

The car flew off the corner and came to an abrupt stop. One tyre and tube were ruined and nearly pushed out of the steel Sankey rim. Simpson was in shock when Ellis suggested they go and have a look to 'see what done it'. They went back to find the road 'studded with little sharp tree stumps' – tyre twisters – barely showing above the dust, 'but as hard as stone and as sharp as knives'.

Around the camp fire at night was really the only time anyone could relax. The culinary highlight of each evening would invariably be an enamel mug of black tea and johnny cakes – one of the many variations of damper – tennis-ball-sized cakes made of flour, salt and water cooked in the coals. Frank was at home out here. The further away from civilisation they ventured, the more relaxed he became.

Not so for Simpson, who was growing increasingly nervous – perhaps paranoid – as to what lay in the Australian wilds. He brought with him a .32 calibre short-barrelled semi-automatic pistol, which, much to the consternation of Birtles and Ellis, he would regularly load and unload, even while the car was moving. Ellis was concerned that the gun might go off. Further, Simpson's chain-smoking habits were of great concern, considering the car was carrying 70 gallons (320 litres) of petrol in tins and quite often he'd be sitting on top of one in the back of the car, attempting to strike a match while they crashed and bounced along the track.

In the past twenty years, the motor car had changed the bush – as Birtles and Ellis once knew it – irrevocably. Roads had been considerably improved. Where once they would meander around obstacles such as trees and thickets, the road now simply went through them. However, cars brought with them a new-found ugliness. Birtles complained of glare flashing from countless discarded fuel tins, motorists having simply thrown them by the roadside.

Water was less important than it once was. In bone-dry regions of the outback, it was sometimes a case of life and death to attempt a 50 mile (80 kilometre) ride with a team of horses. But the modern motor car with 20 gallons (90 litres) of water aboard could cope with the worst conditions. And the Scarlet Runner was suffering the worst conditions.

The car's differential struck a rock, hitting it so hard the Bean came to a stop 'in mid-air', according to Ellis, nearly sending him through the windscreen.

Shortly afterwards, while trying to negotiate a steep slope on a creek, the differential began to make a grinding noise. It had broken a pinion tooth, requiring the replacement of both the crown wheel and pinion. Not a simple job. Simpson, the Engineer, was dismayed. He asked Birtles, 'Isn't there a garage we can tow her to?'

'There is,' came the reply, 'six hundred and eighty-three miles away. What do you want with a garage anyhow?'

Birtles removed the rear axle and differential, found a bent mulga tree and, using luggage straps, suspended the whole assembly in mid-air. The replacement of the crown wheel and pinion took an entire day, with Birtles and Simpson conducting the operation cordoned off with a tarpaulin to prevent all-pervading bulldust filling the differential case. Birtles commented: 'There isn't any job you can't do on a car, so long as you have a box spanner, some fencing wire and a bit of common sense.'

Indeed, the humble box spanner, the kind of tubular wrench with which you'd remove a spark plug, was a particularly useful device.

Just outside Borroloola on the Gulf, the steering rod between the front wheels suddenly sheared in half, resulting in a sudden loss of steering. The disconnected front wheels splayed alarmingly in whichever wild direction they chose. Birtles, Ellis and Simpson were lucky to survive the scenario without ploughing into a tree or rolling the car. Frank removed the two halves of the broken rod and fitted the ends loosely together inside a box spanner.

Looking for something with which to pack the spanner, he rifled through the car, producing some small round metal tins that contained photographic films. Francis had an idea. He lit a small, hot fire and smelted the tins into liquid, pouring it into the spanner. When it had cooled, the broken rod was held rigid; what were once film tins were now a solid solder holding the two broken halves and the box spanner together as one piece. Forward strain wasn't going to be the problem. It would be side-strain of the wheels turning left and right that could see the work undone. This would be a 'belt-and-braces' job.

Once the rod was back in place, Birtles clamped a wire rope along the length of the rod with two u-bolts. It held. Two days later, they found an old iron bedstead in an abandoned house. Birtles cut a section of upright bedstead and fashioned a sleeve covering the whole assembly. They then travelled over 1,000 miles over rough country without a problem.

In the pre-dawn darkness of their campsite somewhere near Tennant Creek, a slumbering Malcolm Ellis felt Dinkum's cold nose on his face. Nine-tenths unconscious and vaguely annoyed, Ellis pushed the dog away, submerging back into a deep sleep until the nose returned, this time with two paws.

Ellis woke with the realisation something was acutely wrong in the camp. Exactly what, he didn't know. He lay silent and still. Wrapped like a mummy in his swag he was formulating mental gymnastics as to how he could calmly and silently reach for his rifle. Through the darkness he could just make out Dinkum's outline as the blue heeler lay down full length next to Ellis. The dog was gazing at the lower end of the swag when Ellis realised the sensation of a live, cold weight across his ankles.

Snake.

What sort of snake or how big it was didn't matter – only how he was going to extricate himself without being bitten. There was nothing to do but try and leap out.

'Should I land on my feet with all my coverings still around me and an angry snake inside doing his worst, or should I come out free? No use thinking about it.' Ellis leapt up. 'I am sure that no hangman ever dropped his victim with greater velocity than mine as I leapt out of those bedclothes, which accommodatingly fell clear away in a heap. He proved to be a fine, fat death-adder, altogether an ugly and unpleasant character of a species addicted to earning its warmth o' nights by trespass.'

Snakes were a genuine threat. Brown snakes, king brown snakes, death adders, taipans – a collection of the world's most deadly snakes were all over the place where the Scarlet Runner was headed. 'Of all the things of the earth he is the most uncanny and the most hated. I know there are blustering fellows who don't mind him, who merely catch him by the tail, give him a good swing round their heads and crack him like a whip so that his head flies off.'

The tougher the journey became, the more Frank was in his element. The car jolted and banged around as he controlled the machine like an orchestra conductor, calmly making it respond exactly as he wanted. His mind was ticking over, relentlessly registering what was happening ahead, simultaneously anticipating cause and effect between the car and the land, measuring distance, processing engine sounds, observing the gauges, tachometer, fuel, amperage. Like a Formula 1 driver, his hand movements were never grandiose, always kept to a minimum, snickering the gear lever back and forth, a slight adjustment with the steering wheel to guide the machine around a tussock. As impossibly uncomfortable as it all might seem, Frank showed no sign of discomfort.

'The first thing you will notice about Francis is that he is without a shirt,' observed Ellis 'firstly because of the tropic heat, secondly because, for some peculiar reason, the continued shower of grass seeds which come over the bonnet pierce and scratch the skin when they strike through cloth, but seem innocuous against bare and perspiring flesh. He has four weeks' whiskers, which make him look exactly like the devil. A cut over his left eye, fresh and raw, adds a piratical look to the deviltry. A long lock of yellow hair matted with grass seeds depends upon his forehead from under his topee [pith helmet]. The back of his right hand, black with oil, is bleeding from a timber gash and swollen from the effects of continual hard work and wheel strain.

'You would probably note, if you were observing us from an eminence, the distinct air of nervous strain in the front seat where Francis and I sit with our eyes glued before us. You would note, too, that we communicate with each other only by a system of signs and nudges which are more certain than words in a high wind, and that we have an air of distinction derived from wearing goggles . . . there would be Francis, iron jawed, hollow cheeked and weather-beaten, one eye fixed on the road, one ear cocked for strange sounds in the engine; and there would be the Engineer perched on a drum of benzine, smoking his cigarette, and Dinkum, high on the luggage enjoying the grass seeds and the breeze.'

It was a rip-roaring adventure – the three pith-helmeted adventurers bouncing along in their overloaded red car, weaving around tussocks, following cattle tracks, dodging wombat holes.

For Simpson, there was no comparison in England to driving in the Australian outback. Frank was teaching him how to use the car in the style of a bulldozer.

'Go through there,' said Francis, 'and keep on in a straight line till I give you the signal. Keep your head down.'

'But how do I get her round those little trees?' asked the Engineer. 'She's not a blooming caterpillar.'

'You don't go round anything any more,' said Francis. 'You've got to make up your mind to go through it.'

'But it was several minutes before we could persuade the Engineer that this was in earnest. It was our first real touch of driving excitement. The timber was small and brittle, but sometimes tenacious of the soil. The way became more and more paved with rocks and sand. The heat became more and more oppressive and insistent. Yet we were too busy to mind it. The Engineer, driving, Francis yelling directions in his ear, certainly was.'

For young Simpson, the drive was frenetic, all senses sharpened, piloting a car across country where there was no road whatsoever. It was like driving across a million square kilometre paddock.

Then, for Frank – the worst. Ellis was (as usual) back-seat driving, and in the calamity of the ride, several times had saved Wowser, who was tethered to the car, from flying overboard. 'At three o'clock, pausing for breath in an open stretch, I missed the bull pup again. He was found hanging over the back of the car, dead as a stone, on the end of his leash. It was our first tragedy, and Francis, who loves dogs a good deal better than he loves men, seemed very near weeping.

'Bump! Bang! Wallop! An ant heap dissolves into powder. Its base disappears under the car, makes friends with the cross steering rod, trundles, muttering, in front of the differential casing and subsides in the dust of its own summit. Three misguided saplings, which happen to be in our path, go down with rifle-shot crackling as we trample them under, and we hear one of them dragging protestingly in the undergear.'

At times it seemed the three were on safari hunting game on the veldt in Kenya. Photographs show the Scarlet Runner parked alongside sizeable water buffalo lying dead – a triumphant pith-helmeted Malcolm Ellis holding a Martini-Enfield rifle, his foot perched on the animal's back. Nevertheless, the majority of the journey was long, monotonous and hard work.

'A whirr of sliding gears and we slip suddenly into a gully and out again. A lightning turn of the wheel, two tons of car and luggage lurch sideways with a sickening swerve. You stiffen to avoid flying over Francis. Over your shoulder you have a hurried glimpse of the Engineer and Dinkum and the

Engineer's cigarette all tangled up with a drum of benzine which has burst its mooring straps. The car stops and goes on in the same movement. We can hear the stump which we so fortuitously uprooted – "by the skin of our teeth", as Francis says – go scraping underneath.'

Frank jumped on the brake pedal, the car instantly locking up and coming to a sudden halt. Inches before the front wheels, the earth had disappeared. In front of them lay a chasm, a creek with its deep sides spectacularly eroded. The other side was vertical. There was no way they could take the car any further.

It was decided that Frank would scout up the creek looking for a place to cross, and Ellis would do the same in the other direction. Simpson would remain with the car. Eventually both Birtles and Ellis returned with a plan to attempt a crossing a mile or so further up. Frank recommended the car be guided slowly through the scrub, and Ellis went ahead 'to the ticklish task of blazing a safe track back to the packhorse "road" from the selected crossing'.

'This is hot work,' he wrote, 'the grass being up to my neck, well larded with snakes and tangled like the hair of the Medusa. Presently I begin to feel uneasy about the Scarlet Runner. I have not heard her moving – she has an open exhaust and roars like the Bull of Bashan when she is really working for her living.'

Ellis gave a 'cooee' – but no reply. He cooeed again and decided to turn back where he eventually discovered the reason for the Bean's no-show. 'The Engineer, tempted by an apparently open space, has desired to feel the exhilaration of a little speed, and has attempted to rush along at the breathless rate of 15 miles an hour. The Scarlet Runner is not now travelling at 15 miles an hour. She is lying at a drunken angle. Her back wheels are buried in a deep-sided washout, one hub below the level of the ground. One involuntarily thanks an inscrutable Providence that the front wheels have jumped over the depression. If they had gone into it, the car would probably have somersaulted and we should have had to use up two or three hours burying the Engineer and a month walking to Darwin.'

Perhaps the most frightening aspect of the journey was the recurrence of fever. Both Birtles and Ellis had previously contracted malaria in their travels in the tropics. Frank had picked up the disease in Africa and had also been diagnosed with blackwater fever. On occasion the symptoms would reappear, unexpectedly, unannounced. The consequences could be terrifying.

'More graves line the great Overland because of fever than because of thirst or any other cause; more murder has been done through it; more friendships broken, more lives ruined. Sometimes it comes in severe form which lays its adversary low and kills him out of hand, but that is generally in the wet season when it joins forces with dysentery.

'In the dry – which means April to October – it creeps upon you like a shadow of terror and anger, bringing loathing and distrust with it. It makes your best friend anathema, the landscape unstable, your food nauseation, and fills your whole existence with an angry poison of unsettlement and vague, unnameable fear. And, if you let it get a thorough grip of you, you lie for nights, dry skinned, aching boned, a sort of human furnace, good for an excursion into the realms of mental instability or, perhaps, even keyed up to murder, if the excuse makes itself for its commission.'

Ellis knew just how out-of-hand tropical fever could get, but Simpson had no idea what happened to a man when in the grip of the illness. 'Francis and I had been through it all before and we knew what to expect. But the Engineer, who had never been one hundred miles out of a town in his life, did not understand . . .'

When fever took hold of Frank, it was a Jekyll to Hyde transformation, where there was no knowing what he was capable of. When Birtles was in this state – off his head with fever – anything could happen. All it would take was for Frank to walk over to the car, pick up any one of a number of rifles or revolvers or an axe and let fly. In terror, Simpson would reach for his pistol – always his first line of defence.

'The Engineer would, perhaps, put some cartridges into his automatic against emergency – for fever, bandits, noises in the dark, suspicious motors near towns and suspicious animal eyes away from them; for donkeys afar on a clear night or approaching black fellows, the Engineer's invariable panacea was that wretched firearm. Generally, the whole dispute would be over in five minutes and its end would be as sudden and insane as its beginning had been precipitate. Finishing a torrent of words, Francis would say calmly: "Well, that's that. I feel better," and would roll himself in his blankets. Dinkum would appear from nowhere and put a pleading paw on his master's arm and a few moments afterwards we would hear these two old comrades at their usual gentle, half intelligible dog talk about the game of the countryside.'

In Darwin, Ellis was finally able to fulfil his desire to study the ratbag, socialist politics of Australia's northernmost frontier in the 1920s. 'Darwin in the grip of Bolshevism. The Territory

Workers' Union was almost in complete control. State officials were compelled to join its ranks and if they did not please it and bow down to its agitators, out they went neck and crop by the medium of the black-list.'

Since the arrival of the iron-fisted Chief Administrator Frederic Urquhart, things had changed. Ellis wrote glowingly of Urquhart, who coincidentally was the former Queensland Police Commissioner who authorised the bayonet charge in Brisbane during the Red Flag Riots of 1919, in which Ellis was complicit. For Ellis, Urquhart was an inspiration, describing the Scottish-born administrator as a '. . . highland type, tall and very broad-shouldered, with a countenance weather-beaten and well branded with the evidence that he has not lived his sixty-eight years free of the punches of men and the kicks of restive horses . . . he might easily be picked out as a bold leader of native police, a pioneer who founded towns, quelled gold rush riots, and who can run his finger over many a line on the Australian map and declare with truth: "I took the first wheeled vehicle or the first pack-horse over that route." He can claim that, too.'

Ellis didn't mention that Urquhart could also claim to be a thug and a murderer who, during his time as a sub-inspector in charge of the gulf, Cape York and Torres Strait districts was responsible for leading a detachment of armed settlers and police against the indigenous Kalkatunga people, where at Battle Mountain near Cloncurry 200 Aborigines were slaughtered. A royal commission in 1899 found Urquhart to have 'an impulsive and exacting temperament' and a 'vindictive and tyrannical nature'.

He had been appointed as administrator of the Northern Territory in 1921 to 'clean up the place', and the militant unions backed off when Urquhart turned up unannounced at their office with a loaded Martini-Henry carbine. Ellis revelled in the idea of gunboat diplomacy. But probably not so, Frank. He steered clear of the administrator – Urquhart had been the one picking up the tab for Frank's bouncing cheques during the Transcontinental Railway Survey expedition back in 1920 with Roy Fry. Frank had no desire to check out the Martini-Henry carbine.

The return journey followed the old telegraph line from Darwin down to Alice Springs, and the trio battled with the car through fine, bottomless sand, and the Depot Hills, north of the Finke River – just as those trailblazers Dutton and Aunger did in 1908. 'We had nothing but load and weariness and sand – sore hands, and our faithful engine.' Eventually, they made their way through the Flinders Ranges in South Australia to Broken Hill in New South Wales, and finally reached the Blue Mountains outside Sydney. After three months on the road, the trio arrived at Wynyard Square at 12.45 p.m. precisely.

'Buses seemed to be charging at us, lorries intent on our destruction. A traffic policeman held us up; a telegraph boy in difficulties with his bicycle delayed us on a corner. These seemed mighty incidents. Then, as the clock in the post office tower in the very heart of Sydney chimed out the quarter before one, we turned to our finishing place, 6,278 miles of travel behind us, all of us alive, dirty, dishevelled and tired, except for the engine of the Scarlet Runner, which seemed to sing with satisfaction.'

In the space of a few months this Bean car had won the Australian Alpine Trial and become the first car to drive from

Sydney to Darwin and back. Could the Bean 14 be the ideal British car for Australia? In time the Bean name would become inextricably linked with Francis Birtles, but for the moment he would keep motoring with the Americans.

17

The Sundowner

In November 1924, Frank was out behind the wheel somewhere south of Darwin, belting along the crude overland telegraph track where he'd once stumbled upon the Dutton, Aunger and Allchurch expedition so many years before. Gone were the days when a journey into the Australian interior was the sort of methodical, painstaking mission a Charles Sturt or John McDouall Stuart might undertake.

It was now the Roaring Twenties, and an old-timer like Frank was doing everything he could to keep pace – right now hammering flat out through the inky darkness of a cold desert night in an attempt to break the speed record from Darwin to Adelaide. He and his co-driver, Brisbane mechanic Rudi Muller, were hanging on to a howling six-cylinder Oldsmobile as it careened along the ruts that ran beneath the rusted telegraph poles, the pair hunched behind a custom-made metal fairing that scooped up from the firewall to where the windscreen should be – an attempt to streamline what was an otherwise unstreamlined 1920-model car.

In typical Birtles fashion, the Oldsmobile was covered with all the paraphernalia needed for a long outback drive – swags, fuel tins, timber fruit boxes filled with spares and, of course, his lever-action Winchester – all of which, no matter how tightly roped down, crashed around at every thundering bump. The rear of the car had been cut down and fitted with a flat-bed, on which were stacked extra wheels for when the going became tough; they could be bolted on as a pair.

Fitted squarely in front of the Oldsmobile's radiator was a large brass headlamp, capable of projecting an enormous field of light on to the track ahead. Yard by yard, the spotlight's brilliance revealed the elusive trail meandering through the desert, vast black shadows flickering from the smallest stump. In the distance, eerie red reflections from the eyes of startled kangaroos gave the motorists an uneasy feeling of being constantly watched. Whatever Rudi Muller thought of the desert's claustrophobic darkness, Frank was right at home; typically, it was Birtles' uncanny ability to thrive on little or no sleep that enabled the pair to break the record.

Frank's winning plan was simple: to drive flat out around the clock, reducing drowsiness by hardly eating – perhaps one tin of peas or fruit per meal. It would mortify health and dietary experts today, but this was the Birtles tried and proven method of long-distance driving, a la 1924. 'Appetites must never be appeased,' Frank wrote. 'A full meal would make us sleepy. Better, for safety's sake, to be always hungry at the wheel than to battle against the sleep fiend. Sleep, instead of being a friend, had to be kept at bay as an enemy. Heavy tired eyelids had to be washed with eye lotion three times daily.'

Indeed, to keep the time down, Frank insisted the pair sleep only two and a half hours per day. Frank never pretended he was a racing driver. He was an endurance driver.

It was a dangerous, relentless and gruelling dash, and not without surprises. 'Our powerful lights awoke white cockatoos which screeching, flew blindly into mystery regions beyond,' Frank wrote. 'Flying foxes flopped silently to the ground, little three-inch high kangaroo mice skipped excitedly and erratically about, confused by the glare. At fleeting glance they looked like frogs. Then from a recent thunder shower the ground became slippery and shiny. Opening up the throttle I "belted" the Oldsmobile along, well knowing that treacherous bogs lay below the surface. A big stick was contracting and expanding across the track – a sixteen-foot snake hunting for frogs. A couple of twists of my wrists and there had happened a serious accident – for the snake.'

Rudi Muller described part of the run: 'In a sizzling downpour of rain our Oldsmobile six ploughed along. Wheels were double banked. The red mud and dead grass hung in shapeless dripping masses – all over the car. The wind had now changed to the south. The cool change cleared our numbed senses. We longed for a hot drink. Stopping the car, the billycan was dipped into a nearby pool, some sticks hastily gathered, benzine poured on a lighted match flung into the heap, and in a few minutes tea was made, biscuits eaten, and the journey continued.'

They shot through Alice Springs at 2 a.m., picking up fuel deposited on the verandah of the grocer, who was deep in sleep. Sleep was a luxury.

Not far south of Alice Springs, the car vaulted into a sand channel 'and was now fast settling down in the quicksands,' wrote Frank. 'The front wheels were on an extreme lock and buried fore and aft above the hubs. We had just reached the limit of physical and mental endurance, and intended to push on to the edge of the sandhill country, have five hours' sleep and get through the heavy country early in the morning. The thoughts of this five hours' sleep had been our mainstay for some days . . .' Every miscalculation, every lost path, every time they were stuck in some bog – cost time.

'Night-time found us traversing a region of open plains. Here I saw a chance of making up time. A roaring blast came from the exhaust as the car thundered across. Nerve-wracking was the intense lookout which we had to keep.

'At 1 o'clock in the morning we speeded into Marree. Friend "Fogarty" the storekeeper was asleep, but we noted that he had left our petrol supplies handy. These we hastily loaded on and scorched away into the darkness. We had gained on our schedule and treated ourselves to two hours sleep. More greasing and oiling at dawn and a hasty pannikin of tea. Adelaide was under 500 miles away.'

Frank recalled their triumphant arrival in Adelaide. 'Through the heart of the city traffic constables gave us the right of way. A cheering crowd besieged we three, Mate Muller, Friend Oldsmobile Six and I. Francis Birtles.'

They had driven to Adelaide from Darwin in 9 days, 9 hours and 15 minutes, having driven 20 hours of every 24.

A newspaper report picked up on just what a toll the drive had on the motorists. 'Lack of proper rest and food naturally had its effect on Birtles, even accustomed as he is to hardships in overlanding and back country trips, and he reached Adelaide a very tired man . . . There were a lot of sceptics amongst motorists in this country, for this transcontinental route for years past been painted with everything that was bad and detrimental to motoring. Since the day when H. Dutton and Murray Aunger first took a Talbot across from Adelaide to Darwin in 52 days in 1908, there have probably been not more than two motorists who have accomplished the full trip from ocean to ocean.' Frank knew all about it.

The success and publicity generated from Frank's Oldsmobile transcontinental run was nothing short of astonishing. An exquisite booklet commemorating the drive was produced by the journey's sponsor, the British Imperial Oil Company, complete with maps of the journey, times, distances, photographs, illustrations – even an autographed portrait of Frank at the wheel. The oil company publicly presented him with an elaborate gold watch depicting a spoked car wheel surrounded by a laurel capped with the Shell logo. It was inscribed 'Presented to Francis Birtles by the British Imperial Oil Co. Ltd. In recognition of his pioneer journey, Darwin to Adelaide, 9 days, 9 hours 15 minutes, 18th to 27th November, 1924.'

The Oldsmobile's speed trial and the ensuing publicity caught the eye of Jack Bean, the general manager of Bean cars in England. He'd been delighted with the coverage the Scarlet Runner had received, but now he was after speed. Jack Bean had also been under the impression Malcolm Ellis was the star of that journey. After all, at every turn he'd been stamping his authority as 'expedition leader'. It turned out this Francis Birtles fellow was the one to watch.

'. . . the British Bean . . . represents the finest product of British engineering, built to stand up to Australian conditions of the very severest kind,' reported the *South Australian Motor* about the Scarlet Runner.

For the Bean Car Company – and the British motoring industry as a whole – the Scarlet Runner's successful drive from Sydney to Darwin and back had been an unexpected shot in the arm. In a land so far dominated by Fords, Chevrolets, Oldsmobiles and Studebakers, the English car had proved both robust and reliable. Further, it had helped put Francis back in the public eye – not in his dubious role as a government-appointed consultant, but as the tried-and-proven outback adventurer everyone knew and understood.

In 1926, Jack Bean was touring Australia on a promotional tour. Thanks to Ellis and Birtles, Bean cars had had a taste of American-style publicity in Australia and Jack Bean was keen to keep the momentum going. While in Melbourne, he entered into an interesting discussion with car dealer Alexander George Barlow, whose Latrobe Street business, Barlow Motors, was the local agency for Bean Cars.

Barlow was something of a colourful entrepreneur, full of bright ideas and 'spin'. (Four years later, when Barlow Motors folded due to the Great Depression, he leased the Lower Melbourne Town Hall, where he set up a miniature golf course.)

Together, Barlow and Bean concocted the kernel of an unusual motorised publicity stunt. The Bean Car Company had a commercial division, manufacturing mid-sized motor lorries, and Barlow was well aware there was an as yet untapped seam of rural truck customers. The Bean truck was as rudimentary as it was austere, a functional yet uninspiring piece of 1920s

British automotive engineering. Nevertheless, the motorisation of Australia saw an exponentially growing demand for trucks just like this, and Bean Cars wasn't going to be left behind.

A promotional idea was devised that would involve both a Bean car and a Bean truck in transcontinental crossings. A Bean truck, carrying a ton more than its recommended maximum load, and a Bean car would depart Melbourne, heading in convoy for Sydney. The Bean car would then be loaded aboard a ship and delivered to Darwin. The truck would continue northwards on its overland journey to eventually team up with the car.

The truck would then turn around to begin the laborious return journey to Melbourne, cementing its place in automotive history by becoming the first commercial vehicle to make the crossing. The car would meanwhile be driven south, flat out with Jack Bean on board, in an attempt to break the overland speed record from Darwin to Melbourne. Bean and Barlow were of one mind. There was of course only one man alive who could undertake such a mission – Francis Birtles, the indefatigable motorist and explorer who had piloted the Scarlet Runner along much of the same route before.

Jack Bean was particularly impressed, and cabled Bean Cars in Dudley to supply and ship a Sports Special to Melbourne for Francis Birtles to drive in the record-breaking attempt. Yet due to sudden business dealings, Jack Bean could not participate. Alexander Barlow insisted his son, Alexander Junior (Alec), accompany Birtles on the journey.

'Whatever happens in the after years,' wrote Alec, 'the moment when my father announced that I was to accompany Francis Birtles on the first truck trip to Darwin – and that I was to race back to Melbourne with him – will always be one of the proudest moments of my life.'

When the car arrived from England, it turned out to be nothing like any machine Birtles had ever driven before. It was a bona-fide racing car – brilliant red, long and thin, with a tapered, streamlined, torpedo-ended body. It was purpose-built. It required the driver and a passenger to lower themselves into a doorless two-seater cockpit, access being somewhat like that of a biplane. The seats were slightly staggered to minimise body width, with the passenger seat not quite in line with that of the driver.

Once inside the car, space was at an uncomfortable premium, two people completely occupying every conceivable inch. Despite the car's ungainly height from the ground, the driving position itself was low, the base of the driver's seat simply fitted to the floor, resulting in the driver's legs being almost flat, straight ahead. Unlike the tourer or Bean 14 sedan, the Sports Special had the gear lever mounted in the more familiar location, directly on top of the gearbox, protruding through the floor between the driver and the passenger.

The car had four massive, mechanically operated drum brakes, with a handbrake lever positioned on the outside of the cockpit. Yet, for all its elegant streamlining, the car was fitted with the Bean truck motor, which differed only in a few details from the standard side-valve, 14 horsepower car engine. It is possible that the truck motor – possessing the same horsepower as the car – was decided upon due to the electrical components being positioned higher on the engine block, a handy feature when making crossings of crocodile-infested rivers.

The Sports Special was as pretty as any racing car of the era. Smaller than the brutish Bentleys and Vauxhalls and larger than the effete Bugattis, it was unquestionably the most attractive car the Bean company had ever built. Yet despite its appearance, as soon as the two-seater torpedo-bodied racer was handed over to Frank Birtles, the bushman, he set to work with a file, a hand-drill and paintbrush in preparation for the journey.

First off, of course, were the exhaust and muffler. Frank replaced these with a four-inch diameter straight copper exhaust pipe that ran full length down the side of the car from the engine bay to the tail. To reduce weight, he had the chassis rails drilled with large holes, and this weight loss was replaced by the installation of a large auxiliary fuel tank situated within the torpedo body behind the cockpit. Two enormous nickel-plated headlights were fitted in front of the radiator.

He then rigged up a series of mechanical linkages that ran forwards from the cockpit, enabling the headlights to be angled from inside the car. Fitted on the external driver's side near the cockpit was a hand-cranked tyre pump with the worrisome brand of Dead-Ezy, and fitted to the passenger's side was a brass Pyrene chemical fire extinguisher.

Frank simply saw the racing car as a blank canvas, and started applying his artistic skills with paint and a paintbrush, with unmistakable depictions of kookaburras and maps of Australia stencilled onto the car's brilliant paintwork.

As for the Bean truck, it was as solid and as stolid as a British truck of the 1920s could be. In an age of speed trials and record-breaking, the thought of slogging it out in a Bean truck from Melbourne to Darwin and back must have been stomach-churning. Ungainly, upright and diabolically slow, the truck sent for the expedition was fitted with an upright timber cab that looked as though it had come from a steam locomotive.

The Bean promotional literature proclaimed: 'Unquestionably there is no finer testing-ground for the commercial motor vehicle than the "great empty spaces" of the Australian continent. If a truck can conquer the manifold difficulties that present themselves on the long journey from Bass Strait to the Timor Sea, the intending purchaser could not reasonably ask for better proof of stamina, for along the Melbourne–Darwin route is admittedly the most hostile trucking country to be found anywhere.'

In selecting this route for a great truck test, the manufacturers of the Bean knew from a previous car trip what lay ahead of them. A full-page advertisement in the Melbourne *Argus*, advising readers to 'Watch for the Birtles, Barlow, Bean car dash from Darwin to Melbourne' depicted a *Boy's Own* style illustration of pith-helmeted motorists in a Bean truck making heavy work through jungle mud, while mysterious all-seeing, all-knowing, spear-wielding Aborigines peered through a clutch of pandanus palms. Just to throw a bit more intrigue and drama into the illustration, a particularly evil, giant, open-mouthed saltwater crocodile was lying in wait.

The advertisement's copy continued the excitement and drama of what the expedition would face: 'It is a dual purpose undertaking, because it is planned to prove the ability of the Bean truck and the Bean car to triumph over the most difficult motoring country in the world – a territory that for the greater part still holds silently aloof, with secrets known only to the wandering black fellow.'

Certainly, these advertisements were designed to grab the readers' attention – unfortunately for Frank Birtles, the ads caught the attention of the wrong person.

For four years, the High Court of Australia, no less, had been looking for him. Frank owed £150 to a Mr Albert Hastings Orchard of Toorak in Melbourne from whom he and Clive had rented the Maxwell car for three months back in 1917 for their speed trials across the country. Frank had on numerous occasions failed to appear in the Supreme Court, and in 1922 the High Court issued a 'praecipe for search' – not exactly a warrant for his arrest but more of a court order to find him. The problem was, every time Francis Birtles surfaced in the public arena, he'd immediately disappear back into the never-never.

One morning, Albert Orchard opened the Melbourne *Age* to read that the famous, money-owing adventurer was about to undertake a motorised expedition across the continent in a Bean car and truck. Orchard now knew exactly where and when the elusive Frank Birtles would resurface from the wilds, and he tipped off the court.

Neither the Bean car nor the truck had been 'run in', their motors being brand-new, so they required careful and patient treatment for the first few hundred miles – that was if they could reach 100 miles. On the first day out of Melbourne, the truck became bogged to the axles, taking a full four hours to extricate. It was going to be a long trip.

Nevertheless, by the time the two vehicles arrived in Sydney they were showing no sign of any problems. Even the truck was 'running splendidly', wrote Barlow, 'averaging 150 miles per day'. In Sydney, Birtles and Barlow farewelled the Bean 14 as it was prepared to be loaded onto the steam ship for Darwin, and joined the crew aboard the truck. In diabolically bad weather, they set off for north-western New South Wales, where just short of Gulargumbone the Bean truck, ploughing through mud and water, put a front wheel into a collapsing rabbit burrow and slowly capsized.

Mercifully, other than a few scratches no-one was hurt. Alec Barlow wrote that he'd been 'buried under two tons of stores and petrol . . . Mr Birtles got out his alligator line, and with the aid of two posts formed a Spanish windlass with which the truck was righted.' The truck slogged its way north, dropping fuel dumps for the return journey at various homesteads and outposts, the last one at Dajarra before heading into the Northern Territory. 'The excitement of attaining and crossing the border between Queensland and the Northern Territory was intense,' Barlow recalled. 'Guns were fired, empty petrol tins rattled, and everyone cheered madly.'

The track north from Katherine had fallen into disrepair since the construction of the railway line many years before. 'Washout after washout was encountered, some of them 10 feet deep,' wrote Barlow. The truck arrived in Darwin 25 days after leaving Melbourne, and two days before the arrival of the steamer carrying the Bean 14 Sports Special. Barlow sang the truck's praises: '. . . the Bean had won through, ably earning its laurels as the first motor truck to be driven from Melbourne to Darwin.'

From the slowest transcontinental crossing, to what would be the quickest. The Bean 14 Sports Special was unloaded onto the dock in Darwin. Frank christened the car the Sundowner. No doubt somewhere along the line they'd turn up at 'an outback homestead in time for supper and a shakedown'.

At 4 a.m. on Friday 23 October, Frank and Alec tore away from their starting point at the Hotel Darwin. 'In spite of the earliness of the hour the atmosphere was unbearably hot, close and stifling,' wrote Barlow. The Sundowner's whopping headlights were on high beam and Frank had the car at full cry. He thoroughly enjoyed driving it – clearly, it was made for him and he was made for it.

They made it to Pine Creek, a distance of 230 kilometres by 12.45, but the track here was so bad Frank gave up on it and drove through the adjacent jungle. That night they passed through gate after gate. In the dark, these were a nightmare. Frank, on the truck journey north, had placed old oil and petrol tins so they'd reflect the car's headlights. Birtles knew what to expect. 'Our headlights caught the glitter just in time to save us from what would undoubtedly become a most unpleasant wire entanglement.'

The drive was harsh and uncompromising, yet Frank and Alec were working remarkably well as a team, Barlow's first drive of the Sundowner came when Frank was simply too exhausted. 'The car felt very strange to me for the first few miles,' he wrote. 'The unaccustomed surrounds and the anxiety of the venture all combined to render me more nervous than I can ever remember feeling. Never had I driven on such a track before.'

The car performed astonishingly well – on good sandy roads, it was attaining speeds of 120 km/h. The pair survived several memorable experiences during their furious drive: barrelling through a violent thunderstorm, an 80 kilometre wrong turn and the terror of being chased by an emu clocked at 'the incredible speed of 40 miles per hour'.

By the time they had reached the massive crowd waiting for them at Martin Place in Sydney, they had been on the road for

6 days, 17 hours and 40 minutes. 'What scarecrows we must have looked,' wrote Barlow, 'as, in Balaclava goggles, silk trousers, singlets, sandshoes, we braved the curious eyes of the crowds.'

Once again, Frank Birtles was about to encounter a fiery catastrophe. At the Taralga turn-off north of Goulburn, a swag fell onto the exposed exhaust pipe running the length of the car, catching on fire and burning through a rubber fuel connection. This in turn ignited petrol in the smaller of the two fuel tanks.

Barlow, who had been asleep, suddenly woke up and yelled for Frank to stop, which he did, 'pulling the car up almost in its own length, although she was hitting 40'.

Even before the car had halted, Barlow had wrenched the Pyrene fire extinguisher from its bracket and emptied the contents onto the fire – the flames now three metres high. Frank leapt out of the Bean and threw handfuls of dirt from the roadside onto the inferno. Then, almost as quickly as the fire started, it was out, although smoke was still pouring from inside the boot.

Frank and Alec doused the car using the water bags, but everything in it was destroyed: cameras, film, food, clothing – all one soggy, soppy mess.

After an hour in Goulburn re-rigging the fuel system, the scorched and blackened car was back on the road. They'd been lucky – if the 200 litre fuel tank had caught fire they'd have been burned alive. Frank knew all about that. 'It was the nearest escape from death I ever had,' Frank said in an interview.

Eventually they reached the outskirts of Melbourne, 'where news of our coming flashed by telegraph caused every town to turn out with a rousing welcome. Cars fell in behind until they numbered scores. Thus escorted, the dauntless Bean 14 completed a journey unique in the annals of Australian motoring.' At 5.30 pm on Saturday 30 October 1926 they arrived at the Melbourne GPO, having made the journey from Darwin in 8 days and 13 hours. They'd averaged around 600 kilometres per day.

The ensuing publicity for the drive was phenomenal. Around the country full-page newspaper advertisements proclaimed their triumph. 'Bean Brings Home the Bacon! Birtles and Barlow

Smash the Record! Outspeeding All Previous Transcontinental Achievements!' Seemingly endless copy was written about the pair: 'Darwin and Back. Birtles' Record Dash! Hypnotism of Engine's Roar!' This was just another addition to Francis Birtles' repertoire of amazing achievements. His name was never bigger.

And Frank was about to collect a sizeable payment from Barlow Motors as a reward – only there was now a slight hitch. While he'd been on the track, the Supreme Court, knowing exactly where Francis Birtles now was, had ordered Barlow Motors – as Francis Birtles' employer – to garnishee the money to repay Mr Albert Hastings Orchard for the rental of the Maxwell car in 1917.

Frank couldn't take a trick.

18

The Proposition

In the long twilight of an English summer evening in 1926, Malcolm Ellis was pouring another wine, having just finished a meal in a Park Lane restaurant. He was now living in Britain as the *Daily Telegraph*'s official London correspondent – a post he clearly relished. From London, he was now reporting first-hand the ever-increasing whirlwind of industrial trouble British industry was being drawn into, and would file daily stories for the readers back home in Australia, relentlessly espousing Britain's parlous state.

Ellis was dining with a like-minded Australian industrialist, Leslie Hinks, a 35-year-old textile engineer from Sydney. Hinks was visiting Europe studying textile mills, his speciality being in their construction. He had recently completed building several mills – one of the most impressive being in Albany, Western Australia. Hinks had just returned from Bradford, the heart of British textile manufacturing, and had been already quoted in the *Sydney Morning Herald*, gravely despairing that 'The textile trade in England is in a shocking condition.' And it wasn't just textiles. Since the war – Hinks spluttered to Ellis – British manufacture as a whole had gone to the dogs. No longer did the stamp 'Made in England' mean 'the best in the world'.

The most potent symbol of the decline of British manufacture in Australia was the motor car. Australia was awash with cars imported from America. You saw them everywhere and they were immensely popular. Why? Because American road conditions were more like those in Australia – long distances over diabolical terrain.

The Americans had stolen the march on Britain – Detroit had its eye fixed squarely on developing nations just like Australia. Britain might have been the United States' best overseas customer in 1920 but, as it quickly transpired, Canada, Argentina, Mexico and Australia – countries that possessed poor communications, huge distances and appalling roads – soon took the lead.

In 1922, Mexico eclipsed Britain as the United States' top automobile export client, and from then on it was Australia, becoming America's biggest export market in 1922 and 1923. And this was after the hefty tariff Australia placed on cars built outside the British Empire. Australia was car-driven. Even though by the mid-1920s the United States possessed around 80 per cent of the world's motor cars – where one in seven of the population travelled in their own car – per capita, next came Australia and New Zealand.

Yet British manufacturers seemed uninterested in the Australian need for a suitable car. Every now and then they'd offer a 'colonial' or 'tropical' version of a standard model, but most people knew this was really only lip-service.

One of the key problems for the export of British cars was the imposition of a horsepower tax on British motorists. In Britain the more horsepower your car possessed, the more expensive your annual registration. Cars with low horsepower were big sellers. The tax created another typically English class divide – only the wealthy could own powerful cars. Yet in Australia, the motorcar was rapidly becoming a symbol of egalitarianism – and for the sorts of distances everyday Australians needed to travel, engine power was everything.

The Australian agent for Morris Cars, Sydney Cheney, had persuaded Lord Nuffield (William Morris, the company's owner) to visit Australia and see why his cars weren't suited to local conditions. If only British industry could get their head around the opportunities to be had in the Australian market. Hinks believed he knew exactly what was needed for the design of a car suitable for Australia. He drew a sketch on the back of a menu.

It was simple: a strong chassis – none of your piddling, fiddly, spidery frames. An Australian-suitable car should be fitted with long elliptical springs that gave both good ground clearance and a smooth ride over rough tracks. On top of that, Australian motorists shouldn't be saddled with gutless four-cylinder cars just because England had a horsepower tax. This was a preposterous imposition on the Australian motorist. Australia was a big country with vast distances that need to be covered in the shortest amount of time possible. An Australian-suitable car should be fitted with a big, no-nonsense, six-cylinder engine capable of plenty of power on demand when barrelling along an open road or up a long hill.

Whether or not it was the wine talking, Hinks suddenly announced to Ellis he was prepared to design and build a car in Britain that was perfect for Australian conditions, which would really stick it to the Americans and help the Empire regain its position in manufacturing. Hinks said that he was going to approach the Bean Car Company to build a car to his specifications, and further, he would personally pay for it.

This was unheard of – someone off the street, walking in to a manufacturer's office and saying 'build me a car and here's the cheque'. It was preposterous. Then again, Hinks did have a lot of money. Ellis later recalled Hinks posing a question: 'Suppose I do build a motor car in England suitable for Australian conditions, how can we test her? The roads here [in Britain] give no criterion. The colonial test course is amusing to an Australian. What is the quickest way to discovering her weaknesses?'

'Drive her across Europe and Asia and down to Singapore or as far as we can get and, if the season is not too late, across Australia,' Ellis replied half-heartedly.

'Will you carry it through?' asked Hinks.

'Give me a car by the middle of December, so that I can leave in the middle of January, and I'll try,' he said on the spur of the moment.

And so it was all set.

The following day, Hinks left London for the Bean car factory in the Midlands, and Ellis headed to the British Museum to study maps.

•

What Malcolm Ellis was proposing was extraordinary. No-one had driven across Europe to the southernmost point on the Asian landmass before. If you looked at a map of the world in 1926, a large portion of Ellis's route across the globe fell under the auspices of the British Empire. From Persia, the route to Singapore travelled through British India, Burma and Malaya and the final leg from Darwin to Melbourne.

At exactly the same time Birtles and Ellis had been plotting the Scarlet Runner adventure on the verandah of Ellis's Cremorne home in 1924, a British Army officer, Major F. A. C. Forbes-Leith, was heading off from England in a 14 horsepower Wolseley Colonial Model in an attempt to become the first person to drive overland to India.

'I decided to make an attempt to reach India by motor car,' wrote Forbes-Leith. 'Aeroplanes had proved their ability to get there on several occasions . . . but no effort had yet been made to bridge the distance by mechanical (land) transport.' Forbes-Leith's journey took five and a half months, and his arrival in India was nothing short of a miracle. Before his departure, he'd been told by his friends he was 'insane' for even thinking of the idea, and as it transpired they probably weren't far off the mark.

Forbes-Leith was extremely lucky to have survived the journey. As he discovered, the further east he travelled, the worse the road conditions became and the more lawless the world grew. Aside from a few near-catastrophic accidents and spectacular mechanical failures, on more than one occasion he'd been attacked by groups of nomads, he'd been shot at, savaged by packs of wild dogs, and would invariably discover unfortunates who had just been robbed, beaten up or worse. Between Damascus and Baghdad, he passed a derelict Model T Ford where the Arab driver and passengers had run out of water. Two of them had wandered off to find help. One had simply vanished into the desert, and the other was eaten by jackals.

Forbes-Leith's accomplishment had opened up the motoring world even further. And further, he had made it that far in a British car. His drive to India gave rise to the possibility of then driving the whole way across mainland Asia to its southernmost point, Singapore on the Malay Peninsula.

•

Malcolm Ellis had another motive for the great drive: politics. For months he had been sounding the alarm to Australians back home on what was taking place in Great Britain, the mother country now in serious decline, the once-great powerhouses of British manufacture being forced to the ground by communist-sympathising – perhaps even communist-driven – trade unions. He'd just witnessed the General Strike of 1926 – how British industry had dissolved into an impasse between the unions, manufacturers and a beleaguered British government. Britain was falling apart at the seams.

But what of the rest of Europe? What was happening in the smoking ruin that was post-war Germany? How close was the Bolshevik menace to taking hold of the ranks of fractured and shattered post-war European nations? And the Empire. How much longer could it hold fast against the forces that sought to destroy it?

Ellis now had the opportunity to see it all – first-hand.

19

The Bean Car Company

The words BEAN CARS LTD are chiselled in curved lines into the ornate stonework above the entrance to the Bean head office in Dudley. The front doorway is framed by squared-off, stylised, granite Doric columns that attempt to give the heavy industrial red-brick factory some sort of classical justification.

Leslie Hinks paid the cab driver and climbed the front steps, pushing open the glass doors to walk briskly across the linoleum-covered floor to the secretary's office window. He announced who he was and that he had an appointment to see Sir Robert Hadfield, chairman of Hadfield's Steel – the company that had in 1926 purchased Bean Cars Ltd.

Shortly, Hinks was ushered into his office. Hadfield stood up from behind an enormous mahogany desk and put out his hand. Sir Robert had had a remarkable career, which equally incorporated business and science. In 1895, he'd become internationally famous with his discovery of manganese steel.

This changed the world forever. His discovery vaulted Hadfield's Steel out of the depression of the 1890s.

Hadfield was always eager to hear from someone with an enthusiastic demeanour, and was particularly interested to hear from the young Australian businessman – he was an avid supporter of imperial trade, particularly with Australia, due to the favourable deal Australia gave British manufacturers over other nations.

With the niceties of the initial introduction over, Hinks got down to business, explaining to Sir Robert that he wanted the Bean company to build him three cars of his own design, at his own expense.

He continued the discussion by painting a passionate word picture outlining Australian manufacturing's role in supporting and maintaining the British Empire, the rugged road conditions in the Australian outback, just how unsuitable English cars were back home, and how Australians would jump at an opportunity to buy an English car over an American one if it was just better thought out. Here was an opportunity for an English car manufacturer to get it right. What Australia wanted was a solid six-cylinder car, representative of all the skill and craftsmanship of tried and proven imperial manufacturing methods. Hinks lit up with a flash of inspiration. That's what the car should be called: the Imperial Six.

Sir Robert was impressed. The Bean Car company was in fact in the process of introducing a small Meadows-manufactured six-cylinder engine for a car which would ultimately be titled the 18/50.

Hinks said he was confident that he would soon be able to establish sales of more than 5,000 of these six-cylindered cars in Australia per year – and he was prepared to put £150,000 of his own money into the venture. Then, to really cap it all off, Hinks proposed one of his new cars – his Bean Imperial Six – would be driven in a marathon expedition all the way across the world, from England to Australia.

A motor car driven from England to Australia! Sir Robert was sold. He had been completely enthralled by the young Hinks's enthusiasm and drive, describing him to his colleagues afterwards as 'full of go and worship of the empire'.

Sir Robert gave the order. Work was to start immediately on Hinks's cars.

Hinks in the meantime returned to London to board an Imperial Airways flight headed back to Australia via Paris. For Sir Robert, Hinks offered a rolled-gold opportunity for his newly acquired company, Bean Cars, and the young Australian's timing could not have been better. There was a change in the wind as far as worldwide car manufacture was concerned. By 1926, Henry Ford's world-dominating company was losing its grip. Ford's own obstinacy in refusing to consider a replacement for the Model T gave his opposition, chiefly General Motors, an astonishing advantage.

As far as a Ford monopoly continuing into the future, all bets were off. Cracks were appearing that could suddenly open wide for new opportunities – perhaps for an English car to fill the void created by Ford. For car manufacturers all over the world, 1927 was shaping up to be an interesting, perhaps even crucial year.

•

Britain might have emerged relieved and victorious after four years of fighting, but all of a sudden British industry found itself wondering where on earth it was going now that the war was over.

Manufacturers who had been on the receiving end of the British government's open cheque book suddenly found it closed. The war had seen British industry operating on a scale as it had never done before, and the armistice of 1918 had abruptly pulled the rug from under it. Heavy engineering works that produced field artillery pieces suddenly ground to a halt. Carpentry shops, once hammering together countless timber crates for countless batches of Lee Enfield rifles, found they had no work.

Foundries that cast the brass elevation handles for Vickers guns, factories producing cork stoppers for troops' enamel water canteens, textile works that produced miles of khaki cloth for soldiers' puttees – all ceased production. Requisitions for thousands of gallons of olive-drab paint no longer arrived. Complicated Edwardian, Heath-Robinson-esque machines that once operated around the clock spitting out millions of rounds of .303 ammunition were now sitting silent. The tank, one of the most remarkable, intricate and expensive inventions of the war, no longer had any purpose or relevance in the new peace. It was as if everyone in industry had been oblivious to how much they'd been depending on the war.

One of the businesses most affected in the post-war industrial wilderness was that of Harper, Sons and Bean, an armaments manufacturer in Dudley, Worcestershire that had produced shot and shells for the Royal Navy.

The company's origins went as far back as 1829, when 42-year-old Absalom Harper set up a rather backward ironmongery at Dudley in the Midlands. It was the arrival of an ambitious young banker, George Bean, who married into the Harper family and jumped aboard his father-in-law's business, that breathed new life into the operation. The revised company, with the particularly cumbersome name A. Harper, Sons & Bean expanded with the onset of World War I. Opportunities arose one after the other as the company was awarded numerous contracts from the Admiralty. Bean knocked down the family home at Dudley and employed German prisoners of war to build a large plant, which was to become the National Projectile Factory. The company then acquired another premises at Tipton to manufacture fuses for artillery shells.

As the money-making machine of war was grinding to a halt in 1918, Harper, Sons & Bean had vast empty workshops. The end of the war to end all wars had ended everything. However, they had factories that could produce monstrous products.

George Bean and his son John (Jack) decided on a dramatic plan. They would make motor cars. But not in the typically English bespoke manner in which automobiles had been produced in Britain – where chaps in flat caps and grey dustcoats tinkered away on handmade car parts with wooden-handled screwdrivers. Harper, Bean & Sons, one of the biggest mass-production outfits in Britain, wanted to churn cars out like Henry Ford.

These Bean automobiles would be the first British cars ever mass-produced. Yet while Harper, Sons & Bean might have understood the mass manufacture of artillery shells, motor cars were a different proposition altogether. In November 1919, the new Bean 11.9 was unveiled at the London Motor Show at Olympia. The company was at pains to stress that its maxim was 'volume production without sacrifice of quality'. Production began in earnest in 1920, and in July 505 units were produced.

Then, just when things were gaining traction, the company ran headlong into a brawl with the trade unions, kicking off soaring wage increases that suddenly threw the company's business plan out the window. It was catastrophic. Car prices were slashed and slashed even further until what was to be the great mass-producing British rival to Henry Ford was suddenly placed in the hands of the receivers. The Tipton production line closed for more than a year but the company still survived.

On 15 October 1923, a new Bean car was announced at the Connaught Rooms in London. It was the Bean 14 –the Scarlet Runner. The 14 would ultimately prove the best model Bean ever made.

Jack Bean, the general manger, claimed one of the reasons the Bean 14 was so robust was that he and co-directors were aiming for foreign and colonial markets. He knew where the car would thrive, and certainly the Scarlet Runner's ordeal from Sydney to Darwin and back proved it in 1924. However, debts accruing from the company's numerous restructuring attempts were driving the business to the financial wall. Sales staff in the London showrooms were telephoned to send the proceeds of any car sales by train to the factory to cover the weekly wage bill. It couldn't last and the company was bailed out by one of its suppliers, Hadfield Steel.

In Australia, the agents for Bean Cars were quickly becoming anxious about supply and support from England. Delays were a key concern, and the product itself was far too expensive.

Desperate, Bean's agency in Sydney pleaded, 'We must supply literature the same quality as that supplied by the Americans. When they send a new vehicle out, catalogues, posters, technical descriptions, parts and instruction books precede it.' They needed to match the Americans in sales and marketing.

While touring Australia in 1926, Jack Bean strongly recommended to Hadfields that it spend £14,000 on advertising in what would be its most lucrative overseas market. Hadfields' board was incensed by the notion. They were quite happy with the advertising Bean's marketing arm produced. Whereas American advertising might depict a Pierce Arrow tourer effortlessly gliding through the Blue Ridge Mountains of Virginia, Bean Cars went for a more esoteric approach. Even looking through the prism of the 1920s, Bean Cars produced some of the strangest advertisements ever devised for the motoring world. They attempted to fuse relatively obscure English historical figures with modern situations in an effort to interest the English public in their cars by somehow connecting the current model Bean with Britain's past. To promote the car as the ideal recreational vehicle, a photograph of an elderly fly-fisherman wearing a flat cap and clutching a pipe looks knowingly to the reader. 'There's one great joy old Izaak never had . . .' read the headline. 'In old Izaak Walton's time there were no Bean Cars . . .'.

Whoever thought of invoking Izaak Walton – the author of *The Compleat Angler*, published in 1653 – as a desirable selling point for a new motor car had a particularly interesting approach to advertising.

In an especially unusual Christmas advertisement published in the *Illustrated London News*, a beautiful Arthur Rackham-style illustration depicts a 19th century village square with Charles Dickens' humorous character Mr Pickwick standing incongruously alongside a new Bean 11.9 tourer.

Bean sales in Australia were shocking. Correspondence from Bean Cars' Australian agencies lists the total car sales for New South Wales between 1 January and 31 May 1927. Of the 13,417 cars sold during that period, 11,160 were American, 1,799 were British and 458 were European. The Americans had 83 per cent of the market. Of the British cars sold – Morris 794, Standard 222, Austin 194, Rover 83 – Clyno, Vauxhall, Crossley, Jowett, Alvis and Bayliss Thomas all sold cars in double figures. Except for Bean. None.

20

The Little Man in Blue

Malcolm Ellis wandered into the map room of the British Museum. There was no question about it – this was the best place in the world to find maps and charts. However, for all the plans held within the museum's thunderous, heavy map drawers, a 21st century Lonely Planet guide what he really needed.

In the days that followed, Ellis was advised by 'Little old men in the British Museum . . . who became young when our plan was unfolded to them. They brought other old men, entomologists, geologists, lean, wise, untidy ancients who all became glorified in the beam of recollection as they told you that here was the spot where they were chased by the elephant.' He faced a myriad of problems, foreseen and unforeseen, in mounting an expedition to drive across the world. The car itself, customs, carnets de passage, language, fuel, spares . . .

The most significant issue the expedition faced was that of weather. It was imperative to avoid a European winter, an Arabian summer and a Burmese monsoon, and success over the weather was contingent on timing. The drive across the world could only be performed at a specific time of year. It was as if the world's weather controlled a secret passage that would open up at a precise moment, allowing travellers to pass through, and would then close in behind them. If the expedition were to succeed, it would be a race to beat the weather.

There were of course also physical obstacles, in particular three forbidding barriers to overcome. Ellis had been warned of the first true trial they would face, the infamous Dragoman Pass dividing Yugoslavia from Bulgaria, the scene of countless Balkan wars, now a viper's nest of murderers and assassins, geographically impenetrable, inhospitable and seemingly impossible for a car to cross. The second challenge was the Lut, the ferocious, desolate wasteland in western Persia where some of the hottest temperatures on earth had been recorded. Not even the murderous bands of nomadic bandits ventured there. Lastly, there was the greatest impediment of all, the Naga Hills dividing north-east India with Burma – a stifling tiger- and snake-infested jungle that covered the razor-sharp silhouette of an unassailable mountain range. After that, the expedition just might succeed in making it through to Singapore.

The museum's great Morocco-bound atlases were certainly impressive and useful, but they didn't give any idea of the simmering, ever-changing, potentially dangerous political world through which Ellis would drive. If he was to undertake this expedition, he needed the best intelligence he could get, and he knew where to get it. Ellis, the former covert agent for the Commonwealth Directorate of War Propaganda (and in later years an operative of the Commonwealth Security Service) certainly had more than a few useful contacts in Britain whom he could draw upon.

His plan to drive across the world was now taking shape as a more of an official, perhaps even military-style, operation. Ellis seemed inclined to inject a bit of 'cloak and dagger' into whatever project he was working on, earning him a reputation as an 'over-zealous amateur'. What is certain is that Ellis was receiving assistance and guidance in preparing the expedition from various individuals in the British military – and possibly the intelligence services – some of whom were even volunteering their services to tag along. 'Close cropped fellows began to drop in casually with a military gait and a fever complexion to whisper they had heard of what was going forward and ask, "Is there any chance?" And it made your heart bleed to have to say "No."'

Sometimes Ellis wrote about his various clandestine rendezvous with mysterious figures in a cryptic fashion. He rarely spelled out who it was exactly that he'd met. It was all a bit of melodrama, but in general, he described his encounters in an off-hand and light-hearted manner. Yet – typical Ellis – all the while dying to let you know how important and well-connected he was.

Malcolm Ellis had influential, high-ranking British military personnel coming and going, assisting him in preparation for the journey. They gave him access to all sorts of useful intelligence as to what might lie in store. Through his contacts, Ellis recorded that he had received 'three hundred feet of maps', and he was able to peruse classified information received through 'one's hired villain', as he said, 'resorting to the something illegitimate'. And the advice he was receiving was second to none.

On a calm Sunday afternoon in September, Ellis was driven out into the Yorkshire countryside by a mysterious, highly decorated retired Royal Navy officer to visit an even more mysterious and secretive major living in a military cottage on an RAF base. 'The naval man' – as Ellis described him – had apparently been decorated by none other than Queen Victoria for some meritorious action that 'happened in the Grecian seas', but according to Ellis, 'He had long since abandoned the practice of firing shells at Britain's enemies to make them for someone else to fire.'

Ellis, the naval man and the major sat uncomfortably in the cottage parlour for some time until there was a knock on the door. The major's black-uniformed batman ushered in a short, blonde-headed man in an aircraftsman's blue fatigues, wearing the badges of an RAF second-class mechanic. Ellis was at first struck by just how tiny this man was, his young and unlined face, and 'the brilliance of his smile and the queer air of authority which made everyone in the room stand up as if something had dragged them to their feet'.

The major and the naval man nervously gave their apologies and left Ellis with the RAF mechanic. The 'little man in blue', as Ellis called him, knew something of some of the regions in which he intended to travel. During the war, he'd had experience in the desert, particularly with campaigning in Rolls-Royce Silver Ghost armoured cars, and they discussed how to 'get them over straight-sided wadis' and their 'phosphor bronze connecting rods'. The conversation progressed to Islam and as to how 'there was no mystery with the Arabs – they were at bottom exactly like ourselves . . .'

Suddenly Ellis froze, dumbstruck as it slowly dawned on him exactly who the little man in blue really was. That he was in discussion with T. E. Lawrence – of Arabia – beggared belief. Ellis, the journo from Cremorne, was in awe, describing his unexpected encounter with Lawrence, the RAF mechanic, who told him that how 'after the war and, worse still, the Peace, he was a worn out man and decided to take a holiday'.

In the years following World War I, Lieutenant Colonel Lawrence, famous for his roles in the Arab revolt against the Ottoman Empire, the capture of the Turkish stronghold Aqaba and the fall of Damascus, sought anonymity in the Royal Air Force as a simple aircraftsman under the pseudonym John Hume Ross. His identity, however, soon leaked out, and he was forced out of the RAF, then joined the Royal Tank Corps under the name T. E. Shaw. Unhappy in the Tank Corps, Lawrence petitioned the RAF to rejoin and only months before the meeting with Ellis was readmitted.

Understandably, Ellis was fascinated by Lawrence. His 'voice was crisp and cultivated; the diction of his phrasing concise and expressive'. He described Lawrence as 'An unusual talker interested in everything, full of strange philosophy, lacking the blasé, sated look of the new, post-war generation with a mind that went directly to the kernel of every question . . . One moment he was saying: "Just now my job is sweeping floors. If you should ever feel the need of the most appropriate setting for contemplation, buy a broom. It is a most soothing occupation. I can highly recommend it."'

Ellis tried to understand why Lawrence was wasting his talents as a lowly ranker in the RAF in this exchange: '"But you have no need to sweep floors," said I, eager to draw him out. "You could be a potentate or a Viceroy. You could succeed in literature, turn Somerset Maugham out of his house in Bryanston Square and appropriate his manservants. As for the lecture platform –"

"'I am sweeping floors," said Lawrence of Arabia, "because I have learned in the east that it is sometimes a greater and more difficult thing to go down than to rise. After all, real life consists in striving to do those things which you find not easy.'"

Ellis was to discover just how prophetic Lawrence's words were.

The throwaway idea sparked over a bottle of wine months before that had been given the grandiose title of the Hinks Imperial Expedition was actually becoming a reality.

Ellis was now engaged in the process of selecting a suitable two-man crew to travel across the world with him in the Imperial Six. Ellis of course, being blind in one eye, couldn't drive, or at least didn't, so while his role was clearly as expedition leader, he needed suitable drivers with mechanical ability.

Without question, Francis Birtles would have been paramount in Ellis's mind. Reports were appearing in British newspapers announcing Frank's success in accomplishing the record-breaking drive in the Sundowner from Darwin to Melbourne. In Australia, Birtles had been feted in a blaze of publicity, full-paged congratulatory advertisements proclaiming the expedition was 'under the command of Francis Birtles'.

Ellis would have rankled at the phrase 'under the command'. One thing needed to be set straight. This upcoming motorised expedition across the world would have Malcolm Ellis at the helm as leader. The uncomfortable possibility of Birtles muscling in on Ellis's trans-global moment in the sun and shanghaiing his glory was too awful to contemplate. As subtly noted in a later biography, Malcolm Ellis 'was rarely inclined to share the limelight'. That was putting it politely.

Ellis made a conscious decision to avoid bringing Frank on board, his rationale being that he had 'hesitated to send for him because, although he was an excellent driver, a first-class rough mechanic, and had a long record of cross-country motor driving, I did not know how he would stand the cold of Europe in winter when suddenly transported from the tropics or how his belligerent nature would react to the vexations of enforced delays among the teeming population of foreign countries'.

This was Ellis at his most churlish. He knew Birtles' history as well as anyone. Birtles had seen far more of the world than Ellis ever had – South Africa, England, Canada, New Zealand. Birtles had nearly drowned in a cyclone in the Indian Ocean and on countless occasions he'd come within a hair's breadth of dying of thirst in some of the most remote badlands in the world. He'd been shot at in war and almost burned alive in peace. To suggest Birtles mightn't cope with a European winter was more than a bit rich. Frank Birtles was one of the toughest men alive.

Ellis instead went shopping for an expedition companion with different qualities, and he found one in Australian-born Captain Eric Walter (Billy) Knowles, a British army World War I veteran from Yorkshire. Knowles had had success in the motoring field in winning a long-distance motor trial, proving he was a dab hand behind the wheel. There was something admirably stoic about Knowles – and that he was a British–Australian war hero only helped to cement his worth in an expedition that linked the two nations.

Ellis described him as 'a little man like most of the great ones, everything in his existence centred round his experiences in France and Flanders where he had a very gallant and, what was rarer, a very unassuming record'. Although Knowles had been severely wounded during the war, Ellis was reassured by the fact that 'he could still sing'. By all accounts Knowles was the life of any party, always smiling and quick with a pun; he had an endearing, effervescent nature. To prove his physical worth to Ellis, one morning Knowles scaled the walls of Tintagel castle. 'After that,' remarked Ellis, 'he was of the chosen'.

As expedition leader, Ellis sang Knowles' praises. 'He was a man of Drake or Nelson material, was Captain Billy Knowles.' Yet time was running out to decide on the third crew-member and despite Knowles' ability to sing and shimmy up castle walls Ellis needed someone with Birtles' track record of producing miracles. Blueprints for the Imperial Six were being drawn up, and very soon the car's construction would commence.

Ellis eventually conceded that Birtles would be a useful inclusion on the expedition – quite possibly at the behest of the Bean Car Company, which was basking in the success of Birtles' Darwin–Sydney overland record in the Sundowner. It seemed everyone in Australia was aware of Birtles' triumph and the word was filtering back to England. For the first time Bean Cars had a publicity coup on their hands. They weren't about to waste it.

Ellis maintained that he cabled Birtles after 'hearing he was so much at the top of his form', making sure to point out that 'he had served under my leadership on the twice across Australia journey in 1924'. But in fact the record-breaking Sundowner was already on its way back to Britain, shipped home for publicity purposes, and with it came Frank Birtles, keen to cash in on his recent success and to pressure the Bean Car Company to supply vehicles for his next expedition into central Australia. Frank was back on the hunt for gold.

'The primary objective of the party,' it was reported, 'which, Mr. Birtles anticipates, will include two British scientists of repute, in addition to other specialists – will be a search for payable mineral fields; but opportunity will be taken to explore thoroughly every mile of the country traversed. Bean motor cars and camels will form the principal modes of transport for the expedition. An aeroplane may be included in the equipment. Two years at least will be occupied in the trip.'

21

The Imperial Six

Work had begun on the Imperial Six with the intention of having it ready to roll by December 1926. Even leaving as late as December meant that the expedition was cutting it very fine indeed weather-wise, and it would be a challenge to beat the unpredictable Burmese monsoon season. A December departure was what was planned. But it was not to be. Blueprint after blueprint continued to be drawn up, and disagreements escalated between Birtles and Bean's design engineers. This was shaping up as a real problem, as the entire premise in building the car was that it was designed specifically for Australian conditions.

Bean's engineers simply did not want to know. Arguments erupted over nearly every aspect of the car – Bean's mechanics ignored Birtles and Ellis's requests for specific, heavy-duty leaf springs, and weren't interested in their views on chassis distortion, something with which the pair had no shortage of experience.

No doubt having the graceless and irascible double-act of Francis Birtles and Malcolm Ellis wandering about the Bean workshop would set any foreman's teeth on edge.

Ellis recalled his and Birtles' frustration with Bean staff who were 'apt, indeed to brush us aside as rather rough colonials who were impugning British workmanship and British material; who were shocked at our insistence that the success of foreign cars in overseas Dominions was due not merely for their cheapness so much as to their construction'.

By Christmas, the car was still nothing more than a heap of parts. Early in January, the engine was fired up on the test bench, and in January the rolling, bodiless chassis was taken out on a test drive. The car with only a benzine case lashed to the chassis was parked outside a pub in Dudley, where a group of children came out to look at it. In a moment of dyslexia, one grubby-faced urchin puzzling over the initials I.S. – for Imperial Six – badged on the radiator called out, 'S.I. – that stands for Scrap Iron! That's what she is, Scrap Iron.' As it turned out, this was to become the most succinct motoring review in history.

The car resembled nothing the Bean Car Company had ever built before. A former Hadfields employee, Mr A. J. Jack, remembered it as 'a ghastly looking car, like a truck . . .' The Imperial Six was indeed a brute. It was a very large and heavy motor car, built on a staggeringly solid chassis from which hung four truck-sized semi-elliptical springs. All this sat on four monstrous disc wheels fitted with oversized block-pattern tyres. Gone was the whimsical egg-shaped radiator of the Bean 14 and earlier models. Instead was a no-nonsense rectangular German silver-plated radiator from which a particularly long square-sided bonnet ran back to meet the firewall.

Despite the car's impressive size, comparable to that of a Rolls-Royce, it had only two doors, and a peculiar bulbous rear-end that incorporated an enormous luggage compartment. The car did possess some of the features desirable for outback motoring: a high ground clearance at 10 inches, a wide 4 foot track, and the chassis a remarkable 8 inches deep.

The engine was still only in its experimental stage, a one-off 3.8 litre overhead-valve six-cylinder motor drawn up by Britain's premier engine designer Harry Ricardo, fitted with the Ricardo high-turbulence cylinder head, also a feature on Bean's smaller 2.7 litre six-cylinder motor. During World War I, one of Harry Ricardo's achievements was the design of tank engines – something the Imperial Six (which weighed 2 tons unloaded – 3 tons fully equipped) could most definitely use.

In theory, the Imperial Six's engine was supposed to have tremendous torque and, coupled with the three-speed gearbox, should 'be able to outperform any six-cylinder car on the market'. But it was hastily thought out, and with only 58 miles of testing on smooth English roads was given a green light to drive across the world.

As this one-off car's construction was drawing to a conclusion, Sir Robert Hadfield made a shock announcement to the Imperial Six crew. He thought it better if there was no publicity surrounding the London-to-Australia expedition. It might be more prudent to conduct the expedition with as little fanfare as possible. No launch, no farewell. Perhaps not even mention what brand of car they were driving. The crew was astonished. Bean Cars had just spent the past few months building a six-cylinder motor car designed specifically for Australian conditions that would be driven from London to Melbourne and they wanted *no publicity*? Why on earth not?

The sudden decision to suppress publicity was the result of another Bean Cars debacle. The company had found itself in a particularly awkward situation when Sir Robert blithely agreed to build Leslie Hinks' Imperial Six. He hadn't thought it through. Jack Bean, the company's managing director, had spent months travelling throughout Australia in an effort to secure dealership contracts, scoring a coup in Sydney with Dalgety & Co, a diverse and powerful business conglomerate that were agents for numerous car brands such as Essex and Hudson, signing them to handle the sale of Bean trucks. Being part of Dalgety's stable was exactly the break the Bean Car Company needed, yet Jack Bean concluded his negotiations knowing nothing of the arrangements that had taken place with Hinks on the other side of the world regarding the construction of a new car.

The psychological effect on Birtles, Ellis and Knowles must have been devastating. They were prepared to put their lives on the line with this new and untried car, ready to drive off the edge of the world. And now they were faced with making the decision to either cancel the entire expedition as Bean Cars clearly wanted, or press on without any support.

Ellis, Birtles and Knowles convened an impromptu meeting to decide what to do. What if they did succeed without the factory's backing? What if, as Ellis put it, 'they [the company] take the battered wreck when we have finished with it and rebuild it as we wish, the result will probably be well on the way to success'. That improbability was so far down the track it was ludicrous to even suggest it at this point.

The delay in finishing the Imperial Six – an extra month – had created a disastrous situation. If they were to go ahead, their plan was now totally reliant on the power and reliability of the untried six-cylinder motor in enabling them to race against the oncoming bad weather in Europe by 'a hurried dash for Constantinople in the last fortnight in January'. They'd then push on through day and night to Delhi, where they'd spend a few weeks in preparation for their assault on Burma. What they weren't to know was that ahead lay the worst winter Europe had seen for 40 years. It was now snowing from France to Jerusalem. Ellis and Knowles looked at Birtles – he was their only hope in ensuring the mission's success.

'My motto's "Chance it",' Frank responded.

Journalist Malcolm Ellis (*left*) with a sizeable water buffalo he bagged with a .303. Simpson, 'The Engineer', measures the buffalo's horns. Behind them is the Scarlet Runner – the first Bean car in Australia.

The Scarlet Runner with some Northern Territory locals. For Simpson, the English engineer, the outback was a different world from Dudley in the Midlands.

The Scarlet Runner crossing the New South Wales–Queensland
border at Hungerford. The overloaded English car performed
remarkably well in the far-flung regions of the outback.

A bush shower offered all the comforts of home.

Frank loved the strength American cars provided for outback motoring. Here, his Oldsmobile seems right at home in the desert.

Billy Knowles, Malcolm Ellis and Frank Birtles aboard the Bean Imperial Six, about to depart Leicester Square for Australia. It was known as 'the secret car'.

The shockingly designed and constructed Imperial Six limping through the wilds of Baluchistan. In India, it would be officially pronounced dead.

Miss Australia, Phyllis Von Alwyn, farewells Francis Birtles outside Australia House on the Strand as he departs for the second attempt to drive from England to Australia.

In Greece, a bridge destroyed by an avalanche required Frank to reverse 8 kilometres along a mountain road.

A Baluchi tribesman. Frank was never sure who was friend or foe . . . and bandits genuinely worried him. 'Brigands murder for as little as a gun,' he wrote.

The Sundowner, Frank's trusty Bean 14 en route to Palestine. In either the Sinai or the Simpson, Frank was more at home in the desert than any city.

The young Canadian traveller, Percy Stollery, who joined Frank in India, clears rocks in a dry creek for the Sundowner to use as a track. The pair had been told there were no roads through Burma's notorious Naga Hills – 'a paradise of headhunters'.

Years of punishing long-distance travel under the most appalling conditions took its toll on Frank, and the epic crossing of the Naga Hills was about the most testing.

Frank manhandling the Sundowner up one of 60 mountains to cross in the Naga Hills. Getting down the other side was just as complicated and perilous.

Frank removed the Sundowner's rear wheels, filed grooves in the brake drums and fitted tyre chains. The tiny diameter of the brake drums gave the car extra low gearing, and the chains dug into the earth, giving serious traction.

Finally, civilisation – an official welcome at the Dunlop office in Rangoon, and badly needed hospital treatment for Frank's hand.

It was the same scene in every city – the overlanders being swamped by well-wishers, as seen here in Brisbane. But on their arrival at the Melbourne GPO, the police moved Birtles and Stollery on, because they were obstructing traffic. They didn't even have their photograph taken!

22

On the Way

Leicester Square had seen countless gatherings of Australians during World War I, but none as strange and quirky as this. Pedestrians walking briskly by glanced at an unusually large motor car – by English standards – surrounded by a small crowd, which had gathered to farewell three raffish Australians in long leather coats and flying helmets who were preparing to saddle up and disappear into the unknown. It was a small affair.

However, the Bean company's 'no publicity' edict didn't stop Ellis filing copy for the *Daily Telegraph* back in Sydney.

**ACROSS WORLD – SYDNEY MEN'S DASH
BEGINS. LONDON, THURSDAY**
Practically unnoticed in the midst of London's throng,
Messrs. M. H. Ellis, of Sydney, journalist, Francis Birtles and
E. W. Knowles, left the Automobile Association Headquarters
in Leicester Square in their Imperial Six, on a journey which,
it is hoped, will end in Martin Place Sydney.

Notably the car is referred to as the 'Imperial Six', the Bean brand deliberately excluded. Future articles referred to the car simply as 'the secret car'. And secret was how it should stay – the car was so raw, untested and unadjusted, even before Leicester Square it was habitually jumping out of second gear on hills and no-one on board was at all confident about its brakes.

The adventurers in the car were squashed shoulder to shoulder unceremoniously on its front bench seat with Knowles behind the wheel, Ellis in the middle and Birtles hard up against the passenger door. With a small Australian flag and Union Jack attached to the corners of the windscreen, they braced for the camera and waved farewell.

The silver-plated Lincoln Imp radiator cap shuddered as the engine kicked over. Round-faced Knowles put the car into gear and eased the clutch, the car edging into London's traffic. The crowd gasped. There was a sudden screeching of tyres and then, bang! The Imperial Six hadn't gone 20 metres and it had clipped another car. The onlookers raced over to see what had happened, as Birtles opened the passenger door and climbed out – fuming. He looked at the scrape along the mudguard. Here they were, still in Leicester Square, and they'd already had their first accident.

Frank drew a deep breath – this was a bad omen. That evening they motored south to the port of Newhaven and checked into the hotel, ready for the morning ferry. Before them lay the English Channel, 'that broad starting line of so many British venturings . . .' as Ellis put it, and after that – it was anyone's guess as to what would happen. It would be a long and uncomfortable journey for three men in one car. Each had his own issues. Ellis was not in a good way. He was sporting a cracked rib and was showing symptoms of a relapse of malaria. Knowles was tentative about the journey – he was leaving behind a wife and young family. And Frank, for the first time in memory, was attempting an adventure without a dog. Dinkum was at that time being looked after by Lady Stonehaven, the wife of the Governor-General.

In the early light of the following morning, the fully laden Imperial Six was driven along the dock and onto a steel tray connected by chains to the jib of a steam crane. The three motorists watched as the crane fired up like a locomotive, the gantry lifting skyward, taking up the slack of the chains, the tray slightly swivelling as it was raised from the wharf. Slowly the crane swung the car over the chasm between the dock and the ferry, a sliver of English Channel only a few inches wide, before lowering the car neatly on deck. Farewell England.

After a hurried meal on board, they wasted no time once the car was unloaded at Boulogne. Birtles and Knowles had quite a job ahead of them in racing to Istanbul if they were to beat the weather. Frank settled into the driver's seat and slowly steered the Imperial Six out of the dockyard, and they were soon underway. '. . . steady miles ticked off in an unaltering style along the unaltering road.'

The feel of this car was nothing like that of the Sundowner. Sure, it had more power than a four-cylinder Bean 14, and so it should. But there was not the altogether cohesive feel of the Bean cars Frank had driven before. Nevertheless, the Imperial Six was capable of covering ground quickly, and before long they were travelling through the countryside of northern France at an astonishing pace. The crisp air of the French countryside was infinitely clearer than the all-pervading winter fug of London's coke and coal they'd left behind. And now their spirits were rising. Knowles, whose key contribution to the expedition – apart from colliding with other cars – was his ability to sing, delved into his repertoire regaled and everyone with a sea shanty.

I thought I heard the old man say
Goodbye, fare ye well.
We're homeward bound
With 12 months pay!
Goodbye, fare ye well.

'Very close home and Australia seemed for the moment,' wrote Ellis, 'just as often home has seemed to a million sailors who have bellowed that old song to end among the coral along the way'. The first impediment they would strike was the ferocious winter ahead. They were more than a month behind schedule as far as the winter weather was concerned, but so far the drive across France had been pleasant enough, the sun shining, the smooth roads and first-rate highways allowing for some seriously fast driving to the point where Ellis pointed out 'The speed grew until I was compelled to curb everyone's enthusiasm'.

Then they struck the first signs of the winter weather. 'Mile on mile of monotony broken by wet winding village streets . . .' remembered Ellis. And as the weather inevitably began to deteriorate, so did the Imperial Six. The car began to run roughly, which was readily pinpointed as a fuel problem. For whatever reason, the carburettor's tuning went hopelessly wrong, Birtles spending hours continually resetting it.

Then, on the open road, they could smell smoke coming from behind the driver's seat, where a short-circuit caused a small fire to take hold. Strapped to the car only inches away were 8 gallons of auxiliary petrol in tins. Knowles began clearing everything in the back of the car away from the fire while Birtles and Ellis used all their strength to try and prise the Pyrene fire extinguishers from their brackets 'into which the genius who had fitted them had jammed them in so that they held like part of the frame'.

On reaching the Rhine, the trio pulled into a queue to pass through customs to enter Germany. Travel through post-war Europe was to prove somewhat of a bureaucratic nightmare. The new Europe, with new boundaries drawn up for new nations, saw nearly 16,000 kilometres of national borders where none had previously existed. Before World War I there were fourteen national currencies. Now there were 27. The green-uniformed customs officer informed them he needed to search the car. 'Nothing of the sort,' said Ellis. 'I have a customs carnet.' Unimpressed, the customs officer responded: 'It is forbidden that motor cars should pass the border without examination.' That's all it took for Ellis to start an argument, and he demanded to see the custom officer's superior.

Ellis's abrasiveness was just a taste of how the weeks ahead would unfold as the expedition attempted to bluster and bluff its way across the world. Ellis wasn't just being difficult or obstructionist – he had genuine reasons why he didn't want the car searched. At the very least, he was known to have a .45 calibre semi-automatic pistol secreted on board, and had in his possession a sizeable collection of detailed military maps.

Further, Ellis, the over-zealous amateur espionage agent, was most probably collating notes while on their travels (his papers in the New South Wales Mitchell Library suggest this). It's unlikely Australia's most fervent anti-communist was on holiday. He was on a political sightseeing tour.

Ellis went to find the custom officer's superior and the discussion finally came to a climax with Ellis taking out his wallet and offering him 'a tip'. The officer's response was not unexpected. Ellis recalled, '"You are in Germany now," he said stiffly. "This is not one of those Latin countries. Here, as in England, you must not tip customs officers. It is forbidden."' Eventually they were allowed through.

Ellis's cracked rib and recurring bouts of malaria meant he was becoming increasingly ill and more cantankerous than usual. On top of this, the deteriorating and freezing weather was proving a nightmare for the car. The radiator began to leak, water streaming from the bottom as it boiled at the top. Trying to keep the radiator functioning became a juggling act, with Frank attempting to fix the leaks with white lead and at the same time having to find unfrozen water to refill it. The radiator was having to be constantly removed to be patched up, and in this freezing weather every time the motor was switched off it became a serious problem. If left overnight, water left within the engine block and oil in the engine, gearbox and differential would all freeze. Ellis described the Francis Birtles method of firing up a frozen engine:

Thaw radiator with boiling water and keep thawed with heated blanket and tarpaulin.

Put hot coals round pump.

Bake spark plugs and surround with hot coals after freeing engine as much as possible with kerosene priming.

Sprinkle plenty of hot ash on engine head.

Fill carburettor with warm benzine and choke with benzine bandage. Fill radiator with water near boiling point.

Swing handle and self-starter in shifts for about half an hour and – if nothing blows up or catches fire in the meantime – you may be rewarded in the end by the cheerful sound of the engine ticking over.

The further they travelled, the worse the weather became, the car ultimately becoming stuck in metre-deep snow. The three attempted to fix snow chains to the wheels, but somehow they lost one of the chains in the drift. They gave up hope of moving the car. Ellis decided he and Frank should stay the night in the village of Böhringen and nominated Billy Knowles to sleep in the car. In the morning, they'd return with shovels to dig the car out.

After a night in a guesthouse Birtles and Ellis returned to find the car – and Knowles – gone. All that remained was a hole in the ice where the water in the radiator had poured out. After much confused talk with the locals they discovered the car had been dragged into a barn. An oxen team and wagon had almost cleaned up the Imperial Six around midnight and a freezing Billy Knowles had organised for the car to be dragged into another village – Drottingen.

It took some time, but Birtles and Ellis learned Knowles had found a hotel, racked up a considerable beer tab from the bar and, having no money, left an IOU for Birtles and Ellis to pay. Knowles then wandered off to another village altogether to find his lost travel companions. Frank found the car in the cowshed and began to defrost it to once again repair the radiator.

Eventually Knowles wandered back drunk and, according to Ellis, was 'merry as a cricket'. Knowles and Ellis would nightly find a beer hall as they progressed across Germany and into Austria, but there's no mention of Frank taking part. No doubt tension was brewing. He was doing the driving. He was doing the mechanical work.

•

They made it into the Balkans, in 1927 a hotbed of political insecurity and intrigue, and exactly what the Hinks Imperial Expedition's leader Malcolm Ellis wanted to see. One morning at 11.00 a.m. Ellis was observing the changing of the guard at the Royal Palace in Belgrade. He was standing directly across the road from the front gates. Exactly what he was doing is anyone's guess; needless to say, he aroused the attentions of the police, who saw a man in a long leather coat watching the front gates for a considerable time. Predictably enough, Balkan police in the 1920s were somewhat touchy about suspicious-looking individuals lurking near government officials. After all, that's what kicked off World War I. They pounced on him, grabbing his right arm to lead him away. Indignant, Ellis demanded to know what was going on. He later recalled the events. A person in the crowd called out to him, 'Sir, you have yet already committed a very great crime. The policeman says that you are [an] assassin. If so it is kaput [all up] with you.' This couldn't be good. He was taken to a police station where he was paraded before a commissioned officer.

'"Take your hands out of your pockets when you speak to me," he said.

'"Take them out yourself!" said I trembling inwardly . . .'

Ellis had good reason to tremble – in one pocket of his leather coat was the .45 semi-automatic pistol and in the other 'the largest clasp knife that I could acquire from Rogers of Sheffield'. His naturally obstreperous behaviour certainly wouldn't have helped the situation and it's probably fair to say Ellis was lucky he wasn't simply taken outside and shot. In the course of questioning, he surrendered the pistol and knife, and probably only survived this – and similar situations that followed – by insisting he was 'a British official'. Police officers would no doubt look at each other and decide it was all too problematic to shoot some foreign diplomat. And so they let him go. Ellis later reflected that he supposed '. . . it was not outside the realms of practical politics that I had a Mills bomb or a jam tin full of gelignite in each pocket . . .'

•

Death was what was awaiting them, or so they'd been told. Even in the British Museum there had been warnings about the diabolically formidable obstacles they would encounter on the drive. Without doubt, the Naga Hills in Burma had been flagged as an impossible blockade, but they'd discover that only if they survived crossing the merciless Lut Desert in Persia.

However, before the Lut was the first of the forbidding barriers – the notorious Dragoman Pass, a geological scar dividing Yugoslavia and Bulgaria that had been a killing zone in countless Balkan wars. Aside from that, the pass was deemed impenetrable. No car had ever driven through it, let alone the slap-dash, homemade monstrosity that was the Imperial Six, struggling through a Balkan winter.

On top of that, the Yugoslavs had warned the trio that the Bulgarians waiting on the other side 'drank blood with their porridge'. Sentries were regularly murdered on either side of the divide, and the pass itself had degenerated into a kind of no-man's land. Since World War I, both sides agreed to let the pass languish, to the point where the road had almost disappeared, parts of it covered with rocks from landslides and overgrown with noxious vegetation. This, in effect, had happily severed the two nations, to mutual approval.

Billy Knowles was keen to climb behind the wheel to attack the Dragoman, but Ellis opted for Frank Birtles. He was a specialist 'weapon' to be used only under extreme circumstances. Ellis had specifically kept Frank in the dark about the perils of the Dragoman. 'I decided to tell him nothing of its terrors and put him behind the wheel,' Ellis wrote. He figured Frank was better off not knowing. The remnant of road that snaked its way down one side of the valley and up the other side was in parts metres deep with snow. No-one had any idea what lay underneath – or even if there was a road there at all. There was no shortage of concealed, sharp debris and rocks easily capable of busting open a sump or a gearbox or a differential. Frank sat behind the wheel and placed the car in gear to begin the long, dangerously rapid descent. The track was narrow and in parts very steep. Some of the time they were actually driving on the ice of frozen hill streams. Even with snow chains fitted to the wheels, the car's weight made it uncontrollable as it bounced and dropped, descending from rock to ice to rock, with Frank doing his best to keep it from capsizing. It was a frightening drive, 'a swaying, bumping medley of men, and gear-breaking bumps, and tossing springs and clanking chains'.

At the bottom of the valley the car suddenly came to a jolting stop with a loud and sickening crash. The engine stalled. The whole car quivered. The men looked at each other, wondering who would climb out first to discover the sump impaled on a rock. As it turned out, it was the front axle that had struck a rock, which had been luckily pushed over sideways and in the process become wedged under the running board. After some pushing and heaving, the rock was removed and the party motored cautiously along a frozen waterway ready for the ascent.

The road eventually resurfaced and cut along the 'side of precipices where a four-foot skid meant death', Ellis recalled, before the path opened up onto broader hillsides. At times, the track became so steep and so slippery that even with tyre chains the car couldn't gain traction. Frank gunned the motor flat out, spinning the wheels to the point where the chains were torn off and the links snapped.

The car, with its bonnet pointed crazily upward to the ridgeline, roared and fishtailed and wallowed, while Ellis and Knowles put their shoulder behind it to try and help. They pushed and heaved, 'perspiring like working bullocks', and with every bit of traction gained, Frank gritted his teeth and attempted to use whatever momentum he could muster to bounce the car forward and upward.

With its engine screaming and wheels flailing, the Imperial Six finally clambered its way to the top and into sight of a

village. Stunned guards clutching their Mauser rifles came running towards them.

They had arrived in Bulgaria, and against all forecasts had conquered the Dragoman Pass – the first car in history to do so.

As it turned out, the Bulgarians were nothing like the fearsome blood-drinkers as billed by the Yugoslavs. Ellis got on famously with them. He was both intrigued and impressed with Bulgaria's stance on communism, the government having outlawed the movement only three years earlier. Like Ellis the Bulgarians took a rather dim view of communists. They simply killed them. In Sofia, Ellis wandered through a public park talking with 'a resident' whereby he noticed unusual notches on tree trunks. He was blithely informed that they were merely bullet marks, the result of a 'Communist hunt'. It was not unusual, the resident explained, to wander into a situation where the police '. . . chased the vermin with their rifles'.

23

Spies in Turkey

For any adventuresome motorist heading east across Europe, Turkey – in particular Istanbul, where Europe meets Asia at the Bosphorus – was *the* milestone. Turkey was a frontier, a crossroads, where any last semblance of European existence was handed over to a world of exotica – a gateway to the unknown, unfamiliar and mysterious worlds contained within the vast expanse of Asia.

Hardly any Australians would have heard mention of Turkey until World War I threw the nation's sons ashore at Gallipoli in 1915. An unexpected legacy of the debacle was that Australia and New Zealand had probably become more aware of the Turks' existence than any other English-speaking nations on earth. Because of Gallipoli and the other campaigns Australians were involved in against the Turks, there was a cautious intrigue about Turkey for the three motorists. 'The sick man of Europe' – as crumbling Ottoman Turkey was known before the war – had given the Anzacs an absolute hiding during the Gallipoli campaign of 1915. The Allies had completely underestimated the Turks' ability and resolve in defending their homeland. Twelve years later, three Australians in a motor car would underestimate them again.

The Hinks Imperial Expedition's entry into Turkey took much longer than anticipated. When checking and stamping their documentation, the Turkish customs officials wanted to know why, out of the crew of three British nationals (Australians were still British citizens then), there was a Frenchman among them. A Frenchman? What did they mean, 'a Frenchman'? No amount of attempted communication could solve the question. They were bundled into the car and taken to see a local chief of police.

Frustrated and impatient, Ellis demanded to see the British consul. The police chief then ordered Frank to be dragged in from the car. Frank stood bewildered as the police chief bellowed questions at him in French. Frank looked about the room explaining to anyone who'd listen that he had no idea what the police chief was talking about. Shortly everything became clear. The word 'Francis' was the Turkish word for French. A corporal at the gate had jumped to the wrong conclusion.

They were appointed a guard to travel with them 'to prevent our chance spying on the Chataldja lines,' wrote Ellis, this being a series of fortifications set up after the Battle of Chataldja with the Bulgarians fifteen years earlier. On sighting the first minarets of Istanbul, the car developed a noise 'like a bad pain somewhere in the interior'. Frank thought the sound was coming from the gearbox, but Ellis and Knowles thought it came from the differential. 'The back axle sounded as if it had a sledgehammer inside it,' wrote Ellis, 'and every mile seemed longer than the last'. The car was placed in the hands of a veritable United Nations of mechanics in a garage – a German, a Turk, a Franco-Italian and a Levantine who all had a crack at repairing the car before giving it the okay.

Before they left the city, Colonel Binns of the British Embassy had appointed a guide named Ismail to accompany the expedition and help them travel through Turkey, somehow squeezing aboard. Thirty-four miles from Istanbul, and the differential started grinding again. Frank removed the inspection plate to discover both the crown wheel and pinion were missing teeth – 'it looked as if it had been to a Russian political meeting,' wrote Ellis, never far from a Bolshevik tie-in.

Frank was certain he could nurse the car to Adar Bazaar some 80 miles away, but it wasn't long before the crown wheel and pinion stripped themselves completely. The car lost all drive – in forward gear it rolled backward helplessly. Knowles saved it just in time by hurriedly placing a chock behind the rear wheel. Ellis set off for the nearest railway, returned to Istanbul and cabled the Bean factory in England for a new crown wheel and pinion – the first of three orders for this part. (The differential was the main design flaw in the Bean car.)

Ellis brought them back to the car, Frank reassembled the differential, and they were once again underway. By some strange series of coincidences, the expedition seemed to run into strife with the authorities in almost every country they travelled through. And for some reason trouble always seemed to revolve around Malcolm Ellis. For the next incident Ellis laid the blame squarely on his guide and the actions of the Turkish police.

Whatever it was that had taken place, the Hinks Imperial Expedition suddenly discovered it had driven too close to the naval town of Izmir on the Aegean. Or so Ellis said. As usual, the Australian 'spy' caught the attention of the *jandarma* (police), who, after checking their passports and documentation, climbed aboard the car with rifles and bayonets and instructed Frank to drive directly to the gates of the naval base. Here they were met by a naval intelligence officer who outlined their predicament, saying, 'I regret to inform you that you are under open arrest'. According to Ellis, the town of Izmir was off limits to all foreigners, and on the advice of their hapless guide Ismail, whom Ellis portrayed as some sort of simpleton, they'd inadvertently strayed too close to the town when they were picked up by police. Izmir may well have been out of bounds due to a recent political incident, but other motorists who'd passed directly through the naval port seemed to have had no trouble.

Nevertheless, the three were placed under arrest and put up as *special guests* in the Hotel Izmir. The Turks weren't throwing them in jail – they were just putting them on hold to make them sweat and see what came out of it. The were introduced to a suave Turkish 'police officer', an intelligence operative who was particularly courteous and apologetic and certain they'd be free to leave – *soon*.

The 24-hour detainment turned into 48 and then stretched to a week. The three motorists were, in fact, in deep trouble – and they knew it.

Only eight months earlier, the port of Izmir had become the focus of worldwide attention due to a botched assassination attempt on Turkey's reformist, war-hero leader Mustafa Kemal – later known as Ataturk. The would-be-assassins were rounded up and after a show-trial, fifteen of the conspirators were sentenced to death. Kemal signed the death warrants and that night the condemned were hanged in various locations around Izmir.

The chief conspirator was executed on a scaffold built on the precise location where he had planned to assassinate the Turkish leader – outside the Hotel Izmir. For weeks, the unfolding story of the assassination attempt, the ensuing show-trial and the executions was flashed around the world.

For Ellis, Izmir – the centre-stage of brutal world politics – would be a 'must see' stop-off point on his personal across-the-world-political-espionage-tour. He had a fascination for rough justice meted out to anarchists, communists and 'civil-disobedients', and the opportunity to see first-hand how modern Turkey was dealing with troublemakers would be just too tempting. The problem was, his naive fascination might just see three Australian motorists handled the same way.

While Frank spent each day working on the car, Ellis began to downplay his insolent, overbearing 'British Official' routine. The Turks were unmoved. 'Of course' they were allowed to write letters and send telegrams to the British Consulate in Istanbul. Yet the telegrams were returned from the post office with the message that the addresses didn't exist so there was no use in sending any more. As for letters, there was a general consensus among the three that they hadn't gone anywhere either.

As the days wore on with no sign of their release, Frank began entertaining the idea of escape and for the first time, Ellis acknowledged the gravity of their predicament. 'This procedure would have inevitably led to his being shot or captured by sentries . . . the result would possibly have been unpleasant for all of us.'

They needed to somehow contact the British embassy and so they devised a plan. Their embassy-supplied guide, Ismail, suddenly 'developed a wife who was very sick' in Stamboul. After a week of 'pining' for his imaginary wife he was allowed to travel to Istanbul by train. Ismail was loaded up with a message for the British Embassy and waved farewell. No-one was sure whether he would ever return.

One morning the Turkish intelligence operative arrived at the door and presented Ellis with the business card of the First Secretary of the British Embassy in Istanbul, and informed him that the Secretary was 'proceeding at once to Angora and will arrange that you be instantly released'.

It is not hard to imagine the calamitous reaction at the British embassy when Ismail arrived alone to announce that the three Australian motorists had been placed under arrest as spies at the Hotel Izmir. Turkish authorities were not averse to summarily executing secret agents outside the hotel's front door. That the British First Secretary needed to personally travel from the embassy in Istanbul to the nation's capital Angora (Ankara) 450 kilometres away to sort out the fate of the Hinks Imperial Expedition gives an uneasy picture as to the sort of serious trouble the three motorists were really in. Yet Ismail's covert mission to the British embassy had worked.

Eventually, their guide returned to Izmir by train from Istanbul bearing messages and supplies from the embassy. In another 36 hours they were allowed to leave.

•

In the Isaurian Mountains, the third crown wheel was beginning to make grinding and knocking noises, and an inspection revealed the head from an internal bolt had sheared off and the teeth were beginning to go. Birtles reckoned he could continue to nurse the car, and might even make Adana in southern Turkey, but another spare crown wheel and pinion they'd sent for was waiting for them several hundred miles further south in Beirut. Once again they needed to find a railway so that one of the party could go and get it. Frank coaxed the Imperial Six mile after mile with as little heavy pulling as possible. Everyone winced. Another tooth was lost on the crown wheel and noises became louder.

To their relief, after cresting a hill they discovered a village on a railway line. It was called Airange Derbend, and it possessed an impressive red-roofed, German designed and built railway station. Here, they would set up a base while they repaired the car. Knowles was sent on the mail train to Beirut via Adana. His mission in Adana was to cable the Bean office (again) in London to send an urgent delivery of a crown wheel and pinion to Istanbul to be forwarded on, and in the meantime head to Beirut to pick up the other crown wheels and pinions supposedly waiting there. Knowles's journey was to be a five-day round trip.

For Birtles and Ellis, it was time to try to give the car a good going over, and they set about a five-day overhaul. The radiator, repaired once again, was leaning against a post. The differential was in pieces, the back wheels removed, the universal joint, drive shaft and other stripped-down parts were laid out side by side to be inspected, cleaned, repaired if possible and refitted.

The days waiting for Knowles to return stretched into a week and then ten days. The pair were becoming edgy, wondering what had happened. In the meantime, Birtles even began contemplating the possibility of somehow cutting the two broken crown wheels lying at the bottom of their tool bag and joining them together.

They received a letter from the parcel agent advising their spare parts might arrive in three weeks, a month or maybe even six weeks. 'That awful summary of possibilities killed stone-dead our chances of completing the journey to Australia,' wrote Ellis. With so many breakages and no doubt so many more to come, and mind-numbingly long delays waiting for spares to replace parts that should never have broken in the first place, there was no chance of beating the weather.

Mail arrived from a friend in Istanbul, which included a welcome copy of the *The Times* from London. In it was an article in which 'a British manufacturer gently reproved us Colonials for our habit of buying American motor cars'. Ellis recalled: 'Francis went out on the plain and shed tears of rage. I was beyond tears.'

After two weeks, they received word from Knowles he was in Adana but sick with fever. The days passed with still no word until one morning the passenger train arrived and Knowles stepped off and onto the platform, the spare parts in hand. Birtles and Ellis were overjoyed.

It must have been difficult for Knowles, sick with fever, far away from his wife and children, and trapped in this shockingly unreliable motor car – sandwiched between Ellis, the political zealot, and Birtles, the gruff, hard-as-nails bushman. In the end, he decided to call it quits and return home. It had been a war of attrition on board the Imperial Six, and Knowles was the first casualty. At the railway station at Aleppo, Ellis bade him farewell. The pompous Ellis referred to Knowles's response when requested to leave by writing: 'He acquiesced as the good soldier he was.'

Knowles climbed on board the carriage, sat down and waved farewell to the pair of mad Australians standing on the platform in the rain.

24

Baluchistan and After . . .

Another of the truly great tests they were to face had finally arrived: the Lut, a vast anvil plateau that stretches across western Persia, where temperatures as high as 70°C have been recorded. It is considered an abiotic desert. Nothing – not even bacteria – lives there, yet somewhere on its edge in 1927 there were two old outback travellers discussing which part of Australia the Lut reminded them of.

Both Birtles and Ellis agreed that some of it was reminiscent of the area around Oodnadatta, except the altitude here perhaps gave it clearer air. Then again, Frank thought some of it looked like the MacDonnell Ranges. They were bracing themselves for a hell-drive across this upcoming inferno when, for the first time since leaving England, the expedition got lucky.

They struck a claypan with a hard highway surface stretching as far as the eye could see. Ellis called it 'the father of all claypans'. It was the sort of find outback motorists could only dream of. No undulations or ruts or stones – just a dead-flat, billiard-table-smooth surface. Frank breathed a bit easier, as there was less stress on the car, although he continued to nurse it along. The Imperial Six was capable of doing well over 120 km/h on a surface like this, but there was no way he was going to tempt fate with the crown wheel and pinion out here.

For some kilometres, the desert had been befuddling the pair with mirages and optical illusions – mountains that appeared on the horizon only to disappear, giant lakes that would vanish, 'a team of camels, upside down, transparent, celestial shadows . . .' And yet it wasn't the mirages and the bizarre desert landscape that affected them. It was the uncontrollable sun, 'like a red-hot hammer beating in one's blood, pulsing on the car's bonnet so that drops of oil on it sizzled in small blisters'.

Frank kept the car powering along, the hefty oversized Dunlop block-patterned tyres perfect for such a drive. The further they travelled into the Lut the hotter it became, the radiator boiling continuously, requiring a complete refill every half hour and therefore ripping through their water supply. They reached a well expecting to find water but found only sand. It wasn't looking good. The pair pressed on for some time, when suddenly, in a world where nothing lives, Ellis spotted a crow flying very low. Birtles took interest – a bird in the desert signified water.

The crow appeared to hover and circle and hover again. Then an object moved on the ground. Ellis thought it was some kind of animal, but as the car drew nearer they realised the shape was human. They climbed out of the car to find a man wearing the familiar Persian black fez and blue, skirted dungarees, collapsed on the sand. He raised his head, his lips horrendously swollen, his tongue black, his eyes blood-red. He put out his arms and pleaded, *'Ab! Ab!'* (water, water). Birtles and Ellis dragged him into the car and laid him out on top of the kit that covered the back seat. Ellis gave him spoonfuls of warm coffee from a thermos. 'I was afraid to give him water, so bad was his state, but he continually raved for it.'

The day wore on, becoming even hotter, when they found the entrance to the Afghan Pass, which would ultimately lead them into Baluchistan. Driving slowly 'between burnt out rock walls which reflected a terrific heat' the thermometer on the dashboard now read 129°F (53.8°C). Ellis recalled, 'the radiator boiled as if it had a fire under it, and we had to stop every few hundred yards in as much shadow as we could find to try and cool it.'

The situation was becoming even more desperate, as their passenger would occasionally regain consciousness, breaking into choking screams for a drink. Every now and then, they'd stop the car for Frank to explore a ravine in hope of finding water. The Persian passenger would invariably get on his hands and knees begging Ellis not to leave him there to die. Frank found what he thought was a water soak, but it was their Persian guest who lifted a piece of rock to reveal a decent trickle of water.

The three set up camp, and after a decent meal their new Persian friend began to tell his story. He was a telegraph maintenance worker who days earlier had left his linesman's hut to walk 100 kilometres through the pass and across the Lut to the city of Bam with nothing more than a pint of water in a bottle and piece of tyre-tread nailed to the bottom of each shoe. His plan to follow the moon at night hadn't worked out, due to the high walls of the ravine, and then the following day's sun had smashed all his sensibilities. When his water ran out, he kept on, wandering further into the Lut, staggering in circles, 'round and round like a horse in a mill,' wrote Ellis.

When the motorists found him, he'd been 65 hours in the desert. The following day they motored on, returning their passenger to the telegraph station from where he started out. His workmates were pleased to see him, although they had not sent out a search party to try to find him. As far as they were concerned, they thought he was either in Bam or dead. 'Such is oriental indifference,' Ellis wrote.

•

Baluchistan was altogether different from the Lut. Rocky, sun-bleached mountains, 'grey or smoky blue or frowning black, worn out, treeless, wolf-ridden, tribe-cursed, crumbling chains of crags'. And worst of all, the Baluchi raider, who with his 'hawk eye, long rifle and three foot Afghan knife' made travelling through Baluchistan all the more terrifying. Driving at night was out of the question, as the car was so unreliable they could break down anywhere.

The pair would hide in their night-time camp and then be on the road as dawn broke, driving in a mad rush, flat out for two hour stretches to cover as much ground as possible, simply to get through the country without falling victim to bandits.

Eventually, with the concerted drive through Baluchistan behind them, Birtles and Ellis were entering the sandbagged, barbed-wired and garrisoned border regions of western India. The threat of Baluchi and Afghan incursions into British India had not been so problematic since 1919, when the British fought 'a quiet war' along the 2,000 mile front. As far as the motorists were concerned, they were able to breathe somewhat easier, being back in British-controlled territory, but their drive was now falling hopelessly apart. Birtles, who had driven the whole way since Knowles departed at Aleppo, was completely exhausted. On top of that, both he and Ellis were becoming weaker with the onset of fever.

On a particularly steep and dangerous hairpin bend, they heard the sound of something breaking underneath the rear of the car. Frank got out to discover three differential bolts had sheared, with oil pouring onto the dust.

Ellis had been in considerable pain for a few days, his heel having developed a sizeable abscess, which he steadfastly refused to lance. He climbed slowly and painfully from the car and hobbled around to Frank to try to be of some assistance, chocking the wheels to stop the car sliding down the hill. Frank put the car on jacks and lifted the rear wheels. He slid underneath, attempting to replace the bolts while lying on his back in the dust. The car was at an alarming angle.

With the new bolts in place, Frank climbed out from under the car – and seconds later it slipped off the jack, the bumper bar striking Frank on the knee. Eventually Frank came good and was able to continue, but it proved that exhaustion was resulting in mistakes.

They stayed for fourteen days in the city of Quetta. Ellis's foot had gone from bad to worse. He was in such pain he was almost delirious. Reality was at last starting to take hold – the expedition was now about survival. Frank was doing everything in his power to get the car to Delhi so they could arrange passage to bail out.

On a long climb out of a valley, the pair was engulfed in a dust storm through which they suddenly heard an unmistakable knocking coming from the engine. It was a big-end bearing, threatening to throw a piston and connecting rod through the side of the cast-iron engine block. Frank muttered that he knew something of this sort would happen as soon as they reached a good road. Covering the front end of the car with a tarpaulin to keep out the talc-like dust, Frank removed the sump. A military car shot past them, raising the tarp and filling 'our crank case with fine sand which jammed the pistons and gave us another hour of washing our cylinders with kerosene,' recalled Ellis.

They pressed on at 20 miles an hour with two engine bearings now in decline. Even though the car – and the expedition – was falling apart, the road ahead continued to throw further challenges their way. At a rest house in Ruchkni, Frank asked the proprietor to help him carry a near-unconscious Ellis onto a bed. Ellis was gravely ill. He clearly remembered Frank saying, 'The poor beggar's gone all right'. The following morning, Frank was keen to stay put so that Ellis might gain some strength, but during the night, as Ellis recalled, his whole leg 'had changed into a pillar of purple streaks and I had lumps under knees and arms and a blinding subconscious pain which seemed to make it advisable to get to a doctor as quickly as possible'.

Ellis had no idea of just how gravely ill he really was, now suffering from a combination of typhoid, malaria, dysentery and blood poisoning. But Birtles pressed on to keep the expedition on the road for as long as he could.

Somehow Frank managed to keep the car alive, following the Grand Trunk Road for another 2,000 kilometres, but despite the careful nursing it was all coming to an end. Birtles, Ellis and the car were fading. They were starting to inhale the fumes of the disintegrating metals as the engine parts wore out.

But they didn't suffer for much longer. Eventually the Imperial Six's engine seized and it was officially dead. Frank had been nursing that car from the day it rolled out of the workshops in Dudley. He, more than anyone, understood just how poorly, thoughtlessly, carelessly, culpably the machine had been thrown together. Frank then simply lost control. He spun around looking for anything that would suffice as a weapon. Frank picked up the car's crank handle and let fly into the radiator as though he was clubbing a buffalo to death. The top tank came off and he ploughed the wrench through the radiator core over and over until it was nothing more than a heap of twisted, mangled copper tubing and nickel-plate lying on the ground. That was the end of it. The Hinks Imperial Expedition was no more.

At Delhi, the motorists parted ways. Ellis, dreadfully ill, sailed for Australia via Ceylon, broken and alone. On returning to Sydney, he met with Leslie Hinks. Ellis laid the blame squarely at Sir Robert Hadfield's door. '. . . the strain caused by Bean's indifference, workmanship and dilatoriness completely broke one crew member, sent another driver nearly off his head with fatigue and that Ellis himself would be lame for the next year or two as a result of his experiences.'

No-one in Britain seemed particularly interested in what Hinks had to say. His vitriolic complaints were simply attributed to a man who the British Board of Trade had assessed as 'not quite mentally normal'. However, his concept of the Imperial Six as a car for Australia was way ahead of its time. A large six-cylinder, three-speed, robust car was exactly what Australians needed. Ultimately General Motors, Ford, Chrysler and even British Leyland in Australia embraced a similar concept.

It is likely that Malcolm Ellis and Leslie Hinks never spoke again.

For Frank, returning to Australia would be admitting failure. It would be just like the failed expedition with Roy Fry. People were all over you when you'd succeeded at something but when you'd failed, that was it. No-one would remember you.

There must be a way to recover the situation . . . The cogs in Frank's mind started to mesh. He had an epiphany.

The Sundowner. It was still in England, having been shipped back there for publicity following the successful Darwin–Sydney dash. Come hell or high water – even if he had to steal it – he would drive the car back to Australia. Or die trying.

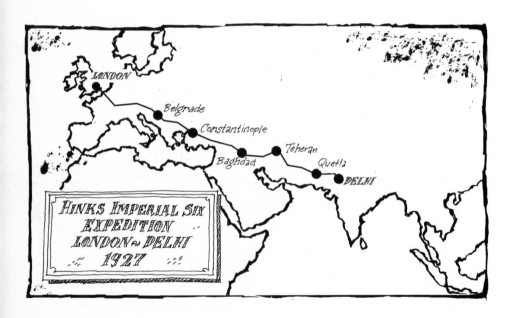

25

Birtles' Return

A bleak pall hung over Liverpool's Gladstone Dock, where the grime-covered brick terminus was readied for another of the seemingly endless number of passenger ships waiting to berth. Long before the stellar international British airports Heathrow and Gatwick, sea ports like Liverpool, Southampton and the East and West India docks in London were gigantic turnstiles for the peoples of the British Empire, with thousands of arrivals and departures every day.

Frank was just one of many shuffling down the gangplank into the shipping terminal who'd suffered the slow journey from Bombay and up through Suez. Frank looked perhaps twenty years older than his 44 years. He arrived back in London in an appalling state. He might have been the last man standing from the expedition – but only just.

However, his appearance and physical condition were not important. It was Frank's mind that had always been his engine room, and it was still ticking over without missing a beat. His arrival in Britain was no whim. He could have returned to Australia with Ellis, who had been broken, was despondent and could easily have died. Birtles had instead booked a passage to Britain with the burning idea that he could make the trans-global drive on his terms. No Hinks, no Knowles and no Ellis to prevent him doing something that could be done. However, he needed money to do it. At the very least, he might be able to tempt Bean or Hadfields into coughing up at least some sort of support.

Birtles' reputation as the indefatigable overlander had taken a hammering. He'd tempted fate and it had hit back. But in his inimitable, unshakable way, Birtles was now even more determined, not necessarily to prove they were wrong, but rather to prove he was right. Frank was raising the stakes. He was going to undertake the drive alone and, furthermore, he'd finish it. Returning home defeated was never an option. As he pondered in his book *The Lonely Lands* back in 1909: 'It's not good to have your name associated with failure.'

In his kit, Frank had brought with him Ellis's maps from the Imperial Six expedition and, having driven over the greater part of the route so very recently, he'd have been confident in retracing his path precisely. But all the confidence and knowledge in the world wasn't going to matter one bit. In order to drive home, he needed both the car and financial backing, yet he knew the Bean Car Company would want nothing to do with him. Sir Robert Hadfield had had his fingers spectacularly burned with the whole Imperial Six debacle. (It had proved wise not to publicise the journey.) Not only could the car have proven an international public relations disaster as it staggered across the world from London to Calcutta, but the expedition almost had the deaths of the three participants thrown in. It could have been catastrophic. Sir Robert wanted no more of expeditions and Australian opportunists.

Nevertheless, one of the first things Frank did after arriving in Britain was visit Sir Robert at his Carlton House Terrace home, ostensibly to discuss 'fresh motor explorations in Australia'. Sir Robert, ever the gentleman, had already agreed to allow Frank the use of the Sundowner, and he had the use of Bean's facilities to work on the car should he wish, but there was no money offered for this expedition.

Frank needed publicity to raise the money. Capturing the press's attention would require some innovative thinking. He knew that the British public had its own perceptions of the archetypal Australian – hundreds of thousands of young Australian men passing through England during World War I had made sure of that. So he opted to play up to the caricature of the naive, fair-dinkum-stone-the-flamin'-crows-cobber mercilessly.

He took the Sundowner on a tour of the 'English outback'. Wherever he could, the Australian abroad, driving his unusual car painted with boomerangs and kookaburras, playfully courted the wire-service press, adopting the tongue-in-cheek angle of the ever-eager adventurer who'd arrived fresh from the antipodes to wonder at the strange customs of Great Britain.

'Australian Motorist to Study the "English Tribes"', read the headline in the *Dublin Evening News*. Birtles explained that his reason for touring the 'English hinterland' was to 'rediscover our country'. Journalists found him eccentric, quick-witted and amusing. 'I'm going up country to study the English tribes. I'm keen to explore the English interior. I've heard they worship the sun up in Manchester; so I'm going there to have a look at it just once before I leave England. What do I expect to find? I am sure I cannot say, but there must be a lot I can learn, I might strike a gold reef. I know there is one at the Bank of England, and I would like to have a closer acquaintance with it.'

Referring to his experiences in the terrible badlands of Australia, Frank reeled the press in, answering to a reporter's question of What do you hunt? 'Why, buffaloes and alligators mostly. It's a curious thing, but in London every time I passed a tube station it reminded me of crocodiles because the smell of a tube is just like the smell of an alligator or crocodile's breath. The buffaloes I hunted in the car. They do 25 miles an hour on the plains; and you've to watch out they don't barge your radiator. But I've discovered just as exciting a sport in London. Baiting taxi drivers. You get in a cab, tell the driver you're in a hurry and to drive hell for leather. Once he's going, you lean out of the window and tell him he's not going fast enough. You do this several times, till he gets rattled; then he fairly zips in the traffic to try and put the wind up you, and the short wheelbase and big look of the London cabs make it appear that they're going to hit things which they miss by half inches. It's most exciting.'

And, as the press appreciated, not only was he quick with a useable quote, Birtles truly looked the part of some antipodean wild man. The *Dundee Courier* described him as 'a wiry little suntanned man' whose 'weather-beaten, travel-stained car, the "Sundowner", had travelled 300,000 miles'. The *Yorkshire Post*'s reporter went on incredulously: 'He told me he's crossed Australia 75 times . . .' The London *Evening News* attempted to explain Frank's quest in undertaking his adventures, concluding in an exasperated tone, 'He just can't help it . . .' This might seem like a throwaway headline from a Fleet Street subeditor, but it was extraordinarily close to the truth.

Almost as an aside, Fleet Street reporters briefly noted that Frank's 'humorous' driving tour around England was in part about his desire to explore his ancestral history and visit the regions where the once wealthy and respected Birtles family resided. Francis would seemingly half-joke about his prestigious ancestry almost as if he was one of the countless disenfranchised post-war European royals traipsing around the world, pining for their rightful place.

Frank's fascination with his forebears in England was not entirely misplaced. The Birtles family did have an impressive lineage, once owning extensive estates west of Macclesfield, Cheshire that could be traced back to the 13th century. Through compounding debt, the land was carved up and sold off during the industrial revolution when Robert Hibbert, a wealthy landholder, bought the most prestigious remnant of the Birtles estates in 1791. The Hibbert clan had made their fortune through African slavery, becoming the largest slave owners in Jamaica, at one point owning half the slaves on the island. Hibbert built a large neoclassical country house on the estate, which he named Birtles Hall, his new title therefore being Robert Hibbert of Birtles.

•

But Francis Edwin Birtles' start in life in fact had been in the bleak slums of working-class Fitzroy in Melbourne, where he was born on 7 November 1881, the third of nine children to David and Sarah Birtles. From the very beginning, this newborn child had it tough. Francis was given the name of his older brother, Francis Henry Birtles, who had died at four years of age that year. His parents came from austere beginnings. Francis's mother, Sarah Birtles, formerly Bartlett, was born in 1860 in the Irish-settled village of Koroit near Warrnambool in country Victoria. Her parents had arrived in Australia from County Tyrone, Ulster, during the potato famine of the 1840s. Francis's 30-year-old father, David, was just four years of age when he arrived in Australia from England with his parents James and Jane, settling in Sunbury, north-west of Melbourne.

With a young family and the reality of ever-increasing industrial action chiselling away at whatever little finances they had, David and Sarah Birtles decided to pull out of the slums. There was no future for a family here. David had already bought land, 72 acres in country Victoria, as early as 1879. The block was near the village of Wandin Yallock in the Dandenong Ranges, some 80 kilometres south-east of Melbourne. For the Birtles children, the transition from Melbourne's slums to the Victorian countryside must have been profound. They were now in tall timber country – thick, rich forests of great eucalypts, broad ferns and wild scrub, where the Birtles kids could grow up, having exciting adventures along the creeks that meandered through the mountains.

Despite the new-found freedom of country life, it was a tough existence for young Frank. His father was a strict Protestant and a harsh disciplinarian. He was also remembered for possessing a heavy hand. The Birtles children were required to attend church twice on Sunday, where if they misbehaved, they knew they wouldn't receive a thrashing on the Lord's Day – that was guaranteed to come around on Monday.

Francis attended the tiny, rough-hewn South Wandin State School until he was fourteen, which was not unusual for the times – that was often considered enough schooling. Yet that was irrelevant, as it so clearly transpired. Frank's education happened on the move. When looking at his life's achievements, his extraordinary ability to write, to draw, to photograph, his astonishing ingenuity, his ability to survive in the most inhospitable conditions and his amazing aptitude for mastering new technologies showed that he had an unusual capacity to teach himself. And in the English summer of 1927 he was learning how to manipulate the Fleet Street press. In an interview with the *Northampton Independent* he signalled his intentions for his upcoming great drive. 'He is now making a tour of England, but the call of the wild to him is so great that he says he feels he is in a glorified prison in returning to civilization with all its conventions and fettering restrictions.'

•

Frank Birtles was not the only Australian adventurer wanting to head home. Bert Hinkler, the famous Australian aviator, was in London, also angling for financial backing in an effort to buy an aircraft and fly back to Australia.

Ten years younger than Birtles, Hinkler had been making a name for himself in aviation circles since the war, flying from England to Latvia and breaking a number of aviation records. Hinkler needed around £2,500 to buy an aircraft, but was having no luck in finding a sponsor.

Perhaps if he had the famous Australian overlander Francis Birtles on board as navigator, he might stand a better chance of securing funds. Certainly a joint Hinkler–Birtles collaboration provided just that bit more incentive for a sponsor to invest. Hinkler approached Frank with the idea of his inclusion in a flight home.

Frank was keen to put his name to Hinkler's project, which suggests how well known in Fleet Street circles Frank was at the time. His name usually appeared first in print: 'Messrs. Birtles and Hinkler's Scheme', 'Mr Francis Birtles, the noted Australian explorer, and Mr Bert Hinkler the well-known Australian aviator, are making preliminary arrangements to fly from England to Australia . . .' If it all worked out, Hinkler and Birtles would fly from England to Darwin in eight hops of about 1,500 miles each, taking a week to cover the distance.

The key feature of this marathon flight would be the non-stop leg from Darwin to Melbourne. This had never been done before. Hinkler wanted to buy a 'Continental type of aeroplane', a newspaper reported, 'as there is no British commercial type of machine capable of flying non-stop from Darwin to Melbourne at a speed sufficiently high to make such a trip practicable . . .' The report went on to sing Frank's praises as a flyer, explaining he had accrued considerable outback aviation experience. As enticing and adventuresome as the newspaper reports made the proposed flight sound, Hinkler still had no luck in snaring sponsorship.

Then, everything changed. On 25 September 1927, it was announced that a French motorised expedition had departed from Paris headed for Hanoi in Indochina under the command of well-known racing driver and long-distance motorist Gustave Duverne. Duverne was attempting to be the first to drive overland from Europe to south-east Asia.

As a rival to Birtles, Duverne was a force to be reckoned with. In France, he was already a national motoring hero, having driven across North Africa, and now he'd departed Paris with a six-cylinder Rolland-Pilain tourer fitted with a trailer. His proposed route was audacious, heading south through Spain, crossing the Mediterranean to Morocco, then driving along the north African coastline through Algeria, Tunisia and Egypt. The journey would be straightforward through Persia and into India. However, he believed his greatest problem would be conquering the mountains of Burma, through which it was said to be impossible to take a car. Duverne opted to see what conditions were like when he arrived, and if need be he'd dismantle the car and employ coolies to carry it over the hills.

And there was another surprise. A further expedition was announced under the command of British army Captain Duncan McCallum MC. McCallum planned to drive a convoy of Buicks south from the British legation in Peking, of which he was commandant, across Asia through Europe to London.

Frank made a decision. He had unfinished business with the Hinks Imperial Expedition. He was going to take the Sundowner and drive home. On 7 October 1927, Frank suddenly announced to the press his intention to 'make the first overland journey to Australia, by way of Europe, Syria, Iraq, Persia, India, Burma, Siam and Malaya, parts of which have never been traversed by car'.

It was an interesting itinerary, with no mention of travelling through Turkey. Perhaps he would ship the car across the Mediterranean. He continued, saying he would leave London in a little over a week. 'The car is the one in which I did the record trip across Australia from Darwin to Melbourne last year. Since my recent tour of England, its camouflaged racing car body is familiar to thousands of people here, and it will be on show at Olympia till I leave.'

He informed the press that he intended to camp out all the way. 'I do not know how long it will take me,' he pondered. 'No-one has yet tried to get all the way down through Malaya by car and I might not be able to do it.'

If anyone could, it would be Frank. On his own, travelling light and quick. In some ways, the failed Ellis–Knowles expedition had been Frank's Burke and Wills experience. Too many people, too ambitious, too under-prepared, too overly complicated. Bound for disaster. This time he'd undertake the journey the way John McDouall Stuart approached crossing Australia's dead heart – as small an expedition as possible, as swift as possible.

26

On the Road

The 1927 International Motor Show at Olympia in Kensington had all the look and feel of a toy fair, only on a bigger and more expensive scale. Every conceivable motor car manufacturer from around the world seemed to be represented. Dodge Brothers and Chevrolet from the United States, Peugeot and Panhard from France, Mercedes-Benz from Germany. And it was where the finest of British manufacturers could make their statement to the international motoring community. Bentley, Morris, Hillman, Austin, Rover, Rolls-Royce . . .

It was where solid British products were presented at their most magnificent, housed beneath mock Parthenons that suggested a Greco-classical setting for machines hammered together in grimy factories in Birmingham, Coventry and Sheffield. Cars from the grandiose Rolls-Royce Phantom down to the bargain-basement two-stroke Trojan were polished and tyre-blacked, gleaming in the bright stage lights.

Sales representatives slick with hair oil and double-breasted suits feted customers as they wandered by, passing them lavish brochures, beguiling them with the wonder of four-wheel brakes, explaining on cut-away diagrams how overhead-valve systems operated. All sorts of individual needs were catered for. The new Talbot was touted as the perfect car for medical doctors 'due to its acceleration and hill climbing ability'. Perfect in an emergency. It was exciting, enthralling, mesmerising.

The motor show exuded a collective, positive feeling for the future everywhere you turned. Everywhere except at the Bean stand. A lone, potential customer stood by the new Bean 18/50 tourer waiting to be attended to, while salesmen stood idly smoking and chatting among themselves. After several minutes the customer shrugged and wandered away in the direction of the Morris stand. What did it matter? The Bean Car Company would be extinct before anyone even knew.

Outside the motor show, Frank and the Sundowner were ready to roll. Compared with the pristine examples of modern automotive brilliance assembled inside, the two-year-old Sundowner with its rag-tag bodywork adorned with crude kookaburra motifs and hand-painted maps of Australia looked like a rolling wreck. And so did Frank. Acquaintances were concerned that he was now tempting fate too much. 'Responsible people along the route had been writing to equally responsible people in England with a view to deterring me,' wrote Frank, 'But I set off, despite their efforts. I had an outback Australian's belief in my ability to meet whatever contingencies might arise.'

Frank pushed the ignition-advance lever upwards to retard the timing. He placed his driving-gloved hand on the gear lever, pulling it into neutral, flicking on the ignition switch and hitting the starter-button on the floor. The Bean fired up. Frank depressed the clutch and put the car into first gear. He was almost on the open road, but he hadn't finished with his obligations yet.

At Australia House in the Strand a more celebratory farewell awaited him. A drive across the world required a bit of theatre to mark the occasion, and so a mock 'bush corroboree' had been set up along with a road sign pointing south-east indicating '16,000 miles Melbourne'. Miss Australia, Phyllis Von Alwyn, posed beside the Bean to be photographed with the valiant Australian explorer. Frank was presented with a parcel containing some of Australia's finest exported foods – bottled fruits and jams and honey.

Even though it was a warm gathering for a homesick expat crowd to wish a fellow Australian farewell, they were no doubt dubious about his chances of success. Bert Hinkler pushed his way through the crowd, smiled and wistfully shook Frank's hand. If it had all worked out the way Hinkler had hoped, he and Frank would be readying themselves to fly back home. But it wasn't to be. Frank – the overlander – had unfinished business with the longest road in the world. Birtles and Hinkler made a bet as to who would arrive back in Australia first. Hinkler gave Frank a three-month head start, promising to beat him to Australia. Birtles took the aviator on, saying, 'I will get a lot of little bumps, and you will get one big one'. As glib as Frank's quip might sound, the memory of this wager stuck with him for the entirety of his journey. The old-time overlander was going to beat the flash, young aviator. Slow and steady wins the race.

Piloting the Bean through London's congested streets simply confirmed Frank's frustration and disillusion with the British motor industry. Countless sluggish open-topped double-decker buses clogged the high street, jostling for space alongside solid-tyred motor lorries belching black exhaust. Minuscule Austin Sevens with their bicycle-sized wheels poked their noses out of Dickensian laneways. Tiny delivery vans darted in and out of spaces occasionally offered between the lumbering red buses working their way through the line of traffic. This was nothing like Australia. London was full of everyday motor cars and lorries designed for short-distance travel over well-made roads. Australia was all about long-distance travel over terrible roads. But these were the very cars Britain was sending to Australia.

At dusk, Frank arrived at Folkestone Harbour and drove straight to the local Bean agents, who had offered to garage the car for the night. He strode into the foyer of the Royal Pavilion Hotel, a magnificent, sprawling red-brick Italianate structure positioned adjacent to the cross-channel ferry wharf.

This was Frank's last night in England, and would be his only night of luxury. From here to Melbourne it would be sleeping rough the whole way. But Frank wasn't idle in his hotel room. He was too angry to be idle. Here he was promoting the British motor industry to the world, and it was as though manufacturers couldn't care less. On a sheet of hotel stationery he began writing a letter to *The Times*.

Sir,

In leaving England on my overland journey to Australia, may I say *au revoir* through your paper to the many new friends I have made? I leave a country where everyone is discussing motor cars, but I go to a country where the motor car is more important than the railway. The car is the key to the Empire's resources. It has enabled lands in Australia, which were valueless five years ago, to be stocked and cultivated. The land values thus created amount to many millions a year. This is why the export trade to Australia is so vital and why it holds such big prizes for the country which can supply what is wanted.

Contrary to popular belief, no radical alteration in the design of British cars is necessary for overseas. The car I am using on this journey – the one that holds 'the record' for the trans-Australia run – is a standard 14 hp Bean, the only modifications being an extra petrol tank, stiff springing, and a less-ladylike body than is common at Olympia. Most British cars might be improved for Australia by means of special adjustments of induction and ignition, construction of the axle-housing so as to avoid wheel-splay, secure anchorage of the radiator, steel instead of aluminium sumps to withstand knocks, a brake lining which does not become useless when wet, a waterproof clutch so as not to slip when going through deep water, and dipping headlights. High clearance is not so essential as clean design underneath.

With attention to such points, I am convinced – and I speak with 21 years experience of motoring in Australia – that the British manufacturer need have no fears for his product. But he must appear to be less apathetic about the Australian market. He could, for instance, go to a little more trouble to cultivate Australian good will; and, if he cannot afford to advertise on an American scale, he could at least do so in conjunction with other British manufacturers. He cannot afford not to.

Yours faithfully,
Francis Birtles.

Royal Pavilion Hotel; Folkestone. Oct. 20 1927

•

Eight months earlier, if you'd have told Francis Birtles he'd be standing at the edge of the English Channel ready to drive from England to Australia for the second time in one year he'd have probably given you an earful. By all rights he should now be in Australia having successfully driven across the world and cooking up a new adventure. Nevertheless, here he was, about to redress what had gone spectacularly wrong in the initial attempt that kicked off the previous January.

The Channel no longer presented the great barrier dividing England and the continent. It was still a potent symbol but technology – in particular, flight – had turned the English Channel into something considered not much more than a canal a bit too wide for a bridge.

Flight – that was where the world was heading. French inventor and self-taught pilot Louis Blériot was the first person to fly across the Channel from Les Barraques to Dover in July 1909. At that time Frank was completing his two-year journey around the Australian continent by bicycle and he had marvelled at Blériot's monumental achievement – all 37 minutes of it. When David Lloyd George, who was to become Britain's wartime prime minister, learned of the Frenchman's success, he glumly confessed, 'Flying machines are no longer toys and dreams, they are established fact. The possibilities of this new system of locomotion are infinite. I feel, as a Britisher, rather ashamed that we are so completely out of it.' Britain seemed to be forever missing the boat in the technology stakes.

It was almost 11 a.m. and the late morning sun was flickering through coal-black smoke belching from the ferry's single funnel. Frank stood at the ship's stern watching the mouth of Folkestone Harbour inching away in the ship's wake. Seagulls circled and spiralled around the rumbling ship as it plodded towards the docks at Boulogne, 50 kilometres away. Farewell Britain.

At the French port, the Sundowner was lowered onto the dock and Frank began the all-too-familiar customs process of having his passport stamped and the car's carnet du passage and insurance documents checked, allowing him to continue. 'For six thousand miles I would have to depend on my own resources,' he wrote.

Frank would attempt to keep interaction with the locals to an absolute minimum. 'I could speak no foreign languages, nor could I understand the devious ways of the many professional nondescripts who acted as professional money changers.' Money was always the problem for Frank – as usual he had virtually none. By camping out and using his own food supplies, he could avoid language problems to some extent. He was wasting no time, and before long was motoring along near-deserted highways branching towards the World War I battlefields of northern France. In typical Birtles fashion, he wasn't stopping. Instead he drove all night through 'gloom enshrouded forests . . . sodden and dripping . . .', the bark and boom from the exhaust-less car echoing through the darkness. He was safe inside the Sundowner's cockpit, and the dashboard lights showed the car was running at its very best. 'The wind howled and as the powerful gleam of my headlamps swept on, I could glimpse big guns, old barbed-wire entanglements and washed out trenches.'

This war he simply could not comprehend. 'As I reverently slowed down a flood of memories came to me . . . Thousands of white painted crosses were around me, seemingly keeping vigil. Over what? I cannot define it – but my best mate lies asleep at Hamel.'

Frank's drive across Europe was extremely swift, covering on average 300 kilometres per day. The Sundowner was running as well as it ever had. In Austria, he happened upon a group of partygoers riding in horse-drawn sledges. They took a shine to the rough-and-tumble Australian bushman and invited him to dinner at an inn, where they plied him with schnapps. 'It tasted like our own outback hotel "Chain Lightning"' wrote Frank. 'I promptly named it "Donner und Blitzen". As "Thunder and Lightning" it will probably be called throughout that district.'

He continued barrelling southward as the roads degenerated into appalling, pot-holed lanes in Yugoslavia, where lumbering bullock teams clogged the tracks in squalid rural villages. 'Barefooted women screeched at long lines of packhorses on whose backs were stowed household furniture. Perched on top of the load were the children and the fowls.' Again, Frank found his way into Bulgaria. While in Sofia, he gave an interview to a British newspaper correspondent explaining the urgency of his drive and how he now planned to be in Calcutta by Christmas: 'I have got to get through by then because of the snow on the Persian Hills, 10,000 feet above sea level.'

Frank finally crossed the border from Hungary into Greece, where he powered along non-stop, racing towards Athens – attempting to cross the country from the border to the city's outskirts in one day. Where the countryside wasn't swathed in olive trees it was broken with rocky cliffs, along the side of which weaved the thin road. As the evening grew darker the road became narrower and steeper, the track ahead difficult to make out in the half-moon light. With the big Smiths headlights on high beam, Frank noticed the road tightening into a series of hairpin bends and had an uneasy feeling. He rounded a corner, which led him onto a stone bridge, where he suddenly stood on the brake pedal, locking up the four drum brakes, the Bean sliding in a skid to a full stop. Before him lay a chasm that disappeared into complete darkness.

The bridge simply ended in mid-air, 10 metres of it swept away in an avalanche. 'I peered down into a crevasse hundreds of feet deep,' Frank recalled. 'Millions of tons of earth and rocks buried the road.' Very carefully, Frank placed the car in reverse and edged inch by inch off the crumbling bridge. He then realised there was nowhere for him to turn around on the single-lane road for miles. With the car in reverse, Frank slowly made his way back 8 kilometres.

The next morning, the Sundowner crested a hill to find the broad, iridescent expanse of the Mediterranean. Below was Athens, with its block-shaped, whitewashed buildings and the postcard presence of the Parthenon and the Acropolis. Frank negotiated the car through the city's streets and alleyways, attempting to make his way towards the waterfront.

Frank wasted no time driving straight for the Piraeus, one of the busiest seaports in the world, eager to secure sea passage for himself and the car. Despite having outlined in London his intended route for the journey across Europe into Asia, this section of the drive was by no means certain. He had announced to Fleet Street's reporters that he proposed to reach Persia from Europe through French mandated Syria and British mandated Iraq and would therefore avoid Turkey, where he, Ellis and Knowles had had so much trouble only months before. Probably, his intention was to put the Bean on a ship to sail from the Piraeus via Crete to Beirut.

It was a popular trade route and it made perfect sense as he could then drive a mere 100 kilometres from Beirut to Damascus and then cross the desert to Baghdad. Curiously, although Birtles makes no mention of it, contemporary newspaper articles report that while in Greece he learned that Turkish authorities had denied him permission to enter Turkey. Driving across Turkey was without question the quickest and most direct land route from Europe through to Asia – it had been for a millennium.

That he'd even contemplated trying to seek permission to re-enter Turkey doesn't square with later accounts of Birtles' experiences there. Perhaps he thought the Turks might have considered Ellis the main antagonist on the previous foray and turned a blind eye to allow him through. Nevertheless, Birtles was held up for a considerable time in Athens due to a problem with his passport stamp when exiting Hungary. It took the British consul in Athens two weeks to sort it out.

Perhaps frustration due to this delay was the reason Frank had had a crack at trying to secure Turkish approval for an overland crossing. But, for whatever reason, his initial idea of 'travelling through Europe and entering Syria' didn't come to fruition. Well, not in such a direct way. After two weeks cooling his heels in Athens, Birtles finally secured passage to cross the Mediterranean directly south for Alexandria in Egypt. He'd make his way to Damascus overland through North Africa. He was not happy. This Egyptian detour added an extra 1,600 kilometres.

27

Into the Desert

No doubt it was a welcome relief to leave behind the throng of peddlers and vendors clogging the streets of Cairo and Alexandria. Frank had no time for crowds; what he understood was the desert. Nowhere was he more at home than in the vast, stark and desolate regions of the world's wastelands. He knew what was involved in living in them, driving across them, surviving in them.

'The great open places of Arabia reminded me of the outback,' Frank wrote. 'Most people speak of deserts with awe. To one who has lived in this type of country, it seems like Paradise after the over-populated regions of England and Europe.'

Unlike Australia's deserts, there was a distinct air of menace in the Arabian wilderness that lay before him. The threat of malevolent nomads and bandits was something over which Frank had no control. The wide-open spaces over the horizon were in effect lawless, and anyone travelling out there was at the mercy of whomever they had the misfortune of stumbling onto.

Bandits worried Birtles. All the might and power of Mother Nature was never going to kill him, but somebody with a gun might. Head down, motor on. The way to cope with such a tremendous drive was not to think about it as a whole. It was a particular mindset. Each day, Frank set out to accomplish his intended distance, and then the following day he would do it all again.

Frank came to the Suez Canal near where it met the Red Sea. The Suez was the lifeline for the British Empire. India, Singapore, New Zealand, and Australia – all of the Empire's territories in the east depended on this trickle that ran from the Mediterranean through to the Indian Ocean. It was the third time he'd encountered the all-powerful canal within a year, and for the first time he observed the progress of the narrow canal's traffic from land. At such a low angle it was a bizarre spectacle, with the vast superstructures of passing steamships projected high above sand dunes that concealed the waterway's presence, giving the impression that the ships were gliding across the desert.

When Moses walked across the Sinai Desert – and much later when Lawrence of Arabia rode across it by camel – it was considered a phenomenal achievement that such a merciless barrier could be conquered. But nobody batted an eye when Francis Birtles, driving a Bean 14, shot across it in two days to reach the Palestine border.

Frank wasted no time – he was headed for Damascus in Syria, and from there he would decide his next move. With deflated tyres, he motored across the sands through to Beersheba and Jerusalem before finally reaching the Syrian border. Frank arrived in Damascus, 'Famous for its steel and its steal,' he wrote. Whether he was in Damascus or Dorrigo, Frank was always having stuff stolen from his car.

Less than ten years before Frank's arrival, the Australian 10th Light Horse had swept through the Turkish-held city hours before the arrival of Lawrence of Arabia. The locals showered the Australians with confetti and rose-water. But not today.

Even in the 1920s the Syrian Desert still possessed an Old Testament, biblical mystique – it was vast, waterless, punishing and potentially deadly. Frank stared at the sunrise. Eight hundred kilometres in a straight line drawn across the burning heart of the desert was his target: Baghdad. Without question, Frank could deal with 800 kilometres of desert as well as anyone on earth, but travelling alone he presented an ideal target for Bedouin raiders on the hunt for money, gold and guns. Except for a small tomahawk secreted alongside the driver's seat, Frank travelled unarmed. 'Brigands murder for as little as a gun,' he later wrote.

Before 1920, no-one had ever crossed the Syrian Desert by motor car. The practice was to skirt around the edges and bypass it altogether, but to drive straight across it from Damascus to Baghdad had been considered impossible. There were no features to take bearings from, no track, no water, and nowhere to set up depots for fuel. The general consensus was that if you took a motor car across the desert, you died. Traditionally the way to drive to Baghdad from Damascus was to circumvent the Syrian Desert altogether.

There were two options, neither advisable. Frank could head north from Damascus up through Palmyra, hook up with the Euphrates and follow the river all the way down to Baghdad. This was the most traversed route, and was the path Frank had taken in the Imperial Six, but it was also by far the longest. And there was an exceptionally good chance of being attacked by desert raiders. A few years earlier an American tourist, Major E. A. Powell, inadvertently drove squarely into a Bedouin camp stretching for seven miles. Powell was chased into a ravine and captured by a rifle-wielding mob to be dragged before their sheikh, whose hatred for Westerners was well known. The American expected to have his throat cut – for the sheik's misdemeanours his camp had recently been on the receiving end of an aerial bombardment from the French and he was looking for any Westerner to punish. Convincing him he was not in fact French, Powell stood up to the sheikh and was eventually able to talk his way free, but only at the sheikh's whim. So the road along the river was dangerous.

An alternative route was to head south from Damascus to Amman, then swing back up diagonally north-east. This route to Baghdad had been attempted by a British army expedition in 1921, driving specially equipped RAF Crossley trucks and Rolls-Royce armoured cars. The expedition barely made it through – attempting to cross a vast petrified lava flow strewn with jagged boulders, giving the expedition grief for hundreds of kilometres. They made it across and back – but only just.

Only five years before Frank's arrival in Damascus there had been a remarkable revelation. In the interests of cutting a deal with the British in Iraq, a gold smuggler named Ibn Bassam had approached the British Consul in Damascus with information he thought he might be interested in. Bassam was aware the British were keen to find an overland route from the Mediterranean to Baghdad and then to India. An unexpected byproduct of the success of the Suez Canal had been the collapse of overland trade and the traditional routes used for that purpose. Bassam knew the British were frustrated with the two options that circumnavigated the Syrian Desert, and he had something to suggest.

Bassam had for years been using an ancient, secret smugglers' route that passed through the heart of the Syrian Desert in a straight line from Damascus to Baghdad. Using caravans of camels to carry his gold, he had crossed the desert countless times, although camels were slow and bandits always a threat. Bassam was rich enough to pay off marauders. In 1923, he dispensed with camels and began experimenting with convoys of motor cars, smuggling along the long dangerous northern route following the Euphrates. Cars made it easier to evade attacks from bandits, and with shorter travelling time his turnover could be increased.

The northern arc following the river was a particularly long detour. Bassam had a revelation – why couldn't he drive on the old smugglers' route straight across the desert? If you knew where to find it, the trail was an effective way to cross the wilderness. It was like a highway – smooth, hard ground, very few hills and surprisingly little sand.

Exactly what Bassam wanted from a deal with the British isn't clear – perhaps a blind eye to his operation – but he was angling for them to carve out a reliable trade route across the Syrian Desert. He offered to show the consul how to cross the heart of the desert to Baghdad. The consul understood the implications. This new route could link the empire from the Mediterranean through to the subcontinent. Excitedly he informed London. The British government was astonished. They immediately commissioned an expedition to test the proposal, and a team comprising Bassam, the British consul Palmer and a particularly interesting inclusion, Captain Duncan McCallum, who would become Frank's rival in driving across Asia in just a few years.

The result of commissioning the smugglers' route as a highway across the desert was that it ran more or less like a railway. It was the best way to avoid catastrophe. Aside from the risk of breaking down or becoming lost, motorists would be at the mercy of desert raiders. Once word had leaked out that this new direct motor route was in operation this 800 kilometre stretch of no-man's land became a hunting ground for thieves and murderers and open season on motorists. As a safeguard against these dangers, authorities from both French Syria and British Iraq insisted motor cars travel across the desert only in armed convoy.

It was forbidden for motorists to travel out there alone.

•

An hour before dawn, Frank was already on the road, leaving the miserable, dung-smelling caravanserai (roadside inns) far behind. These fleapits made the corrugated iron pub at Borroloola look like the Savoy. He later wrote: 'I was fearful of the interior of those huge stone or mud-walled caravanserais. For hundreds of years they had been occupied each night by travellers, and the brand of fleas had practised on pilgrims for three thousand years.'

Frank had the Sundowner hurtling across the desert at a more than reasonable pace. He chanced a quick look at the dimly lit speedometer, not daring to take his eyes off the road ahead for anything more than a sliver of a second. Fifty miles per hour. Not bad.

Birtles was only content when he could feel the wheels turning below. Like a doctor with a stethoscope, every stone, every bump, every vibration was telegraphed from the wheels, into the steering arm, along the drag-link rod, up the steering column to the steering wheel and into his hands, where he could monitor the car's progress over every inch of the 20,000 kilometre journey. And he wasn't even close to being halfway.

Frank braced himself for the inevitable cold snap at daybreak. People said it was always coldest just before the dawn, but that wasn't true. As far as Frank was concerned, it was unquestionably colder just after dawn breaks. It didn't matter. He was on the road to Baghdad, the headlights exposing the stony highway as it raced flat out beneath the wheels. Nothing could catch him.

In the darkness of the desert's pre-dawn, the first hint of light drew a fine, blood-red line across the horizon, silhouetting two de Havilland DH9A biplanes slowly ascending from the graded gravel runway at RAF Hinaidi, the Royal Air Force aerodrome in Baghdad. As the aircraft laboured higher, the loud, flat bark of their 12-cylinder Liberty engines seemed completely at odds with the eerie cry of morning prayer echoing across the city from Baghdad's ancient minarets. This was a duel, held at dawn every day – a contest between occidental modernity and oriental antiquity in which neither side was giving in. Dawn patrols like this one were all part of the British Empire's everyday housekeeping regime in Iraq, chatted about in colonial circles under the seemingly innocuous, broad-brushed euphemism of 'policing the empire'.

During the 1920s, Britain ruled more than half the world's Muslims. This was in part due to the post-war carve-up of the Ottoman Empire in which Britain, on behalf of the League of Nations, was given a mandate to oversee the former Turkish colonies of Iraq and Palestine. To those in the West, this mandate sounded like a terribly good idea. To those in the East it sounded decidedly like old-time Imperialism.

British occupation and administration wasn't at all what post-Ottoman Iraq thought it was getting after the war. There'd been much talk of President Woodrow Wilson's 1919 Fourteen Point Plan, in which Point 12 proposed, '. . . other nationalities which are now under Turkish rule should be assured an undoubted security of life and an absolutely unmolested opportunity of autonomous development'.

The Iraqis had been led up the garden path and they weren't happy. The problem of a permanent occupation for Britain was that it was expensive to maintain. Garrisoning troops, their equipment, their transport, food, health, pay – everything was guaranteed to blow out. In 1921, the RAF proposed to the British government that it could garrison Iraq at a minimal cost – the use of aircraft largely replacing the drain on manpower, resources and the public coffers in maintaining a British army presence.

Soon, Iraq became a showpiece for the inexpensive and effective use of airpower in controlling non-compliant colonies and protectorates. They were so successful, in fact, that the RAF's role expanded to sort out a variety of municipal problems, where dropping the odd 25-pound bomb encouraged even the most recalcitrant Arab tribe to pay tax. The RAF admitted their tactics relied on 'frightfulness in a more or less severe form'.

For marauding bandit tribes who preyed on travellers chancing the desolate road to Baghdad, the sound of a de Havilland biplane's engine announced an upcoming firestorm, the aircraft bringing with it a Vickers .303 machine-gun and two Lewis guns. Their ability to rattle off 600 rounds of .303 per minute each, combined with the de Havilland's ability to putter along at a mere 100 knots, created the ideal, lethal combination for chopping those on the ground to pieces. And, in the nine years since the armistice of 1918, the RAF had refined the worryingly inaccurate art of aerial bombardment into a science of something slightly less inaccurate. There were very few complaints about the problems of precision bombardment in this region anyway. No-one had much to say after a load of high explosives had been dropped in the centre of a Bedouin raiders' camp.

As the two biplanes droned beneath the fiery ball of a rising desert sun, their unmistakable shadows flickered and danced on the irregular landscape below.

Seven thousand feet above the road to Baghdad, the lead pilot spotted a dissipating plume of dust in the distance, pinpointed at its head by what must be a car travelling at high speed. For the patrol, the sight of a single car belting across the desert warranted an immediate investigation. The biplanes peeled off into a rapid plunge, the aerial observers dragging the Lewis guns' cocking handles towards their chests. Safety catches off – they were ready to engage.

Frank knew perfectly well that he wasn't permitted to travel the Baghdad road alone but, as always, he took his chances. He sheepishly confessed later: 'Solo-motorists were not permitted the desert route to Baghdad . . . but I eventually found myself speeding at fifty miles an hour over open plains.' He generally subscribed to the idea it was always 'easier to ask forgiveness than ask permission'. But there were times when this rule-of-thumb maxim could backfire.

Intently concentrating on his battle with the road to Baghdad, Frank was completely oblivious to what was shaping up behind him. Only a few kilometres back, the two de Havillands were now powering along towards him, a mere 200 feet above the road. Not knowing whether the vehicle they were closing in on was friendly or otherwise, the Lewis gunners sat primed and ready in case of a required squeeze of the trigger.

Suddenly the Bean was engulfed in a huge black shadow as if from some giant bird, and Frank was awoken from his driving trance, jolting bolt-upright as if having received an electric shock. The aircraft flew past him low overhead, the undercarriage seemingly so close it could have brushed Frank's flying helmet. For a split second, Birtles lost concentration and then dramatically reclaimed the steering wheel, keeping the car on course. Another shadow flashed low over the Bean, this second overtaking aircraft clearly intending to unsettle him. As the plane trailed away, Frank could see the rearward-facing gunner, intently looking at him through the Lewis gun's large aerial sights, the machine-gun's barrel trained on him.

Frank watched as the two aircraft banked away and repositioned to come back head-on. He was well aware that his reaction now might make the difference between the pilots' friendly acknowledgement and someone deciding to let fly with a machine-gun. He eased off the accelerator and knocked the Bean back a gear to lower his speed. He ripped off his flying helmet and goggles and propped himself higher in the seat so that he could be easily seen.

The de Havillands were on the return run and Frank raised his arm in the air and slowly waved at the oncoming patrol. The aircraft tore past low over his head, the resulting cloud of oncoming dust stinging his eyes. The Bean continued to coast along in third gear, with Frank still holding one hand in the air, his other firmly on the steering wheel. He turned to watch the aircraft banking again for another run. Back they came, but this time not overhead, instead flying almost level with Birtles to one side, the pilot giving a firm wave, signalling that Frank was okay. Frank waved back. One of the Lewis gunners aimed his index finger disapprovingly towards him and shook his head, meaning, 'You were lucky'.

Frank brought the Bean to a stop and drew a deep breath before putting his flying helmet and goggles back on. He watched the aircraft until they had completely disappeared into the blue sky. 'The Arab does not love the air patrols – the eyes of the desert,' wrote Frank. 'They upset the sporting raids which have been his right since the dawn of history.'

28

Into Persia

Late at night, the Bean's headlights illuminated the mud walls of a Foreign Legion-style desert fort. Birtles was only 40 kilometres from the outskirts of Baghdad, but the fort's officials refused to allow him to proceed any further. 'The bandits of the road had declared, at present, open season for motorists, especially at night-time,' wrote Frank.

At daybreak, he was allowed to continue, and soon arrived in Baghdad, crossing the Euphrates over a rickety bridge of boats, where he was descended upon by a swarm of guides and market sellers. It was Baghdad fresh out of an adventure novel, the hapless explorer and the exotic locals vying for his custom, 'I recognized them as the descendents of the Forty Thieves, but they had multiplied exceedingly.' Frank posted a letter to the newspaper wire service in London – it was the last communiqué with the Western world he would make for weeks. Eager to make up time, Frank was in and out of Baghdad within a day and headed straight for the Persian border.

A flustered RAF pilot officer wearing an oversized pith helmet and tropical-issue shorts emerged from the border office holding Birtles' passport high in the air. He pushed through the crowd, his eyes scouring the throng to find its owner. He locked onto the Bean and made his way towards the car. He pushed his way through the orange sellers and vendors, and fronted Frank, pressing the passport into his hand. Everything was in order here, but the pilot officer wasn't convinced of Frank's chances of crossing the border into Persia. There'd been an outbreak of cholera on the Persian side and they were talking about quarantine.

The pilot officer shook Frank's hand and wished him luck. Whatever little protection the notion of a British Empire afforded him in Iraq, Birtles was now entering a country where he was again truly on his own. Frank eased the clutch and the Bean moved slowly through the crowd towards the border gates. Frank noticed the Bean was the only motor car in a long, bedraggled line comprising primarily heavily laden camels and donkey-drawn carts. The Bean gradually inched ahead until it was in line with a cluster of Persian gendarmes manning sentry boxes at the gate. Eventually, it was Frank's turn in line. A gendarme moved on from a merchant's dray to the Bean and demanded to see his passport. Frank sat quietly as the policeman commenced leafing through the document.

Birtles understood the policeman's lot from his time in the Transvaal – boredom, the dread of insufferable complainants and the terrifying possibility of someone suddenly pulling a knife or a gun. And so he was able to talk his way through.

●

An hour before sunrise, Frank had fired up the Bean and shot out of the mud-walled city of Kermanshah, in present-day Iran, now well and truly on the road heading east. He wondered how long his luck would hold before the winter caught up with him; the onset of winter weather would of course be a problem, but it was just one of any number of situations that could destroy any expedition.

The smallest incident could bring an adventurer's entire world to an end. In 1933, five years after Birtles passed through Kermanshah, a German motorcyclist named Walter Tonn was attempting the same route in the hope of being the first to ride a motorbike from Europe to India. Tonn had ridden his 750 cc Indian Mabeco all the way from Hanover. He had struggled through mountains and across Iraq's desert sands to arrive in Kermanshah. Here, he was bitten by a sandfly and contracted sandfly fever, which developed into typhus – and he died within a matter of days. He was buried in a small grave on the edge of a Muslim cemetery on the outskirts of the town. Only a few weeks later, two young German motorcyclists attempting the same challenge discovered Tonn's bike, flat-tyred, derelict and half-stripped.

The Bean pulled up in the mountain village of Kangavar, just ahead of the Asadabad Pass. Birtles was in two minds about tackling the pass again. He had driven up it with Ellis and Knowles and remembered it distinctly. It was a steep and hazardous drive – a loose, stony track that climbed to a height of more than 2,000 metres.

The altitude had really knocked the three of them around. Ellis had complained, 'As soon as you climb the Asadabad Pass, the high, hot-cold, rare-aired plateau has even a more deleterious effect upon the constitution and temper than the sweltering plains of Babylon.' Besides, the altitude played merry hell with the car. The higher the altitude, the thinner the oxygen, which would then muck up the fuel mixture. Frank could see the snow-capped red mountain range on the horizon, and made the decision to avoid the pass, turning instead off the main road to head south-east and cross-country for Isfahan, the idea being he'd be able to hopefully avoid the snow line and wind his way around the mountains north to Sultanabad.

It wasn't long before this side road closed in to become more of a cart track, rising more steeply by the metre. Frank noticed it had been some time since he'd seen any sign of civilisation. Back at the turn-off, some nomads herding a group of camels and mules were the last people he'd seen. The breath from Frank's nostrils fogged his driving goggles. The temperature was dropping, the air growing colder – the Persian winter was now snapping hard at the back wheels. He remembered the trouble they'd had with the Imperial Six when the three of them blundered their way through the European winter.

The trick through the mountains was to keep the car running for as long as possible, at least until he could find shelter. While the engine was ticking over and hot, it was still alive, and Frank could keep the journey's momentum. In this deteriorating weather, switching the car off for a time could easily see the water in the radiator and in the engine block freeze solid.

As the car pushed higher along the narrow, rutted road, Frank kept an eye on the tachometer on the dashboard, which was reading a steady 300 revolutions per minute. The altimeter was now indicating he was approaching 6,000 feet (1,800 metres) above sea level and still climbing. Holding in third gear, he dipped his head to the side, listening intently to the whine of gears meshing in the gearbox, humming their constant, shrill tune. So far – with the car at least – all was good.

The skies over the red mountain horizon ahead began to darken. Frank's eyes narrowed as he watched thick grey snow clouds seemingly turn inside out. He was about to drive into a maelstrom. He adjusted his goggles and flying helmet and yanked the collar of his leather jacket across to button it up in preparation for the evil weather into which he was about to disappear. The only part of his body left exposed to the elements were his lips and the tip of his nose. He swung his thick woollen scarf around his face and was now completely encased, ready for whatever the weather would throw at him.

The road twisted further skywards, Frank's leather driving gloves gripping the Bean's large steering wheel as he carefully guided the car higher up the vague, stony track. As the temperature dropped degree by degree, Frank suddenly became aware of tiny flecks of ice tapping his goggles lenses: sleet. He dragged his heavy-gloved index finger across his goggles, wiping the glass clear, the sleet now increasing by the second and beginning to impair his vision of the road ahead. Frank needed to find cover very soon, yet there was nothing. He passed a kind of dugout on a hillside but it would be hopeless as shelter. He took stock. He could well freeze to death.

Once the blizzard started in earnest, Frank lost all visual contact. 'The snow came down softly and fast,' he wrote, 'eddying around the car. The mountains were blotted out. I was enclosed in a white nothingness. For hours it kept on. Bushes standing up above the snow were my guide. Then the bushes disappeared. Straining my eyes I peered into the silently eddying whiteness and kept the car as near as I could to the general direction of the track. I could not tell downhill from uphill. Glass worms seemed to be floating before my eyes.'

Snowflakes raced from left to right and darted up and down, zigzagging back and forth like schools of frightened fish, completely disorientating Frank, who had to pull the car up. He couldn't see the road. Was he still on the road? For all he knew he could be on the edge of a cliff. This was a nightmare. With the handbrake on and the engine still running, Frank climbed out of the Bean and shuffled through the worsening storm to where he guessed the track should be. Through the white-out, he established that he was at the base of a steep section of mountain road. He would need to put the snow chains on the wheels and have a decent run-up to make it to the top. Frank trudged back to the idling Bean, which by now had developed a 'miss' – a slight stutter – indicating it was having trouble igniting the fuel.

The snow was now higher than the axles. Frank had unwittingly driven into a snowdrift, and the Bean was stuck fast. He removed the shovel lashed to the car's side and began scooping away the banked-up snow. He rummaged through his equipment in the rear compartment of the car's ducktail body to produce the bottle jack, a wheel-brace and two copper snow chains. He then jacked the car up and removed the rear wheels. However, in order to apply the chains around the tyres and then screw them up tight, Frank needed to remove his gloves.

The sudden shock of the icy, sub-zero wind on his unprotected hands caused him to take a sharp breath. He picked up a snow chain with his bare fingers, the freezing copper links instantly burning into his skin. There was no option. Painfully, Frank peeled the frozen chain from his fingers, leaving them raw.

Back behind the wheel, he depressed the clutch and dragged the gear lever across and down to engage reverse. The gearbox growled as the Bean pushed slowly backwards through the snow, stopping in readiness for the charge towards the peak. With snow still falling heavily, the car's bonnet was now lined up squarely with the mountain track. One of his options was to try to charge flat out at the snow-covered mountain path, getting the car up to speed in, say, third gear, and hope the momentum would carry him to the top. Or he could leave the car in first gear and keep the power on; the engine would be revving its head off, but the low gear and chains would do all the work. He decided on the second option. A top-speed assault was way too risky. Who knew what lay under the snow – boulders, ruts – and when the car's momentum ran out he'd be needing to do some fast and precise gear-changing on a slippery surface. If he missed a gear and hit the brakes, he would lose control of the car. To get to the top, Frank needed a combination of engine control, low gearing and the traction of the snow chains.

He put the Bean in first gear and flattened the accelerator, the engine roaring as he released the clutch, and the chains on the back wheels gaining traction through the snow. The car slowly began its awkward, painful ascent, Frank hanging on to the steering wheel, his eyes aligned with the full length of the bonnet, which bounced skywards as the long leaf springs soaked up the shock of the rocks beneath the wheels. The car jolted from one rock hidden beneath the snow to another, each turn of the wire wheels engaging the snow chain with the

earth, with snow and mud churning as the Bean slithered its way up the track.

Frank's eyes glanced at the tachometer – the engine revolutions were way over redline. He ground his teeth hard as the car continued to struggle along the track towards the top. He braced his heel to the floor to stop his foot bouncing up and down on the accelerator. The engine was now in full scream and the back wheels were somehow finding their footing on the steep track, until the Bean finally reach the top.

With the blizzard still throwing snow in all directions, Frank was now in a full sweat. He felt uneasy, and turned around. 'Looking back along the car tracks there seemed to be a trail of blood. The underlying red soil had been churned up with snow by the chains on the wheels.' There was something unnerving about this place. As the blizzard grew worse, Frank was fully aware that shelter was now his priority. Through the storm, he could just make out what was most probably a large, snow-covered rock. If he could position the Bean next to it, he could string the car's canvas tarp between the two as a kind of tent, using his camera tripod as a centre-pole. Frank drove the Bean alongside the rock, only to discover that what he'd thought was a rock was in fact another motor car – half buried in snow.

He stood back to try and take stock of what he'd discovered. It was a large, upright, four-door sedan. The car must have broken down – most probably unable to cope with the altitude. Frank scraped his heavy gloves through the snow to reveal a mudguard and followed its swooping shape down towards the running board. His hand found the engine cowl, then the windscreen and door, and what must have been the window. With a heavy wiping motion, Frank pushed the snow away until he was scouring the glass. He lifted his goggles onto his forehead and put his face and hands to the window to peer inside. He fell back in shock – a pallid, translucent face stared back at him from the other side of the glass. It was a young woman – her eyes wide and dead, her mouth open, her skin a wax-like blue-grey.

Frank scrambled and stood up, his heart racing, taking deep breaths to calm himself. He nervously put his hand on the door handle. Holding his breath he turned the handle downwards, wrenching the door open and catching the young woman's body as it slowly toppled from the car. He peered within. Frank had discovered a tomb. Inside were seven bodies, well-dressed and neatly seated as though they had been out on a Sunday drive – all frozen solid. Whatever had happened within the confines of that car as one after another perished was too horrendous to contemplate. Who knew what was racing through the mind of the last person to die?

Frank closed the door and turned to the Bean, removing the canvas tarpaulin lashed across the back of the car. With the blizzard still howling, he tied one end of the tarp to the steering wheel and the other to the side-lamp on the snow-covered sedan. He unstrapped the camera tripod from his car and pushed it up under the tarp to create a centre-pole. The blizzard raged.

Tonight, under a canvas tarp tied to a motor car filled with seven dead, this would be home.

•

Frank peered over the edge of a large flat rock to watch a long line of nomad tribespeople travelling through the valley far below. They were heading from the winter-ravaged mountains to warmer climes in the lower lands. The nomads were wild looking, several of them carrying wide-mouthed flintlock blunderbuss-type weapons.

'There were bad men among the band of drovers – robbers and cut-throats – the British consulates had warned me about them,' Frank wrote. More than ever, he was aware of the region's lawlessness. With the sun barely up, Frank had the Sundowner fired up and, powering along over a broad, flat, frost-covered plain, was making good time.

In the distance, he could see a grey mass milling before him that turned out to be a long column of ragged and weary soldiers, some of whom were injured. On reaching the limping stragglers, he invited a group of seven to jump on board. 'We could not understand each other, but judging by their travel-worn condition, they must have marched a long way – they may have been out hunting bandits.'

Frank wrote: 'The Sundowner, with a warlike crowd of deadbeats, all whiskers and dust, rifles and fixed bayonets aboard, looked as though it was just back from the action front.' They drove a further 30 kilometres before pulling up at a fortified village. His passengers disembarked, one of the soldiers thanking him with 'a hand to head, mouth and heart movement'.

Frank was aiming to make it into the hills before nightfall. By evening, the Sundowner became stuck in a series of sand drifts, Frank climbing out to scout around the area to try to find a way through. When he returned, he discovered someone had ransacked the car. All the luggage straps were undone and all his blankets, waterproofs and warm clothing were stolen. Frank found footprints leading away into the darkness. This was disastrous. It was now becoming seriously cold and there was not a skerrick of wood in sight to make a fire.

Frank made the decision to start the car and head back to where he thought he'd seen a turn-off for a village. With the big headlights illuminating his previous tyre tracks, he motored through the night, with the temperature falling. Eventually, in the early morning hours he arrived at the solid timber gates of a mud-walled fort. By now Frank was suffering hypothermia. A cautious gendarme opened an access door in the gate and came out to talk to him, followed by another policeman, and they both climbed on board the Sundowner, guiding Frank through a maze of deserted mud-walled streets.

Eventually they arrived at the doors of a British mission hospital, where the resident, seeing his condition, immediately found him a bed and made him coffee. It took him two days in the hospital to recover from the freezing drive. Upon leaving, the hospital supplied him with new blankets and a sheepskin coat.

Back in form, Frank pressed on through the desert and over giant sand hills, where the car suddenly became engulfed in a sandstorm. 'Streaming torrents of sand shut out all vision,' Frank recalled. 'My car stopped dead, axle-deep in a drift where it would soon be buried.' Frank quickly deflated the tyres and put his new blankets under the rear wheels to give traction on the fine sand, eventually reaching firm ground. The blankets were blown away and were only just saved after Frank sprinted after them.

He pressed on towards Sultanabad, where thick snow covered the ground in every direction. 'The whole world seemed to be blanketed in snow,' he wrote. 'I crawled along, roaring in low gear, mile after mile. Above the sound of the engine rose that of hard snow crushing, and ice splitting under the slowly revolving, chain-skidded wheels. The copper exhaust pipe – racing type – was red-hot from end to end, and a plume of steam spiralled from the radiator cap. Icicles were hanging all over the bodywork and chassis.'

In Australia and in England, people were starting to worry that no-one had heard from Francis Birtles for weeks. Was he alive? Was he crook with some disease in some makeshift hospital? Had he been kidnapped? Had he fallen foul of thieves and murderers? Fleet Street began to sound the alarm.

WHERE IS BIRTLES – AFTER BAGHDAD?

A letter received in London three weeks ago from Francis Birtles, who is motoring from England to Australia, stated that he had left Baghdad for Persia. Since then nothing has been heard of the intrepid Australian motorist. Birtles cabled on 14 December that he was due to reach Calcutta by Christmas. No tidings have been received at Delhi or anywhere else along the route and Birtles has not been reported since he left Baghdad on 28 November.

Perhaps he'd become a victim of the punishing weather – sandstorms or snowstorms. Who knew? Newspaper reports could only speculate. 'In view of earlier references to heavy snowfalls in the regions he had to traverse, it is feared that he may have been caught in one of them. On the contrary, he may have been held up at some remote spot from which it is very difficult to communicate.'

His disappearance was of great concern, 'One of Birtles' backers in England views the situation seriously, and has informed the Australian Press Association that he, personally, is worried. His only hope, he said, was the viewpoint that Birtles, being Birtles, would overcome all adverse conditions, and turn up somewhere.'

This rationale was hardly irresponsible or glib. It was sound advice. 'Birtles being Birtles' summed up the inexplicable machinations of how the Australian bushman worked. He'd disappear into some God-forsaken region of the world, only to resurface at the eleventh hour. No-one had any idea how he did it. It's just what happened, time and again.

29

North West Frontier, India

Harsh, bleached, lonely, cold and miserable. That was the best that could be said of the landscape out in the wilds of Waziristan and Baluchistan near India's North West Frontier. Stunted briar-like shrubs, something like Australia's outback mimosa trees, were the only sign of life in the stony valleys near the border.

Frank motored on, '. . . seeming to be the only person alive in a world of rocks, mimosa-bushes and snow. I was traversing those lonely desert valleys at the foot of the gigantic mountains of the Afghanistan frontier.' Frank had been through this miserable tract not long before, and knew what to expect. There was only one course of action. Get in and get out.

Due to an increase in bandit activity, North West Frontier political officers had prohibited travelling through the region, yet Frank was carrying papers issued in London authorising entry. Birtles was more uncomfortable about banditry in India than anywhere else. In particular, he was worried about the

Dacoit bandits. The Dacoit bandits were ruthless and merciless – perhaps even psychopathic – for whom murder after robbery was simply a whim. In an interview as far back as the Balkans, he'd announced, 'I am travelling alone, and I am taking no arms with me until I get to Calcutta because the Dacoits kill you all the sooner for the sake of any arms you have got. Dacoits are creatures I don't like.' For all Frank's bush experience, nothing could predict the outcome of encountering the Dacoit. Frank gave his clear intention of 'buying a heavy-calibre revolver and a high-velocity rifle' as soon as he reached Calcutta.

These snow-covered passes were a far cry from when he and Ellis almost perished of thirst during the sun-hammering summer months. That was a battle royal with the infernal Imperial Six in its death throes, but the old Sundowner was showing no signs of fatigue.

The sitar perhaps was more likely, and the last sound anyone would expect to hear in the wilds of India was the bagpipes. Early one morning on the approach to Calcutta, Frank could clearly hear 'the skirl of the pipes' and 'to the tune of "The Cock o' the North," the famous Black Watch marched by with swaying sporrans and chequered kilts.' Frank had driven squarely into British Army manoeuvres. 'The mists parted on the plains and revealed a modern mechanical army on the move, marching with that steady click-click only the Tommy Atkins can achieve.'

Birtles was treated to an extraordinary display of the British army's might in India: columns of troops marching with bayonets fixed, light tanks, Indian cavalry and 'gurkhas with their famous snickersnee knives'. This was exactly what he wanted to see – Britain committed to looking after her dominions and keeping them safe. Before long, Frank was driving through dust and dense smoke in Calcutta's outskirts, his progress reduced to walking pace as he motored through vast crowds attempting to mingle with the motor traffic. In the confusion, he had absolutely no idea of where he was going until he was eventually spotted by a Shell oil representative who had been sitting in a car waiting for him to arrive. Birtles was to follow him to the Shell office, and on behalf of the Shell company invited Frank to stay. The Sundowner was placed on display at Shell's Calcutta office and Frank spent the next few days servicing the car.

While in the city, Frank met a 23-year-old Canadian, Percy Stollery, a fellow cyclist and adventurer. Stollery had been on the road cycling for almost a year when his bicycle had been stolen while in Calcutta. Stollery was fit, footloose, had no money and no means of transport. Both Birtles and Stollery arrived at the conclusion he'd be a valuable asset to the expedition's attack through the Naga Hills.

'I warned him that there was a chance of his head being the chief decoration on the top of a wild Naga Hillman's spear,' Birtles wrote. 'He looked quite hopeful at the prospect, so I accepted him as a companion – and he proved to be a good mate.'

Indeed he was. The inclusion of Stollery turned out to be a wise decision. The challenge through the Naga Hills demanded the eyes, ears and strength of more than one person. Frank was strongly advised not to undertake the journey, and wrote: 'We were told by most intelligent persons that we were attempting the impossible; roadless jungles, impassable mountains, tigers, elephants, headhunters and fever lay ahead.'

Further, the Shell office received a telegram from the Automobile Association in Rangoon. 'We notice that Mr Birtles proposes to do Calcutta–Rangoon section by road. Does he know there is no road? Information received tells this is an impossible feat even for a well-prepared party, let alone a man alone. Even in fine weather the jungle is impenetrable by car, and the danger from wild animals and headhunting natives is extreme. He should reconsider.'

The mission's chief detractors, those working for the Shell offices in Calcutta, eventually resigned themselves to the fact that no amount of advice would deter Frank, and so they presented him with a rifle and cartridges. For Birtles and Stollery, this firearm would have been a sobering statement, warning of the dangers they were to face in the jungles of Burma's mountains.

Frank had no shortage of experience with firearms, particularly the large-calibre, centre-fire rifles he had used in the Boer War. But this firearm was something else. The monstrous and unwieldy double-barrelled rifle presented to Birtles was an 'elephant gun' that chambered a .450 calibre 'nitro-express' brass cartridge a full 10 centimetres long. The Kynoch brand cartridges packed an almighty wallop – intended for felling a charging, rogue African bush elephant if you were brave or stupid enough to stand in its path and try to land the .450 projectile between its eyes.

30

Headhunters

There were good reasons to be worried about what lay within the dense jungle forests of the Naga Hills. The whole mysterious region had been a dangerous and recalcitrant corner of the British Empire since the first colonials set foot there in the 1880s. The way everyone spoke of the Naga Hills, from the President of the Royal Automobile Club through to Calcutta newspaper boys – telling of its man-eating and venomous wildlife, and the homicidal hill tribes that would appear from the undergrowth, butcher and behead any trespasser before melting back into the jungle – they had all the ingredients for a 19th century bone-chilling gothic horror story.

The problem for Birtles and Stollery was that all these over-the-top tall stories were in fact true. There had been a long history of British expeditions entering into the wilds of North East India and Upper Burma resulting in dire consequences. Well-prepared and well-armed parties had ventured into the forest's darkness, never to return. The region was inhabited by a fractured collection of warring tribes whose only alliance with each other was a combined hatred of intruding aliens.

They, somewhat correctly, believed that the difficult terrain in the jungle-clad mountains gave them some sort of immunity. The going was so rough that it was only Gurkhas who could handle the conditions while on patrol. The first inkling of just how barbarous things could be in the Naga Hills came in 1888 with the murder of two British army surveyors whose heads had been acquired as part of a ransom for a chief's wife held hostage by a neighbouring tribe. Despite numerous campaigns mounted to subdue the area, British attempts were unsuccessful, with troops thwarted by dysentery, malaria and the accuracy of the tribesmen in dropping boulders on the heads of their adversaries.

Even as Birtles and Stollery were preparing the Sundowner in Calcutta, British political officers with armed patrols were clambering through the jungles of the Naga Hills from village to village in an attempt to free slaves and stop the practice of child sacrifice. Tribal chiefs struck a deal with British political officer H.E. Mitchell by biting on a tiger's tooth – each elder declaring they'd be eaten by a tiger should they break their vow. However, Mitchell upped the ante by substituting the biting of a tooth with a .303 bullet, then giving them a demonstration of the destructive qualities of a Lewis machine gun. Mitchell claimed it was 'a real eye opener' for people who'd only ever seen flintlock muskets before. It must have worked to some degree – in 1928 only two child sacrifices were reported. These forays into the forests didn't even scratch the surface in subduing the Naga's hill men, though.

In 1928, vast regions of the mountain jungles were still completely unknown, hopeless to access, and the people therefore impossible to subdue. Even as late as World War II, British anthropologist Ursula Graham Bower described the Naga Hills as 'a paradise of headhunters', and American airmen flying over Burma were advised if they were to crash-land in the mountain ranges on the Burmese–Indian border to avoid the hill men at all costs. At that time, fifteen years after Birtles and Stollery, the USAAF regarded the Naga Hills as being neither under the control of the Allies or the Japanese – instead it was ruled by 'active head hunter villages' and even in 1942 some of these villages were calling for skull-taking raids on foreigners.

•

'So we started off from Calcutta one bright morning on an attempt to motor through to Rangoon . . .' wrote Frank. Once again he was diving head-first into the unknown, severing all communication with the Western world, and would hopefully, somewhere, reappear. The pair headed east, trying to find a viable way to cross the River Ganges, but when standing on its banks they found the water was far too wide and fast-flowing. They reconnoitred for about half a day before hiring a bamboo rowing punt used for transporting cattle.

Putting the Sundowner on board was a tricky operation, with the car slithering along slippery and greasy loading planks and the ferry tipping and swaying with its weight. The car was balancing nicely enough on the bamboo floor when halfway across the river the ferry began to list and take on water, and would have capsized if they hadn't made it to the other side in time. It was nerve-racking, to say the least.

The journey across the Ganges on the bamboo punt took three hours. If they were to continue heading directly east, Birtles and Stollery were faced with many more crossings like this. They would be attempting to cross the Sundarabans, a hazardous series of deltas, swamps and tributaries at the mouth of the Ganges. After several more risky river adventures where they had placed the car on jerry-rigged barges that were simply canoes lashed together, or sitting the Sundowner precariously on flimsy green bamboo rafts that rapidly lost buoyancy, they decided that once they'd crossed the Brahmaputra River (or rather the rivers that become the Brahmaputra) they'd head north towards Assam.

For six weeks, the Sundowner slogged along jungle tracks that connected village to village, with Frank at the wheel and Stollery carrying the elephant gun. It was remote and dangerous territory. 'We were out spotting for tiger, leopard, and other spit-cats,' Frank wrote. They made their way up into the far-flung, remote and mountainous pocket of the north-eastern India region, where finally one night they reached Imphal, the capital of Assam.

They rested here for a week, looked after by the small white community living in the town. This was the end of the line, for now they were on the threshold of crossing into the Naga Hills. Right from the word go, as far back as Malcolm Ellis wandering around in the great halls of the British Museum, anyone qualified to give an opinion on the drive from London to Singapore was stumped when it came to this mountain range on the border of India and Burma. Birtles and Stollery were as prepared as they were ever going to be. The locals presented the pair with a sizeable stock of food supplies, which they stowed in the rear of the torpedo body, on top of which was coiled 100 metres of rope, a crowbar, pick, shovels and an axe.

Birtles followed a cart track, which then became a one-man path much narrower than the car. Then, when driving around a bend in a valley, their world changed, before them 'looming way up into the blue skies, a jungle-clad mountain with wisps of cloud tipping the top'. The single-file path before them had begun to increase its incline to be seemingly almost vertical, zigzagging skyward at alarming angles to disappear up the mist-covered mountainside. It was a goat track that corkscrewed its way into the clouds. 'Just to put the wind up us,' Birtles wrote, 'we saw streaks of yellow earth in a series of hairpin bends'. Birtles and Stollery climbed out of the car and stood silently facing a monumental challenge. They had reached the barrier of the Naga Hills. If they were to get through, 60 mountains just like the one before them had to be conquered. The hills would now swallow them up and hopefully spit them out at the other end. For however long, these 60 mountains would act as a colossal, dank, green jail for the motorists – or perhaps become their tomb.

If they were to survive, Frank knew that every inch of the journey would need to be carefully planned. One miscalculation, one wheel in the wrong place at the wrong time, and their lives would be over. But they were going ahead. The pair pitched camp by a creek and spent the next week plotting their assault. The plan was to hand-carve a section of the ascent, bring the Bean to that point and then carve another section, gradually working their way through the hills. The pair made a careful reconnaissance of the first 5 kilometres of mountainside, studying and surveying each corner of each hairpin.

With pick, shovel, axe and crowbar they set about building a road – removing boulders, cutting down trees, chopping away at the cliff face to widen the track. Within 2 kilometres the track rose 350 metres. They widened several tight hairpins in the hope Frank could skid the Bean around the corners without losing momentum on a one-in-two incline. Up these hills, momentum was everything.

With the first section of road more or less ready, Frank set to work on the car. He stared at the mountainside towering above him. How on earth would the car make it up that? For it to be able to climb such breathtaking grades required much lower gearing than the three-speed gearbox the Bean possessed.

Frank stood deep in thought. Sometimes with the old Model T you'd need to drive the car backwards up a hill, thanks to the very low reverse gear. Yet there was no way he could reverse up that goat track. If only the Bean had that low reverse gear to move forward. Frank had a flash of inspiration. He jacked the car up and removed the rear wheels. Stollery helped him remove the whole differential and rear axle assembly from the rear springs and they flipped it upside down. The differential would now turn in the opposite direction, meaning Frank now had four reverse gears and one forward. At full power the Bean's top forward speed was now 15 km/h.

Birtles and Stollery stripped the Bean of everything that could be removed. The spark plugs were then taken out and cleaned, the ignition points reset and the engine was tuned to within an inch of its life. They were ready. Stollery stood a kilometre up the mountainside at the first bend of the cleared section of track. Frank reversed the Sundowner for 100 metres in preparation to let fly at a run-up. He floored the accelerator and the Bean's engine screamed at full power. Now underway, the howling car reached its maximum speed of 15 km/h, 'roaring as though doing 80 miles an hour' – the certified top speed. Birtles wrote, 'The car climbed the first grade, with its incline of one in two. We were ascending the first of the hills – there were sixty waiting for us.'

Only 100 metres past Stollery was the first hairpin bend, and Frank braced himself to throw the car sideways into a broad slide and power the car around the corner and keep climbing upwards. His chief worry was a dubious piece of ground on the corner that had the potential to break away and possibly roll the car.

Frank wrenched the steering into a hard lock, the rear wheels went into a slide, skidding violently before they found traction, and the Bean rocketed out of the corner onto the next incline. With the engine flat out Frank hung onto the steering wheel, the car's momentum causing it to shudder violently over the stones and washouts. With the cliff wall lining one edge of the track and a sheer drop on the other, Frank piloted the car dead ahead with hardly an inch to spare on either side. It scraped the cliff wall and Frank was showered in scree. At the next bend, the Bean came to a stop. The corner was just too tight to negotiate the long, cigar-bodied car.

Birtles made a Spanish windlass, the primitive form of winch he'd used countless times – doubled-up rope with a thick stick inserted in the middle and turned. This they attached to the dumb-irons at the front of the car and a tree stump, and by jacking up the rear wheels and winding the winch, they slid the car on bamboo skids inch by inch around the corner.

At one point the pair built a 4-foot-high sloping ramp out of stones, something like a ski-jump. Frank backed the car up and gunned the engine, giving the Bean a flying start up the hill ahead. When the car finally stopped, the incline was so steep that engine oil poured out past the rear of the crankshaft. The higher they climbed, the steeper the inclines became. Sometimes even chains on deflated tyres with all the brakes applied wouldn't hold the car. Its sheer weight combined with the near vertical gradients saw it slide uncontrollably on the wet jungle soil.

Whenever they committed to an ascent, they couldn't stop until they'd reached the top. The pair devised a system that worked as follows: a rope was attached to the dumb-irons at the front of the car and as Birtles began the drive skyward, Stollery, who stood at the summit, took up the rope's slack. If the car started to plummet out of control, Stollery immediately roped his line to a tree as an anchor.

The two men developed quite complicated techniques using ropes to swing the car around should the track slope outwards as well as down. They would tie a short rope on the dumb-iron secured to a tree, and by releasing the brakes the front of the car would be drawn sharply in as the car swung around due to gravity, and the line pulled taut.

As the rope became increasingly worn, it developed the tendency to snap. 'Most grimly I had to hang onto hand and footbrakes,' Birtles wrote, 'while my mate scrambled breathlessly on the steep hill among jungle vines and thorns, to find secure anchorage. Had he failed me, the Sundowner and I would have gone down the mountainside.' As their equipment wore out, so did their chances of survival. Daily they were being pushed beyond their limits. On conquering one mountain, they'd look across to the next, perhaps even larger, steeper, more dangerous. Birtles wrote: 'We would get up each morning wondering – I speak the truth – if we would be alive at sundown.'

The days that followed were both frightening and nerve-racking, offering the same dangerous routine. Every day started with a reconnaissance, followed by hours of path clearing with the shovel and crowbar, carrying their kit on their backs up the steep tracks. The final part of their efforts would be the ritual of firing up the car and attacking the mountainsides, the bonnet pointing skyward, the outside wheels flailing, sometimes barely in contact with the edge of the precipice, Birtles glimpsing the jungle far below through gaps in the swirling mist.

31

Is Frank Dead?

The press were becoming anxious. For the second time in a matter of weeks Frank had disappeared. He was no longer in the freezing deserts of Persia – now he was in the steaming jungles of Burma. It was hard to keep up. For some Fleet Street and Australian reporters, it seemed fair enough to conclude that Frank had probably tempted fate just that once too often. Sooner or later his luck would run out, and newspapers were already working on obituaries to publish. While not technically obituaries, some articles published about Frank's disappearance were the next best thing.

As far as one newspaper was concerned, he was gone for all money.

> Francis Birtles, whose disappearance somewhere in Burma on his 16,000-mile motor trip from England to Australia has been reported, will probably in later years be remembered for his long-established habit of putting to the supreme test

of endurance the various means of locomotion that were popular before mankind generally took to the air.

Birtles left the air to others. He did fly on a mission to central Australia in recent years, but he preferred terra firma for his conquests, and he picked on the wildest and most uninviting bits of scenery that he could find to throw down his challenge . . . He has been mostly on the go ever since. In the course of his wanderings, he has extensively advertised certain tyres, a make of bicycle, various makes of cars, and Francis Birtles . . . He was next announced to be leaving for Australia by car alone.

He made good progress as far as Athens, but after leaving that place had many delays. He was missing in the Persian desert for some weeks, but turned up unexpectedly in India. He left Calcutta a few weeks ago for Burma, and once more no trace of his whereabouts could be ascertained . . .

Matters became more serious, and before long suggestions were being put forward for the Australian government to put together a search and rescue party.

NO NEWS OF BIRTLES. ANXIETY IN LONDON. MATTER OF SEARCH DISCUSSED

There is some anxiety in London concerning Francis Birtles, the Australian explorer and overlander, who left London for Melbourne by car about six months ago. There has been a lack of news since he left Calcutta on 19 January, and there are fears that he may have met with difficulties in the jungle. If nothing is heard from Calcutta within a week, it is proposed to ask Australia to organise a search for the traveller.

How exactly 'Australia' would organise a search and rescue mission to find Birtles in the far-flung regions of northern Burma wasn't exactly fleshed out, and no-one had come up with concrete plan.

•

'Nights were eerie,' wrote Birtles, as each evening a strange mist would rise from the valley floor and weave through their campsite like the fingers of a pervading, ethereal hand. Everything in the jungle was damp, and the tiny amounts of timber they could find were rotten through. Camp fires, therefore, were out of the question. Dark and motionless, nights in the hills were uneasy, with unexpectedly loud and worryingly close noises coming from unseen wildlife. Mosquitoes were rife, and every night the pair slept under nets. Yet sleeping was always light – Frank had the elephant gun close by, just in case of tigers or headhunters. He also kept a two-gallon tin of petrol and a box of matches on hand to douse the scrub around the camp perimeter and set it alight in an emergency.

One morning, just as the first hint of dawn silhouetted the shark-toothed skyline of the mountain range, Frank woke with a start. 'Something big, heavy, and soft-footed struck the ground near Stollery's mosquito net!' he wrote. Frank lay silent, listening intently. He heard whatever it was then pad around close to his own mosquito-net-covered head. 'My nostrils were filled with a nasty wild-piggy odour.'

Frank slowly sat up, reached for the elephant gun and climbed out from under the mosquito net. By now Stollery was awake too. Frank reached up to switch on the spotlight attached to the Bean's windscreen. 'I swung the spotlight round and its ray gleamed for an instant on the striped body of a tiger as it slipped away into the undergrowth.'

As the days turned into weeks, the hillsides became even steeper, and Frank's ingenuity came further into play. Even with the Bean's extra low gearing, due to the reversal of the crown wheel and pinion in order to overcome the preposterous ascents asked of the car, Frank set about devising new levels of bush mechanics. In a stroke of genius, he removed the rear wheels and, with a small hand file, spent hours filing grooves in the brake drums around which he could attach chains. The chains' links were locked into the grooves and then the whole assembly was tightened with bolts. With the rear of the car sitting at an alarming angle on the small-diameter chained drums, Frank now had even lower gearing, the chains digging into the soil like cleats on a tank's tracks. Once the car was in gear, the brake drums spun like mad, the links gaining purchase, and the car was able to jolt and climb up spectacular angles.

Whatever the Naga Hills threw at him, Frank had an answer. As yet, he and Stollery had seen little sign of the notoriously terrifying Naga Hill men; that is not to say that the hill men weren't aware of two white men trying to push and pull two tons of motor car through their mountains.

Eventually, the mountain hunters revealed themselves. They were amazing to see. They were quite small, broad and muscular, with blue tattoos on their arms and chests and a long, narrow shock of black hair running along the back of their skulls.

They wore black loincloths and were armed with *dahs* – long metal knives held in wooden sheaths. They stood silently in small groups, watching Birtles and Stollery struggle with the car. When Frank fired up the engine, they were taken aback. Frank wrote, 'They reckoned that the Sundowner was packed with *Nahz* – friendly devils from the insides of dead men.' This was Frank in his element, able to hold his own with people completely alien to the world of the 20th century and, with no understanding of their language, or they of his, Frank could get to the bottom of the story.

Frank wasn't put off by their reputation – he could tough it out with the best of them. One evening, he and Stollery had had no option but to put on hold their attempt in attacking a diabolically steep grade where the car simply didn't have enough power to make it to the top, and no amount of winching could move it any distance before nightfall. It was far too dangerous to continue after dark; the car's bonnet was pointing towards the stars and its tyres were perilously close to the edge of an abyss.

With the windlass still in place and the car lashed almost vertically to the side of the cliff face, Birtles and Stollery decided to make camp. At midnight, Frank's eyes opened. He could hear heavy movement on the jungle track above, the snorting and braying of large beasts plodding down the mountainside towards them. Hundreds of buffalo were shuffling through the night along the narrow path, herded by blue-tattooed hill men, armed with long spears and the formidable *dahs*.

The leading buffalo abruptly came to a stop where the Sundowner was lashed on the track. Frightened of the machine, they refused to move any further, the whole cattle drive beginning to bank up. There was only room for one buffalo at a time to pass between the roped-down Bean and the edge of the precipice and the cattle were stubbornly refusing to move.

The hill men pushed their way through the mob to suddenly find this strange tied-down object blocking the path ahead. Angry, one of them unsheathed his knife to commence chopping through the Bean's ropes in preparation to send the car over the edge. While furiously hacking away with his *dah*, the hill man suddenly looked up to find the muzzle of the elephant rifle squarely in his face, with Frank at the other end, squeezing the trigger. Frank meant to use it; if the car lay as a twisted wreck at the bottom of the chasm 300 metres below, then he and Stollery were as good as dead out here in the jungle, so it didn't matter what happened now.

The hill man understood the situation and backed off; there needed to be some sort of compromise. Birtles and Stollery covered the car in bushes to disguise it and the cattle slowly began to file past one by one. It took all night. Frank noted that even though the hill men were known as headhunters, the term, as far as he was concerned, was 'a mere euphemism'. Instead, the purpose of their manhunt was to prove their own manhood by cutting off the genitalia of their dead victims, 'which, after being dried, are presented to the hill man's loved one to adorn her necklace'.

By now, rations were starting to run thin and the pair was in need of a decent feed. At least the two men were not afraid to try something new. They began yearning for meat, 'white man's tucker – juicy steaks', as Frank put it. He took the elephant gun and shot a monkey, then skinned it and cooked it in a two-gallon petrol tin. 'As he boiled' Frank wrote, 'the victim's grinning face, with teeth showing and little clasped hands, made me feel like a cannibal.' Native superstition told that killing a monkey would bring bad luck. That's all they needed.

As they continued manhandling the car up and down the mountainsides, deeper into the jungle, they were often passed by the traffic of generally uninterested hill men, returning from the hunt, and in the course of their adventure, Birtles and Stollery were taken to a village concealed in the thick jungle. The village was set out more or less like a stockade or fort, surrounded by 3-metre poles sharpened to a point to deter bears, tigers and any belligerent tribes on the warpath.

To enter the compound involved crawling under a heavy trapdoor of sharpened bamboo and emerging from a tunnel. Birtles and Stollery were invited to sit on mats laid out on a balcony overhanging a precipice with a sheer drop of hundreds of metres. The view was spectacular, a 'glorious panorama of valleys and ranges – all purple, darkening into the glow of an amber sunset'.

They were given rice whisky served in sections of upright bamboo as cups. The cockroach-like black insects floating on top Frank likened to a hill man's version of a glacé cherry in a cocktail. Nevertheless, they drank it, Frank claiming 'it had a kick like a backfiring motor'. They were then served the village speciality: roast puppy. The locals loosened up as the night wore on, no doubt due to the rice whisky, Birtles and Stollery smiling and subtly pouring it through the cracks in the balcony floor.

The tribe's elders listened to the local news broadcast by a sort of minstrel, who wandered from village to village, picking up and relaying the local gossip. He prattled off everything he could remember, accompanied by his aide on a bamboo flute.

Every news item had to be succinct and performed in one breath. 'It was quite an art,' Frank wrote.

This strange invitation to see the hill men up close was a brief interlude in the daily grind of pushing the car through the mountains. Frank had cut his hand badly. In an age before penicillin this could be catastrophic. The monotony of carving their own road simply became part of Frank and Stollery's existence, almost as though they were serving a prison sentence and, in time, they'd be up for parole.

Finally, their time arrived. They had reached the summit of the last of 60 mountains and gazed upon the thick green jungles of Burma's Kabaw Valley far below. In 28 days, they'd travelled 58 kilometres and had broken the back of the greatest physical barrier for the overland drive from London to Singapore. It was an astonishing feat. The French and British expeditions of Gustave Duverne and Captain Duncan McCallum conducted the same year had written off the overland route through the mountains as impossible, and instead decided to bypass the Burmese sections altogether by placing their cars on trains and ships. Birtles clearly infuriated McCallum, who'd maintained that a passage through the Naga Hills was impossible; the experienced English explorer, the commandant of the British legation in Peking, had been walloped by an Australian bushman trying his luck in outback Burma.

In his book *China to Chelsea*, recounting his adventures, McCallum discussed in considerable detail the difficulties in crossing the Naga Hills by car. He outlined all the reasons why he avoided a land-crossing attempt – weather, roads, lack of information. Ultimately, he conceded a sort of reluctant acknowledgment of Birtles and Stollery's improbable and astonishing achievement, although he never mentions Birtles by name, only ever referring to him as 'the Australian': 'A great part of this route would have been quite impossible in the wet season; but even in the dry, the recent experience of an Australian has proved that, if possible, it is scarcely practicable in a reasonable sense of the term.'

McCallum skilfully avoided using the word 'success' when it came to the Birtles–Stollery crossing. However, he wanted it put on record that he'd actually come up with the idea of crossing the Naga Hills, too: 'in a report issued in Calcutta, I suggested that, with a little patience and hard work, it might be possible to take a car through. The Australian certainly found need of patience and hard work. He literally had to cut his way through jungle-bush, and those 69 miles [111 kilometres] took 36 days to accomplish!' Bizarrely, McCallum even included a large fold-out map of what his 'proposed' route would have been (the same path as Birtles', by the way) if he'd have done it, which he didn't, just so everyone knew that he'd thought of it too.

As far as Captain McCallum was concerned, Birtles' achievement proved nothing: '. . . in the light of the attempts of the Frenchman coming west and the Australian going east, it may not unreasonably be claimed that, under present conditions, Burma very definitely denies the motorist a thoroughfare from Siam to India'.

That is, unless you were Francis Birtles.

In England, Bert Hinkler had managed to scrape together enough money to buy an aircraft – an Avro Avian Cirrus Mk II biplane – described by the press as a 'baby aeroplane'. It had financially cleaned him out. Like Birtles, he was virtually broke. Hinkler had tried to take out a 'sporting insurance policy' with Lloyds of London, a curious arrangement – more or less like a bet – where he would be paid a sum 'increasing in mathematical progression' for each day whittled off the 28-day record achieved by Ross and Keith Smith in 1921. But there was a premium of £150 to pay and he simply couldn't afford it.

Hinkler trawled London looking for sponsorship 'but the response was about as good as if I had been trying to sell rotten fruit,' as he exasperatedly put it. With no fanfare, no farewells from Australia House, no staged corroboree under mock gum trees, his wife waved farewell as Bert Hinkler took off in his little plane from Croydon aerodrome, headed for Australia.

•

Travelling through the jungles of the Kabaw Valley was no easy task. There were hundreds of miles of country to be traversed through which no motor car had ever been before. Their plan was to try to hook up with the Irrawaddy River and follow it all the way down to Rangoon. The going was rough – the humidity in the giant teak forests was stifling and the leaf litter on the jungle floor concealed enormous holes and obstacles discovered only by smashing into them.

Frank described the Kabaw as 'a nightmare for any motorist.' It had become an all too bizarre world for the exhausted pair – the jungle was alive with snakes and haunted by the alarming, furtive shapes of large black monkeys watching the raucous, dilapidated car crawl by.

Birtles pulled the car up. He saw something on the mud track ahead. Stollery had no idea what Frank was looking at. Can it be? Frank climbed out of the car and strode ahead, intently looking at the mud in front of his feet. '. . . with yells of delight,' wrote Frank, 'we noted that there was the track of a motor car.' At last, civilisation.

They arrived in the village of Tamu in the Kabaw, where the message of Birtles and Stollery's reappearance into the world was telegraphed to Calcutta and then to Australia – newspapers around the nation went wild with the news that Francis Birtles was still alive. *He should be dead! A thousand times over! How does he do it?* The public had become enthralled with Birtles' real-life cliffhanger yarn.

And just to compound Frank's sensational reappearance there was some other breaking news: Bert Hinkler had done it – he'd successfully flown solo from England to Australia, becoming the nation's greatest aviation hero. The press scrambled to capitalise on the delightful coincidence of the pair of Australian adventurers simultaneously popping up, recounting Birtles and Hinkler's wager before Frank left London as to who would reach Australia first. The Overlander or the aviator? Flight had won.

On their arrival in the Burmese capital of Rangoon, Frank and Percy were reported in the international press as looking 'somewhat of a wreck'. Frank's infected hand had deteriorated into an appalling condition and at last he could receive urgently needed medical help. But not before he could say to the world, 'The fact that I am here means that the so-called English "impossible" has been achieved. I had to run the gauntlet of bandits, wolves, raiders, Hillmen, leopards, tigers, and wild elephants. So far I have not lost any "bark", but am feeling tired. The car is perfect.'

The white community in Rangoon feted them royally. They were described as 'Petrol Pioneers' at a civic reception and at Dunlop's office, banners welcomed 'Captain Birtles who has driven his Bean car to Rangoon on one set of Dunlops.' After a week, Frank's hand was showing some response to treatment and he reckoned he was fit enough to move on.

Then the monsoon struck – hard and with a vengeance. It was as if nature, riled at the motorists for having conquered the Naga Hills, had not finished with them yet. The monsoon's storms unleashed a thunderous ocean of tropical rain, and the landscape flooded quickly in every direction – paddy-fields, roads, rivers – forcing them to stop.

Marooned, Birtles and Stollery huddled under the Sundowner's canvas roof for several days. The rain just did not let up. 'Between storms, mosquitoes and anxiety we had plenty to torment us,' Birtles wrote. Waterlogged, the Sundowner crawled along, attempting to make for the peninsula's west coast. The rain didn't show any signs of easing and the whole expedition was in danger of collapse. Their clothing was beginning to rot with mildew and their sodden blankets were growing toadstools. Their biscuits had gone soft and were covered in a blue-green mould.

On top of that, both Birtles and Stollery were beginning to show signs of malaria. Soon the rivers and streams would swell exponentially and any sort of drivable passage would be completely obliterated. As it was, they were trying different routes to continue south – they had to turn back from the Siamese border just short of Moulmein and then opted to try southward, following a path through lower Burma along the edge of the Andaman Sea, but all the river crossings were in flood. It was hopeless. At one point the car's cockpit was ankle-deep in water, the exhaust pipe submerged and the sump full of river water.

Frank learned there was a ship at the port of Mergui in Burma's far south that was due to leave for Penang. He made the decision to try to catch it and put the Sundowner aboard. Stollery was becoming quite ill and the only thing left was to make for the ship. The monsoon had beaten them, even though in the dry the terrain through here would have been easily negotiable by motor car. If the timing had been right, they could have made it without loading aboard the ship. Nevertheless, the steamer journey south was a welcome relief, the two men and the Bean car arriving in Penang on 24 May.

The Sundowner slogged south. It never, *ever* stopped raining. And then it happened. Finally Singapore, the southernmost point on the Asian landmass, was within reach.

The Sundowner powered through the city's outskirts, yet Singaporean newspapers described the two motorists as being in 'a terrible condition' and 'suffering the effects of privation' but at this moment that was irrelevant – they had truly achieved the impossible.

In conquering the Naga Hills in Burma, Francis Birtles had become the first person to drive from France to Singapore – the western edge of the European continent to the southernmost tip of the south-east Asian mainland.

Frank had driven 21,500 kilometres overland. And survived. With Stollery's condition deteriorating, Frank drove straight to Shell's office to find out when their next ship would be leaving for Port Darwin. Coincidentally, the Shell freighter *Unda* was in the process of having hundreds of cases of benzine hoisted aboard, and was being readied to depart almost as soon as they arrived at the wharf.

It was hard to believe. Next stop Australia – home. Just to think of it. Frank knew every inch of the drive from Darwin to Melbourne, every track, every creek crossing, every jump-up, every gate, every bloody currawong sitting in a bloody scribbly-gum. As far as Frank was concerned, Darwin was Australia's front gate and the road to Melbourne was just a long driveway. If Bert Hinkler received such a hero's welcome for taking two weeks to fly from England, then what sort of a reception would Frank Birtles receive for *driving* the whole way?

He was about to find out.

32

The Final Stretch

The *Unda* stopped very briefly at Borneo and two days later the Australian mainland appeared on the horizon. They had arrived just in time. Stollery was by now quite ill with malaria and Frank wasn't too far behind. Exhausted and penniless, they planned to stay in Darwin for as long as it took Stollery to recover enough to travel. However, their stopover looked like it might take some time.

After unloading the car at the wharf, Darwin customs officials notified Frank they were impounding the Sundowner until he paid import duty. Import duty? He wasn't importing the car, he was bloody well driving it home from England. Duty on the car had been paid when it was imported to Australia the first time. In fact, this very car had already sat on this very wharf once before when it had been shipped from Sydney for the Darwin to Sydney speed record run with Alec Barlow in 1926. The customs officer was probably even the same bloke on duty then.

Frank went ballistic. He'd just driven a car from England – the first person ever to do so – and the first Australian to greet him when he arrives home was some would-be copper who was trying to wring money out of him. No doubt about it – Francis Birtles was back in Australia all right, and he was going to make these pen-pushers' lives hell. He went straight to the offices of the *Northern Territory Times*, where word got out to the wider world while Frank continued to do his block. Headlines surfaced all over Australia about his plight. 'A Tale of Woe – Birtles at Darwin – Car Held By Customs'. 'Birtles Returns, Car Seized. Duty Demanded.'

Suddenly the bureaucrats at Customs House in Darwin didn't know what had hit them. Frank had put a spotlight squarely on their offices. 'Mr Birtles says he has had more trouble in Darwin than in any other place in the world, and the red tape of the officials and his treatment generally made him ashamed to have to admit that he was an Australian.'

The *Sunday Times* in Perth went to town: 'We can imagine the lurid indignation of Frank Birtles when a Customs pirate at Darwin demanded duty on his car. Frank can swear in Australian-ese, Aboriginal-ese, Chinese, Japanese, journalese, and-best-of-all in Birtles-ese. We guess that Darwin dingo felt the cutting blast of the expert Frank until his pelt was burning. Even the benighted heathen in coloured Asia worshipped his car and gave it a push along, through jungle and morass, and it was only when he reached his native land that he was held up for tariff plunder. And, behold! The car is the one that he took away with him – it had already paid the Australian customs duty when first imported. It is a wonder the pirate did not want to collect duty on Birtles' old pants!'

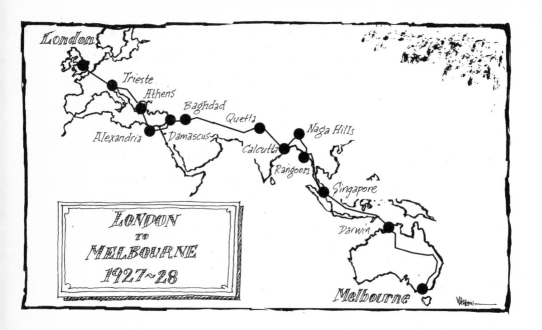

London

Trieste
Athens
Baghdad
Quetta
Alexandria
Damascus
Calcutta
Naga Hills
Rangoon
Singapore
Darwin

LONDON
TO
MELBOURNE
1927~28

Melbourne

Still on the warpath, he decided to go straight to the top, sending a telegram direct to the prime minister, Stanley Melbourne Bruce, pleading for the car's release. Bruce, who had been a minister in Billy Hughes' cabinet while the Roy Fry debacle was running riot, would have no doubt done anything to keep Frank at arm's length. The prime minister sent a telegram back to Customs House in Darwin stating simply, 'Release the car.'

Within a week, Stollery was feeling well enough to travel and the pair set off for the long drive to Melbourne. Although glad to be on the move once more, Frank was bitter about the treatment he'd received in his own country, compared to the Hollywood-style adulation afforded to aviators like Bert Hinkler.

The *Townsville Bulletin* ran an article about Frank Birtles, 'who draws a scathing comparison of the treatment of aviators arriving from overseas and that meted out to him by the authorities'. Ironically, placed alongside the story is another about Mr and Mrs Bert Hinkler visiting the town of Stanthorpe in Queensland, where 'they attended many receptions in town today, and received a great welcome wherever they appeared in public'. The article lists the myriad engagements awaiting them around the state. 'When Hinkler returns to Brisbane he will be presented with £1,100, the proceeds of the Mayoral Fund.'

People weren't interested in overlanders any more – now aviators were well and truly the rage. As he motored through the outskirts of Darwin heading towards the interior, it must have occurred to Frank that he could have sat in the navigator's seat with Hinkler on the flight from London. He could have been feted and lionised as a national hero, shaking hands with the governor-general and the prime minister, as was happening with the famous flyer right now.

Frank's decision not to accompany Hinkler home to Australia resulted in a completely unforeseen outcome. By going it alone Hinkler had suddenly, and unexpectedly, captured the Australian public's attention by becoming the first person to fly solo from England to Australia. Hinkler was now a star of international proportions.

On his return Hinkler received an impromptu government-funded prize of £2,000 for his spectacular solo effort, presented to him by Prime Minister Bruce on the steps of the brand-new parliament house in Canberra, where troops saluted him at the present arms. 'You have added to the lustre of our race,' enthused Bruce, 'you have contributed greatly to the science of aviation; but above all you have strengthened our faith in the future by your amazing demonstration that the men of Australia possess all those qualities that make the greatness of a nation.'

Indeed Hinkler had, but all Frank Birtles got from the prime minister was the okay to release his car from customs at the wharf in Darwin. In Canberra, Hinkler was a guest of the governor-general, he was a guest of the commandant and staff of the Royal Military College at Duntroon and was given a standing ovation in the Senate and the House of Representatives.

Yet, fundamentally, it was his solo flight they were applauding. Frank's decision not to travel with him had inadvertently jackpotted Hinkler's fame. Frank and Bert had made their bet in London as to who would arrive back in Australia first. Hinkler's stunning arrival meant he had well and truly won the bet.

As Birtles and Stollery were battling their way south from Darwin, following the old overland telegraph line track, the premier of Queensland was feting the great Australian aviator Bert Hinkler – the state's most famous son – at the Queensland Aero Club Dinner. After a cheery, upbeat speech, the premier then finished with a macabre sense of foreboding about the aviator's future, saying, 'I hope you will not be inveigled into some dangerous flight that will mean the loss of you. I do ask you, if you do attempt such a flight, to see that your route is well patrolled, so that you will have a reasonable chance of preserving that life that has been so valuable to Australia.' In five years, Bert Hinkler's body would be found by Italian *carabinieri* in the wreckage of his aircraft on the slopes of the Apennine mountains between Florence and Arezzo.

Birtles and Stollery motored south-east through Longreach in Queensland, where Birtles reflected on the impact the motor car had had on remote Australia. 'The car has altered the meaning of life for the men and women – and children – of the interior. It has brought them comfort, given them social opportunities, given them better chances in case of sickness and childbirth, and widened their whole mental and physical horizon.' It was true. Frank had lived through it all – from the horse to the bicycle to the internal combustion engine.

He'd seen the far-flung regions of Australia gradually brought closer together by the prevalence of the motor car. And Frank had been there from the start – Dutton and Aunger with their Talbot in the desert, Syd Ferguson with the Brush, the Model T, the Hudson Super Six, the Oldsmobile, the Scarlet Runner and Scrap Iron – the Imperial Six – the car for Australia.

Through all this, it was the mighty Sundowner that had performed above and beyond the call of duty. Frank sang the car's praises, subliminally comparing the Sundowner to its disastrous sibling, the Imperial Six, 'The old Sundowner should, by all the builders' rules of stresses and strains, have been scrap iron, thousands of miles back along the track, but it left Darwin humming "Home, Sweet Home" in a voice that, if mechanical, was true in every note.' (Scrap Iron, as Frank cryptically put it, was still thousands of miles back along the track in India.) 'I marvelled at that engine. It was a much-used piece of machinery when I took it to London. Since then it had covered over 13,000 miles [21,000 kilometres] of rough pioneering, overloaded, and at an average crankshaft speed of 2,500 revolutions per minute. I worked this out roughly at one hundred and twenty million revolutions for the journey.'

Despite Birtles' disappointment with his reception in Darwin, the publicity over his blue with customs had in effect given him tremendous advance publicity for his arrival into Brisbane.

BIRTLES ARRIVES IN BRISBANE. THRILLING DETAILS. TRIBUTE TO BRITISH CAR

A large crowd assembled in front of the G.P.O. this afternoon to witness the arrival of Francis Birtles, the celebrated overlander, through Europe and Asia and across Australia from Darwin, by motor car.

Upon reaching Brisbane Birtles had traversed 18,000 miles, of which 16,000 were covered by car. Accompanying him was a young Canadian, P. E. Stollery, who had joined him at Calcutta. Immediately Birtles and his bespattered car were observed coming up Queen-street a volley of cheers rent the air and when the intrepid motorist came to a stop he was given a rousing welcome.

•

'The most hazardous journey ever!' read the headline on the double-page spread in the *Sydney Mail*. Frank and Percy were given a rousing reception in Sydney before continuing on the final leg of their monumental drive.

'He's done it – that Francis Birtles has done it! He's driven from England and he's made it! I never doubted that he would – even when he went missing in Burma – or was it Persia? He's a daring cove, that Birtles . . .'

They were finally in the heart of Melbourne, where bystanders ran onto the road in their hundreds, swamping the car as it reached GPO in the centre of the city. Trams had come to a complete stop as the crowd doubled, then tripled, then quadrupled. Traffic was in gridlock, men threw their hats in the air, cars sounded their horns. The sound of the crowd was exhilarating. It was bedlam. Percy Stollery hung on as people jostled and clambered to take hold of his hand to furiously shake it, patting him on the back, punching his shoulder in congratulations.

Frank pressed the horn and nudged the car forward until he'd finally made it to the steps outside the post office. Black-helmeted policemen then elbowed their way through, yelling to Frank that he was obstructing traffic and to move on. The police jumped onto the car and told him to get going. He didn't even get his photograph taken. Welcome home, Frank.

Birtles and Stollery were ushered through to Melbourne's Parliament House, where they were heartily received by the premier and his wife. At last Francis Birtles was being given the accolades he deserved. Newspapers placed him alongside Charles Kingsford Smith in the pantheon of Australian heroes.

'Two more notable achievements go down in history in the credit of Australia. The conquering of the Pacific by Captain Kingsford Smith and his gallant crew, and the blazing of an automobile trail from England to Australia by Francis Birtles are two remarkable records that will stand for all time. Their times will no doubt be beaten, but their great pioneering efforts cannot be eclipsed.'

There were those who clearly recognised and understood the significance of Francis Birtles' astonishing achievement. Somehow he'd produced a miracle for the British motor industry, this Australian colonial chap and his roaring Bean 14 having crossed the world, smashing all obstacles before them. Birtles had revealed a glimmer of hope for British industry in perhaps stopping the onslaught of the American automotive juggernaut.

Surprisingly, one of the first to congratulate him was the pessimistic Sir Robert Hadfield, thrilled with Birtles' success and with the possibilities for the British motor industry and the future for Bean Cars. He was quoted in newspapers all over

Britain, adding his enthusiasm to the celebratory air: 'We can compete with and beat the American productions.'

Yet there were those who weren't quite as enthusiastic. For Malcolm Ellis, Frank Birtles' success was the realisation of his worst nightmare. As far as Ellis was concerned, his initial paranoia in bringing Francis Birtles onboard the Imperial Six expedition had been more than justified. Birtles had taken Ellis's idea of driving across the world, successfully completed the mission, received the glory and then painted the expedition's instigator and chief architect out of the picture.

Everyone was talking of Francis Birtles piloting the Sundowner across deserts and over jungle-covered mountain ranges, but nobody knew of Malcolm Ellis, leader of the unknown Hinks Imperial Six Expedition aboard the 'secret car'. He was now an invalid at his home in Cremorne on Sydney's north shore, bitter and hostile. He could only read of Birtles' triumph in the newspapers. Ellis, the prodigious writer, attempted to have the last word on the trans-global drive, hammering out a manuscript about the Imperial Six expedition, the published book titled *Express to Hindustan*.

The first sentence in Ellis's preface makes his intentions perfectly clear. 'This volume seeks to tell the story of an attempt by three Australians, under the author's leadership, to reach Australia by motor car . . .' Within the book, Ellis portrayed himself as the urbane and generally unflappable leader, Captain Billy Knowles as the finest of stoic companions, and Frank as a rough and simple Australian outback colonial abroad. As rip-roaring an adventure story as *Express to Hindustan* is, in truth Ellis's leadership saw the three motorists perpetually harangued by police and in one instance placed under arrest for three weeks.

That they weren't executed as spies was nothing short of exceptionally good luck, due to some fast footwork from the British embassy in Instanbul. The fine Billy Knowles had in reality been of little value to the expedition and in some instances was simply a nuisance, who was simply 'let go' in Aleppo. It was Francis Birtles who had in fact performed the vast bulk of the driving and had carried out all the mechanical work on a car that was beyond useless.

While not ever criticising him directly, Ellis's portrayal of Birtles was generally, subtly unflattering and at times bordering on cruel. In his book, Ellis took delight in recounting Birtles remonstrating with a Dunlop representative in England for not knowing who he was: 'I'm a king in Australia – the King of Arnhem Land – where no white man has ever been. And you never heard of me?' He wrote of Birtles shouting his disparaging opinions of Britain as being a 'Hell of a country! Like driving down a blooming sewer.'

Birtles' experiences while touring Britain suggest exactly the opposite. Determined to leave his mark, Ellis finished his book's preface by stating, 'Even though we did not succeed, I left behind me a skeleton organisation and a basis of information which will lighten the task of any other party attempting a journey in the future.' Here he had his final swipe at his old driving companion by letting everyone know that technically, by crossing the Mediterranean, Francis Birtles too had failed. 'Already, one member of our party, using it, has tried unsuccessfully to achieve the complete journey, but at almost the very outset was compelled to omit 2,000 miles of the direct route from Sofia onwards. My assistance is at the disposal of any other sporting adventurers who care to try.' In other words, Birtles' achievement was null and void. Who would care to have another try? However Ellis's toxicity didn't really matter because reviews of his book pigeonholed it as old-fashioned adventure literature, the critics unaware of the fury behind its creation.

33

The Later Years

Little more than a year after Frank's drive from London to Melbourne, the Western world was shut down by the Great Depression. At its worst, 29 per cent of Australians were unemployed. Frank was at wit's end. By all rights he should be an independently wealthy man by now. This unbelievably capable individual had had a crack at turning a quid by doing everything he knew best. He'd gambled his life for success.

Since he returned from South Africa all those years ago, he'd written non-stop of his adventures, his stories having been published countless times in newspapers and magazines. He'd written books. He'd photographed the Australian wilds and taken extraordinary cinematograph footage of an era in the Australian outback that had now vanished – due in no small part to the efforts of overlanders and adventurers like himself.

For a brief moment, he'd had his own film company and he'd even been employed by the prime minister, no less, to give his views on the future of the nation. He'd flown in aircraft and driven a motor car across the world. It had been an astonishing life packed wall to wall with adventure that people should have paid good money to hear about. But at 50 years of age in 1931 he was penniless. Fame didn't necessarily equate with fortune. His name would appear in the newspapers every now and then – sometimes with a new expedition in mind. 'Mr Francis Birtles, the Australian overlander, is contemplating a motoring trip to New York. He is making arrangements to leave Canberra in March in an eight-cylinder sports car, and will go overland to Fremantle, ship to Cape Town, and thence go overland to Morocco. After crossing into Spain and France he will drive across Europe and Asiatic Russia. Crossing the Bering Straits he will continue down the North American west coast to San Francisco, and thence across the United States to New York.'

But who, during the Great Depression, was rich and naive enough to sponsor a Frank Birtles expedition through Africa, Europe, Soviet Russia and across the Bering Straits to Alaska and on to New York? Besides which, in reality, the gruelling trans-global drives had knocked his health. Frank needed to think of his welfare. It was now every man for himself.

Frank went back on the hunt for gold. He always knew in the back of his mind that if he put his knowledge and skills to the test, he might just strike it rich. 'I spent a number of months in Arnhem Land working alone,' wrote Frank. 'I had a feeling in my bones that it was here, in this little-known part of the country, that fortune awaited me.' After some months prospecting over an area covering several miles, Frank found what he was looking for. 'Dish-washing gave good traces of the yellow metal. The indications were too promising to leave.' Frank continued to work the site, staying in Arnhem Land for the duration of the wet season before returning to Sydney to try to raise capital to open up the lease.

He managed to raise enough to form an expedition and in 1933 he 'left Sydney in charge of a party of six men, with the necessary equipment . . . Although everything looked promising, there was a good deal of anxiety for me.' To secure the capital, Frank had to hand over the greater proportion of his share.

The Arnhem Land Gold Development Company was formed and listed on the stock exchange. However, as Frank was the original vendor, the law prevented him from share transactions for six months. Frank hit the road publicising the mine, he maintained, as a 'hosing-down' exercise, 'so as to put a stop to all bulling of the market by giving publicity to the extent of our developments and demonstrating there was nothing as yet to warrant a boom'.

In other words, Frank was simultaneously talking the mine up and talking it down. Then, for some reason, he just went bush, spending time alone way out in the never-never while testing continued at the mine site. 'Then disaster came to me,' he wrote. 'I lay on my bunk with my two legs swollen, my left arm paralysed, and my nerves stretched to the limit. I was ill with the dreaded beri-beri. Months of living on bad flour and mouldy rice had brought it on.'

By chance an Aborigine wandered through the camp, and Frank scrawled a note for help, asking for it to be delivered to a white camp some miles away. One morning, Frank heard the drone of an approaching aircraft, and he limped from under his canvas tent, lighting a fire from a rubbish heap, which gave a column of smoke as a signal. The plane flew low overhead and then circled, the pilot leaning from the cockpit, staring intently at Frank each time he flew past. 'I know now that he was making sure of my identity,' Frank wrote. 'There came drifting down a stick to which was tied a letter.' The pilot watched Frank pick the letter up, waved farewell and banked away. Frank opened it – it was from his brother-in-law, whom he'd left in charge of his affairs.

The gold mine had struck it rich. 'My shares, on exchange, had increased many times over in value,' Frank recalled. 'One lease that I had held had been sold outright. I was a rich man, independent for life. I looked down at my bedraggled person – and just couldn't believe it,' Frank wrote in his memoirs.

'All my life I'd been a battler, either cutting the deck with nature in her more grim moods, or else stroking a reflective chin over the problem of how to pay my own way. I'd been broke a dozen times. And now the grand climax of my hopes came to me, sick, in my lonely camp in the Never-Never . . . And that's my story. I am now enjoying being a man of means and of leisure. I've got some of the things I've always wanted – the sort of things a man of my tastes dreams of owning when he hasn't got a cracker. There's a motor caravan that has cost me as much as I could have lived on for five or six years in the old days. And there's a little fleet of sporty two-seater models fitted with every possible refinement. I've got a photographic – and cinema-photographic outfit – that couldn't be improved upon. It includes everything and everything is of the best.'

Fate had smiled on him. Frank had finally landed on the elusive winning square at the end of the great game of snakes and ladders that was Frank Birtles' life. He'd fought hard, struggled on – and when almost on his deathbed a message fell from the heavens telling him he'd finally earned his just reward.

•

At least that's the story Frank wanted to leave his followers with anyway. The reality was somewhat different.

On 14 March 1935, the independent member for the Northern Territory, Adair Macalister Blain, demanded a full inquiry, perhaps even a royal commission, into the Arnhem Land Gold Development Company, claiming its flotation on the stock market 'constituted one of the biggest scandals in the history of goldmining in Australia'.

According to Blain, the company had tricked investors into buying shares and leases in a worthless mine by producing bogus gold samples. Blain claimed that samples taken from the mine were most likely 'salted' – gold had been added to deceive potential shareholders. Further, he claimed that the first prospectus stated the company 'had a lease of a mining area which had been worked for two years by Mr Francis Birtles'.

It later transpired that the company had no lease in the area at all, though it said that one could be inspected at the office of its solicitor, who also happened to be a promoter of the mine. Blain claimed the prospectus was 'untrue from end to end', and that it was under investigation in the Territory. According to the prospectus, the gold find was supposed to be on a field unknown to anybody until Francis Birtles revealed it to his business partners in February 1933, yet prospectors had been crawling all over the site for fourteen years.

Two tons of ore supposedly carrying free gold were taken from a shaft and sent to Port Kembla for assessment, where it was concluded the gold found in the sample had in fact been lying on the surface as long ago as 1922. The gold in the sample didn't come from the excavation.

As Blain said, 'There must in those circumstances have been grave suspicion of salting'. He continued, saying that at present no-one was making anything out of mining in the Northern Territory except go-getters and scoundrels and the iniquitous Sydney Stock Exchange, which, he said, appeared to have no morals when there was a commission to be earned. He started pointing fingers. 'How much have the Territorian battlers who discovered the place made out of it? Certainly not as much as Francis Birtles, who has bought six large motor cars and has been staying for months at a fashionable hotel out of his proceeds from the business.'

Frank had teamed up with two well-known, colourful business partners, John Bailey and Frank Green, both of whom had form. Bailey had been the president of the Australian Workers Union and at the time of the mining company's formation was the vice-president of the New South Wales federal branch of the Labor Party.

At the 1923 state Labor Party conference, Bailey was accused of being complicit in tampering with delegates' votes by using ballot boxes with sliding panels – a debacle that became infamous as the 'sliding ballot box scandal' – something for which he was temporarily expelled from the party. Green, a former alderman and deputy lord mayor of Sydney, had been sacked after being found guilty of bribery in connection with the construction of the Bunnerong Power Station at La Perouse in Sydney. Blain proclaimed, Green 'did not stand before the world as a person of so unblemished a character that a graft transaction was the last thing with which he was likely to be associated'. He claimed these 'Labor men' had taken £80,000 of 'promoters' shares' out of the company, but the mine so far had only ever produced £54 worth of gold, and that he could not find a single statement on a material matter made by the company or its manager which was not fraudulently untrue.

The demise of the Arnhem Land Gold Development Company had little bearing on Frank's future. He'd sold his share, he had the money, and he was set for life. The blowtorch put on him by Blain under parliamentary privilege eventually fizzled out, and Francis Birtles was content and lying low. With his new-found wealth he no longer needed to disappear into the outback to keep creditors and summons-wielding local sheriffs at bay.

In the thick of the Great Depression, Francis Birtles had miraculously found wealth. Money had brought an air of respectability, and at 54 years of age Frank decided it was now time to have a crack at settling down. He suddenly found a wife – 40-year-old Miss Nea McCutcheon from Curlewis, south of Gunnedah in northern New South Wales. Frank's impromptu marriage was the last thing long-time Birtles-watchers were expecting.

Nea McCutcheon was an attractive and confident woman, and was known for her penchant for heavy, garish make-up, which, coupled with Frank's new-found wealth, was enough to set tongues wagging. The pair married at St Mary's Cathedral in Sydney on 11 Februay 1935, and attempted to settle down, buying a house in the Sydney seaside suburb of Coogee. As Adair Blain had pointed out, Frank had bought a 'fleet' of flash cars, including a sporty two-seater Singer Nine Le Mans and an impressive Vauxhall Hurlingham Speedster – a whopping movie-star's kind of car fitted with a voluptuous boat-tailed body and twin v-shaped aero screens. Less than 50 Hurlingham Speedsters were ever made.

For all the trappings of a wealthy existence after so many years of travelling through the wilds of the Australian outback, the gentrified and cashed-up Frank Birtles decided to kick off his new life with his new wife by heading back out beyond the black stump again for the umpteenth time. Frank bought a new Ford V8 light truck fitted out as a campervan – a sort of Jurassic-era Winnebago – and before long Mr and Mrs Francis Birtles were on the road: perhaps Australia's first grey nomads. Photographs depict the happy couple preparing for some outback adventure, Nea very much in the spirit, wearing jodhpurs and boots and a broad-brimmed hat, coiling a length of rope to be placed in the open boot of the Ford truck.

Frank still had the desire to prove his worth to the nation, and once again wrote to the government asking for support for his latest expedition into the outback.

> The Hon Mr Paterson
> Commonwealth Minister for Interior
>
> Dear Sir,
>
> It is my intention to leave Sydney (per motor caravan) for the Gulf of Carpentaria – Northern Territory. I propose to depart about the middle of May and proceed along the projected railway route from Bourke to the Barclay Tablelands NA . . . and investigate the pros and cons in connection with development of the regions adjacent . . .

It was old-time Frank Birtles trying to ramp up the government as he had in Billy Hughes's day. The letter continued for a full three pages, expounding Birtles' latest intentions and theories about what needed to be done in the outback and how he'd venture out and report back. Sixteen years after the catastrophic mission with Roy Fry, Frank was still hanging on to his unrequited – unwanted – views on the now-shelved transcontinental railway. He just couldn't let go.

On the left-hand corner of the letter the minister, unimpressed and uninterested, simply marked in pencil his sentiment, for his departmental secretary to formally respond: 'We have better uses for our money than Birtles.'

Things weren't as they should be. Frank's new wife was never popular with the rest of the Birtles family. There was suspicion she had married Frank for his wealth, and claims that she deliberately kept him away from other family members. Certainly Frank's contact with his brothers and sisters tapered off.

Probably newspaper reports announcing Frank had presented his new bride with 'a goldmine as a wedding gift' did little to engender bonhomie among the Birtles family, who were surviving the Great Depression. In the years that followed, Clive's wife Olive, the girl to whom Frank's brother had written so passionately from the Gulf of Carpentaria all those years ago, had no time for Francis Birtles. Clive spoke little of him, but nevertheless, never had a bad word to say about his brother.

In 1935, Frank wrote a memoir for the publishers Angus & Robertson, titled *Battlefronts of Outback* – a sort of omnibus, reminiscing about his life's adventures. The 300-page book gives a good outline of the sorts of amazing exploits Frank had experienced – his Boer War service, crocodile hunting, time spent with the Aborigines, his cycling and motoring feats. The book is all the more fascinating for what Frank's life story doesn't include.

Frank neatly moulded his narrative, omitting some particularly important details. He failed to mention mechanic Syd Ferguson's role as driver and expedition leader on the first latitudinal crossing of Australia by motor car. Frank, hired as a navigator on the 1912 Brush journey, painted himself as the expedition's key proponent, with Syd Ferguson as a sort of 'hanger-on'. Frank also failed to mention that his brother Clive, a motor mechanic, was actually the driver for many of the first motorised journeys into the outback. Naturally, he doesn't expand on the fiasco that occurred around Roy Fry, and his own 'pure indifference', which probably caused the accident and the irreparable fallout with an unforgiving government.

Yet even more startling was that not once did he ever mention the irascible Malcolm Ellis, with whom he had shared both marvellous and terrifying times. Ellis, whom he had first met with Clive on the Brisbane to Sydney Speed Trial back in 1917, and with whom he had travelled with 'the Engineer' across Australia aboard the Scarlet Runner. Ellis, who was responsible for the whole idea of a trans-global drive in a motor car, and with whom he had shared the rolling catastrophe of the Imperial Six.

It was as though Malcolm Ellis had never existed. In fact, the entire Imperial Six expedition might as well have been surgically removed from Frank Birtles' life – he never mentioned it once. And Frank didn't detail how the dubious Arnhem Land Gold Development Company generated its money. Those who are mentioned in the book are those who played lesser roles, who, while not portrayed as exactly obsequious, play second fiddle to Frank in an adventure. Nevertheless, his story was in print and there for the record.

Frank and Nea were still on the road fifteen months after their wedding when they were interviewed for a newspaper about their overlanding in the Ford motor home. Clearly, Nea was now the spokesperson. '. . . according to Mrs Birtles they are still on their honeymoon trip. The couple have just finished a 7,000 mile trip through Queensland and the gulf country. Mrs Birtles confessed that she had many unenviable experiences in the great outback, but is confident that her husband can overcome all difficulties. "We own our own home at Coogee now," said Mrs. Birtles, "and naturally I look forward to settling down . . ."'

Frank was more melancholy in his reply. '"It's a good place to leave and a good place to go back to after travel. When I think of the old method of travel it makes me wonder how such great distances were traversed," he said. "Coming over from Wilcannia, I had visions of the old mail coaches, jogging along. Now the air mail caters for the districts, but it traverses the old coach routes."'

The overlander's reflective response certainly wasn't the Frank Birtles of old. He had found the respectability he always craved, but with that came responsibility. He was now financially secure, with a wife and a house in Coogee, but somehow the spark that perpetually fired up Frank Birtles had been taken away. It was as though he had lost the fight in him.

He was no longer the strapping scout on the open veldt, no longer the mile-smashing cyclist, no longer the tireless long-distance motorist – no longer 'Australia's greatest overlander'. He was Francis Edwin Birtles, 54-year-old husband, from Beach Road, Coogee. And he hated the suburban way of life.

Years later, Nea recalled Frank's frustration and intolerance of attempting the most simple chores. Mowing the lawn, tending the garden – complete anathema to him. Simply – Frank yearned for his youth.

Sometime in 1936, Frank walked through the doors of the Griffiths Brothers Tea Rooms near Sydney Town Hall, where his eyes fell on a young waitress with long black hair. She had the most beautiful smile he'd ever seen. The girl was full of personality and life, and he couldn't help staring at her as she moved from table to table, taking orders, delivering meals. Frank would turn up regularly to the tea rooms just to see her, and eventually she noticed him and they started talking. Her name was Warilda Hawkins – everyone called her 'Rillie' – and he was? The famous overlander – yes she'd heard of him.

Before long, Frank had become infatuated with 21-year-old Rillie – who was more than 30 years his junior – and he did his level best to impress her. She radiated youth and exuberance – the things Frank had now lost. One evening she told her father how this explorer fellow Francis Birtles was regularly coming to see her at the tea rooms. Francis Birtles! Her father was impressed, insisting she invite him over for tea one weekend at the family home in the Sydney suburb of Epping.

It was all a bit awkward. Everyone knew the famous Francis Birtles was recently married – and where was all this supposed to lead? Besides which, she had a boyfriend. Nevertheless, Rillie's dad was adamant – he wanted to meet the famous overlander. When Rillie asked Frank, he jumped at the chance, turning up the following weekend driving his Singer Nine Le Mans sports car, and taking Rillie and her aunt tearing around the district.

Frank became a regular visitor to Rillie's house, ignoring her 21-year-old boyfriend, trying to make an impression with his extraordinary accomplishments. To drive home his fame he gave her a selection of photographs of his adventures intended almost as a Francis Birtles Self Promotion Kit. There were photographs of his outback journeys, of Frank filming in the desert, of Aborigines in the wild, of the Sundowner parked outside Whirley Old Hall at the Birtles estate in Macclesfield, and another of Frank behind the wheel of the flashy and expensive Vauxhall Hurlingham.

Boiled down, these photographs represented exactly what he aimed to say about his life in the book. Adventure, drama, fame, prestigious ancestry and wealth. Frank continued to pursue Rillie until one day she announced she was engaged to marry her boyfriend, Eric. It was a shock for Frank. She never saw him again. What had he been thinking? What would someone so young have ever seen in an old warhorse like Frank Birtles anyway? He simply wanted to impress someone. He just wanted to feel young again.

But people were no longer impressed with old stagers like Francis Birtles. He'd acted like a celebrity, but people thought he was a novelty. The world had moved on from old-time adventurers making silent films in the outback. Now Europe was the place everyone was talking about when leaving the newsreel theatres.

In 1940, American film director Clarence G. Badger was in Sydney casting roles for a new feature film, to be called *That Certain Something*, for Argosy Films.

A movie gossip column outlined the difficulty Badger had in casting for a minor role. He was confronted with the problem of securing an Australian bush type for the picture. He wanted a man whose face was lined by the hot sun and wind of the Australian outback, and he wanted him to be the real thing. Mr

Badger had interviewed dozens of applicants for the part and had not found his man, when it was suggested to him that the very man he required was in Sydney. The man was Francis Birtles, famous throughout Australia for his travel and exploration in the Commonwealth over the past 30 years.

According to the National Film and Sound Archive, the plot for the film is this: 'An American film director wants to make a film about pioneering women. He searches Australia for a woman with "that certain something" for the lead role. A young man uses trickery to get his girlfriend the part.' Frank had a walk-on role as an old-time bushman wandering into a modern, luxury hotel. But, as usual, Frank was never comfortable in front of the camera.

The gossip column explained, 'Someone asked him did he feel that he wanted to get back to the bush again, and this bushman who had been weathered by the strongest sun of the tropics, and had gone quietly through cyclone and the dangers of thirst in the desert, said: "Yes, I'd like to get away from the heat of those lights in the studio."' *That Certain Something* was released in 1941. It was poorly received. The film and its trailer still exists in the National Film and Sound Archive in Canberra.

That Frank was prepared to take a walk-on part in a B-grade romantic comedy shows what he had become. He wasn't the star anymore – he was the guy who looked like a bushman. Remember bushmen?

Frank and Nea continued to travel in the motor home, during which time he began having trouble with his heart. He'd been in and out of hospital several times and was on the road to recovery when he and Nea drove to the Blue Mountains on a camping trip. They discussed a plan for a further trip in Queensland.

On their return, they called in to visit friends in the Sydney suburb of Croydon. While there, Frank suffered a massive heart attack. On 1 July 1941, Francis Edwin Birtles was dead. He was 59 years old.

The *Sydney Morning Herald* ran a small story on page 11 reminding readers of his exploits. Similar stories were published in newspapers around the country but they were never anything more than a couple of paragraphs.

Frank was cremated at the northern suburbs crematorium and was buried at Waverley cemetery in Sydney's eastern suburbs – halfway between the house in Coogee he bought when he was rich and Bondi, the beach he cycled to after his first transcontinental bicycle ride in 1908, when he was flat broke. There was no death notice.

Nea later remarried, becoming Nea Long, the wife of a doctor. She again became a widow, her last years spent in the house in Coogee where she rented out a room in the garage for boarders. She was remembered as being a lonely figure, never without her garish make–up, and was keen just to have a chat with tenants as they walked up the driveway. Sometimes, over a glass of white wine, she'd tell them of her incredible first husband and of the things he did. But they'd never heard of him, and on learning of the amazing Francis Birtles would wonder why they never had.

Frank Birtles was never officially recognised. There was no knighthood. And unlike other contemporary Australian hero-figures such as Don Bradman, Charles Kingsford Smith or Bert Hinkler, no-one even wrote a cheery song about him.

There are no memorials to Birtles except for three streets named after him – one in Canberra, one in Melbourne and another in Sydney. Of his films, only one survives, *Coorab in the Island of Ghosts*, held in the National Film and Sound Archive. Of his photographs and stories, collections held in numerous cultural institutions including the National Museum of Australia, the State Library of New South Wales and the National Library of Australia hold testimony to his adventures.

His heroic drive from London to Melbourne was without question the pinnacle of his adventuring career. His success in crossing the Naga Hills simultaneously infuriated professional explorers and delighted the Australian public. The drive from England to Singapore would not be reprised until almost 30 years later when a joint Oxford–Cambridge university expedition drove from England to Singapore in a convoy of Land Rovers. They were able to use remnants of the Ledo and Stillwell roads carved through Burma by the Americans during World War II. In 1928, Frank and Percy didn't even have this luxury. Nor did they have a four-wheel drive.

The Sundowner Bean 14 was presented to the Australian government in 1929 and placed in the care of the Prime Minister's Department. For decades it was left to languish in various government sheds around Canberra until it was saved by two enthusiasts, Garth Fisher and Des Rees, in the 1960s. The car was in an appalling state; parts had been stolen, it was missing its radiator, was sitting on perished tyres. In time the car came back together. Today it is part of the collection at the National Museum of Australia, where in 2000 it received a complete strip-down and rebuild. It is a fully functioning, drivable motor car – conserved, not restored.

However Francis Birtles' true legacy is not something physically tangible like films and books and motor cars. What he did was open up Australia for everyday Australians. In his lifetime Frank changed travelling into Australia's dead heart from a perilous explorer's expedition into a holiday with his wife in a campervan. He showed Australians, ignorant and fearful of the continent's interior, what was inside their own enormous backyard – and it was something unlike anywhere else in the world. The outback was unique. And it was unusually beautiful.

Exactly how many times Francis Birtles crossed the nation isn't really known – some reports state 70, others say 88 – but it doesn't matter. He helped Australians understand that trans-continental travel was achievable and in doing so, helped plant the seed for overland travel and outback adventure. Today, as cattle trains and cars with caravans tear along the long, smooth, Stuart Highway from Alice Springs to Darwin they are in fact following the old overland telegraph track. If you stop and step off the bitumen it's as wild and untamed as it ever was.

There's a special place, somewhere along that road, where in 1908 three pioneer motorists boiled the billy with a wild-haired cyclist: Australia's greatest overlander.

Acknowledgements

There are many people to thank, all of whom have been an important part of my learning about the Francis Birtles story, and writing this book.

Firstly to the relatives – Francis Birtles' niece, the delightful Muriel Tait, daughter of Frank's sister, and his fascinating nephew Calvert Birtles, son of Frank's brother Clive. Muriel and Calvert revealed some astonishing first-hand information which gave extraordinary insight into the adventurer's often impenetrable personality. I'm grateful for their time and knowledge. To Terry Birtles, a relative of Francis, who compiled an extraordinarily comprehensive list of research notes for the National Museum of Australia. Terry, an accomplished author and historian, had pieced together much of Francis Birtles' life – as unruly as it was – and his document was of inestimable value. To Trevor Bartlett, related to Frank's mother, who contacted me after the screening of the ABC TV series *Wide Open Road*. Trevor's indefatigable capacity to successfully rifle through archives and family tree records proved vital in establishing Frank's background. Trevor turned up a wealth of information – death certificates, land title deeds – all of which contributed to piecing together the story.

To two very special mates, old-time motor-racing chaps, mechanics, veteran and vintage car enthusiasts, Lynne Brown and Geoff Simmons (known in their motor racing days as *Team Partyhouse*) who stripped my Bean 14 and oversaw its resurrection. Many weekends were spent with the three of us skinning knuckles with Whitworth spanners on the machine. During this process I was able to gain an understanding of the workings and construction of Francis Birtles' most famous car. Their technical advice was essential. Geoff and Lynne would receive telephone calls at any hour asking 'Reversing the differential – it doesn't make sense. So how could Birtles . . . ?' and so forth. I bow to their knowledge, patience, wisdom, and cherish their comradeship. (Thanks too, to Trish and Anna for letting us play.)

To Bean 14 owners and enthusiasts Alec and Anne McKernan (from whom I bought my Bean car) whose knowledge of Bean motor cars is unsurpassed – Alec, the owner of a magnificent Bean 14 Tourer, was able to furnish extraordinary details about the car and the marque.

To Bob Lamond. Bob is perhaps Australia's foremost Francis Birtles expert – particularly on the subject of the 1912 trans-continental Brush drive. Bob's assistance and generosity in sharing documents, photographs and information has been tremendous. Bob drove his own 1912 Brush car across Australia to commemorate the centenary of Ferguson and Birtles' crossing.

To Carol Leggett, daughter of Rillie Hawkins, the young waitress Frank Birtles had his eye on back in the 1930s . . . Carol's chance phone call one day to the *Daily Telegraph* resulted in the revelation of a completely unknown tangent of Francis Birtles' story, and a treasure trove of photographs he'd given her mum.

To Gordon Fisher, who approached me at a vintage car show and produced Francis Birtles' passport from his drive across the world from London to Melbourne in 1927–28. In it, Birtles had written his occupation as 'explorer'. Years ago, Gordon's father had been given various pieces of Birtles ephemera, which included a cartridge from the elephant gun presented to him in India.

To David Kirk, who had once boarded at Birtles' house in Coogee, located its whereabouts for me and could tell me firsthand about his landlady, Frank's widow, Nea.

To Associate Professor Andrew Moore of the University of Western Sydney, an expert on Malcolm Henry Ellis. I had already studied Andrew's essay 'From the Strand to Boorooloola: Malcolm Ellis as Pioneer Motorist', when one day, through strange happenstance, I met him at an Australia Day Rodeo in Taralga, New South Wales. (I remember Andrew saying, 'I'd never imagined being at a rodeo talking about Malcolm Ellis and Francis Birtles'.) Andrew's generosity in sharing his knowledge and some of his personal files encouraged me to explore Ellis's tempestuous relationship with Birtles, and the ensuing debacle that became the hushed-up Imperial Six Expedition.

To Dr Georgine Clarsen of the University of Wollongong. Georgine's knowledge of early Australian motoring and outback life is astounding. Our long discussions on outback conditions in the 1920s prompted me to pursue Francis Birtles' evolving views on Aborigines.

To Pedr Davis, the doyen of Australian motoring historians, who has written so much about Francis Birtles – and other pioneer motorists in Australia – and can answer pretty much any question about motoring history straight off the top of his head. (Just don't start him on the differences between a Talbot and a Clement Talbot . . .) His knowledge and generosity helped enormously. Dr Meredith Burgmann, a great and wise friend with whom I had many lengthy conversations about Australian politics during the 1920s. This really helped set the scene.

To the staff at the National Museum of Australia who generously presented me with a copy of all their files on Francis Birtles and allowed me to sit behind the wheel of his Bean 14 – the Sundowner. Many thanks to the extraordinarily helpful and effervescent Laura Breen, the car's wonderful old-time curator Col Ogilvy, Denis French in the copyright department and two old mates, Dennis Grant and Guy Hansen. And all you other blokes out at Mitchell! Your assistance has been phenomenal.

The staff of the Mitchell Library, Sydney, hold an extraordinary collection of Francis Birtles' material including his personal scrapbook – a national treasure. Many thanks to all the staff with whom I worked on the 'Lost and Found' series, who guided me in the right direction.

And thanks also to the National Library of Australia, and the National Archives of Australia – they were invaluable sources of information, and all their staff were unfailingly helpful.

To everyone at the *Daily Telegraph* who's put up with me, in particular Paul Whittaker and Mick Carroll.

Thanks also to Keith and Louise Brodie, Paul Clarke, Rob Coombs, Roger Coombs, Anthony Eden, Mal Garthon, Lana Hurst, Lang and Bev Kidby, Troy Lennon, Mick Matheson,

David and Katherine Medina, Lynne and Neil Shaw, Andrew Snelling, John and Bronwyn Sullivan, and Jane Summerhayes.

To the earbashed Birtles-story-listening-committee, Brett Martin, Sturt Krygsman, Mark Southcott and Graeme Leech.

To the Australasian Primates, particularly the authors amongst them, Judy Nunn, Bruce Venables, Paul Ham, Bob Ellis – thanks for your encouragement and camaraderie. Wassail!

To old mates Steve Pizzati with whom I served two seasons of *Top Gear Australia* on SBS; Pat Sheil for his knowledge of the Overland Telegraph; and fellow cartoonist and author Bill Leak, who was dropped on his head as an adult.

Thanks to another old mate, my radio producer Stuart Duncan, on whom I'd sometimes test out a few pages of the book to see what he thought. Stu's been particularly enthusiastic all the way through the writing process, and would come up with some challenging observations. He should write that book about the gun one day. Clever bloke.

To my brother Gordon, who travelled with me one weekend up to Bingara near the New South Wales–Queensland border on a mission to pick up an old jeep. With Gordon as a captive sounding board, the trip up and back was a great way to formulate how to put the story together.

And to my sister Narelle for her larger-than-life personality, and for her sounding-board qualities as well.

Many thanks to my agent, James Laurie – wise, attentive and a marvellous guide. As always, it's been a great journey – home, James.

To the editors at Hachette Australia, who brought everything into shape; and also those who did the brilliant work on some appallingly aged and weathered photographs, and for the marvellous cover design.

An extra special thank you to the urbane Matthew Kelly, my publisher at Hachette Australia, who initially approached me to write this book. Matthew has been an absolute delight to work with and even when he's made serious editing decisions he is still prepared to listen to a protest. Never once were six-guns ever placed on the table. It has been a pleasure, Matthew, and thank you for having faith in me.

To my beautiful son Oliver who, as this book was going to press, announced he wanted to grow up and become an explorer. At five years of age, this is the best time for exploring the world.

And to Tanya, my wife, the love of my life, the most amazing person, my best mate – the greatest thanks of all goes to you. Thank you for holding things together, listening, being there . . . and for being you.

Warren Brown

Sources

In the research and writing of the Francis Birtles story, I have relied heavily on many Australian newspapers of the day – both metropolitan and regional. It has been of immeasurable assistance to have so many of them digitised and available through Trove, the online resource of the National Library of Australia. I refer to many newspapers in the pages of this book – and I accessed almost all of them through Trove. In addition, the records of the National Archives of Australia were invaluable.

In addition, I relied on many books, both those published in Birtles' day, and also more recently. Below is a list of the most important. The books and articles written by Birtles himself have been especially valuable – and I have relied on them a great deal in the telling of this story of his life and times.

The books I have found most useful are:

The Age of Motoring Adventure – T.R. Nicholson, Cassell, London, 1960.
An Anthology of Classic Australian Folklore – A.K. McDougall, The Five
    Mile Press, Victoria, 2004.

Any Colour so Long as it's Black, Designing the Model T Ford 1906–1908 – John Duncan, Exisle Publishing, New Zealand, 2008.

Ataturk: The Rebirth of a Nation – Patrick Kinross, Phoenix, London, 1964.

The Australian Dictionary of Motoring – Pedr Davis, Pedr Davis Pty Ltd and Bookworks, Sydney, 2001.

Australian Transport: An Illustrated History – Max Colwell, Paul Hamlyn, Sydney, 1972.

Australians at War, For Queen and Commonwealth – Time Life Books, Sydney, 1987.

Australians on the Road – Pedr Davis, Rigby, Adelaide 1979.

Battlefronts of Outback – Francis Birtles, Angus & Robertson, Sydney, 1935.

The Bean – Jonathon Wood, Shire Publications, Buckinghamshire, 2001.

The Bicycle and the Bush – Jim Fitzpatrick, Hesperian Press, Carlisle, Western Australia, 1980.

Britain's Motor Industry: The First Hundred Years – various authors, Haynes, London, 1995.

The British Empire, Issue 75, Lawrence and his Legacy – Time Life Books – BBC Publications, Netherlands, 1973.

The Burma Road – Donovan Webster, Farrer, Straus & Giroux, New York, 2003.

'Business and Investment Strategies in the Inter-War British Steel Industry: A Case Study of Hadfields Ltd and Bean Cars' – Geoffrey Tweedale, *Business History*, Vol. 29, No. 1, 1987, pp. 47–72.

China to Chelsea – Capt. D. McCallum, Ernest Benn Ltd, London, 1930.

The Complete Catalogue of British Cars 1895–1975 – Culshaw & Horrobin, Veloce, Dorchester, 2006.

The Decline and Fall of the British Empire 1781–1981 – Piers Brendon, Random House, London, 2007.

An Epic of the Outback – A.A. Barlow, Melbourne, 1926.

First to Damascus – Jill, Duchess of Hamilton, Kangaroo Press, Sydney, 2002.

Five Roads to Danger, The Adventure of Transcontinental Motoring 1919–1930 – T.R. Nicholson, Cassell, London, 1960.

Ford Model T: The Car That Put the World on Wheels – Lindsay Brooke, Motorbooks, Minneapolis, 2008.

Francis E. Birtles – Overlander – Terry Birtles, notes for National Museum of Australia, 2000.

Frank Hurley: A Photographer's Life – Alasdair McGregor, Penguin Viking, Melbourne, 2004.

'From the Strand to Boorooloola: M.H. Ellis as Pioneer Motorist' – Andrew Moore, *Journal of Australian Studies*, No. 81, 2004.